crazy

dead

people

By

Joni Mayhan

Cover design by Joni Mayhan

Crazy Dead People 2019 by Joni Mayhan. All rights reserved. No part of this book may be used or reproduced in any manner without written permission from the author.

Any resemblances to actual places, people (living or dead) are purely coincidental.

Also by Joni Mayhan

True Paranormal Non-fiction
Haunted New Harmony
Ghost Magnet
Spirit Nudges: Allowing Help from the Other Side
Signs of Spirits – When Loved Ones Visit
Ruin of Souls
Dark and Scary Things – A Sensitive's Guide to the Paranormal World
Ghost Voices
Bones in the Basement – Surviving the S.K. Haunted Victorian Mansion
The Soul Collector
Devil's Toy Box
Ghostly Defenses – A Sensitive's Guide for Protection

Paranormal Fiction
Lightning Strikes (Angels of Ember Dystopian Trilogy– Book 1)
Ember Rain (Angels of Ember Dystopian Trilogy – Book 2)
Angel Storm (Angels of Ember Dystopian Trilogy – Book 3)

The Spirit Board (Winter Woods – Book 1)
The Labyrinth (Winter Woods – Book 2)

Acknowledgements

This book means more to me than any book I've written. Mostly, it's because the characters have been with me, inside my head, for almost twenty years.

When I couldn't find an agent for my first book, I put Shelby and Fugly in a box on my shelf and continued writing, hoping the next book would be the one to finally launch my writing career. As it turns out, I never ended up getting an agent. I took control of my own destiny and learned everything I needed to know to do it myself. I haven't looked back since.

I'd have to go back twenty years to properly thank everyone who's made this dream a reality for me. From my high school creative writing teacher to my first writing group to my current troupe of dedicated beta readers, you all have my gratitude.

Thank you to Gare Allen, my fellow author and friend, for reading every word as I wrote it and offering your stellar feedback. Thank you to Paula Bundy, Clarissa Powell and Susan Landry for your feedback and essential edits. An extra thanks goes to Jim Budziszewski for not only reading and editing, but also sharing that crazy bat story with me, which ended up in this book. I'd be remiss not to thank Shaman Michael Robishaw for keeping all the creepy crawlies out of my space while I wrote.

To my readers, you'll never know how much I appreciate your support over the years. As I've said before, the best way to thank an author is to write a reader's review. I hope you enjoy this. I'm including an additional story about this book at the end, so keep reading.

Prologue

He was coming.
She moved to the back corner of her cage, praying he wouldn't see her.

There was nothing to hide behind, so she pressed her back against the cold metal bars and tried to shrink down as small as possible. She just wished she could make herself invisible like Marjorie in Room 303.

She'd never seen Marjorie disappear, but she believed her. Marjorie was the one that told her they'd lock her up the next time she bit an orderly and she'd been right. The only thing Marjorie didn't tell her was that they'd pull all her teeth first.

Maybe he'll take someone else this time.
She'd lost track of how long she'd been down there. All she knew was that someone came down twice a day to give her water and replace her bucket. If she was lucky, they'd also throw a heel of stale bread at her.

I won't bite this time.
She wanted to scream the words at him, but she kept them to herself, fearful it would draw him to her. "I have to bite. It's the only way to stop them from doing the bad thing," she whispered instead.

Beside her in a cage just like hers, a man moaned.

"Take me. Just take me and get it over with," he wailed.

She pressed her hands against her ears, trying to block out his voice. Sometimes he howled all night long, the words slithering into her head like worms trying to eat her brain.

The doctor took his time coming down the stairs. She could hear his black shiny shoes click against the treads.

She ran a finger inside her mouth, feeling the gummy holes where her teeth used to be. They still bled and oozed, even though it happened several days ago. Sometimes the ooze tasted like tuna fish and it made her stomach icky.

Go away, man! Go away!

She chanted the words inside her head with her fingers still pressed inside her mouth. She could hear the click of his shoes, walking and then stopping, walking and stopping.

"I don't have the devil in me," she whispered, as a memory drifted into her head. When she started having the shakes and nobody could stop her, not even by holding her down, her daddy said she was filled with demons. The preacher tried to bless her, but she still kept getting them, so her daddy brought her here.

"They can help you here," he told her, prying her hands away, but his words were a lie.

"A lie!" she said a little too loud.

The doctor with the shiny shoes and the black eyes continued down the row, not stopping now until he got to her cage.

"Hello, Janine. I have something for you," he said.

She didn't want to look, but she had to.

What if it's chicken or meatloaf? What if it's CANDY?

She opened her eyes and found him standing in front of his cage with something in his hand. She wasn't sure what it was, but it looked like an ice pick.

"Don't worry. It will only hurt for a little while."

That was a lie too.

Chapter 1

I drove down the tree-lined street, taking in all the signs of a quickly disappearing summer. The maples, with their paper-thin helicopters hanging in bunches, were beginning to turn. The edges of the crimson leaves caught the sun, making them look almost iridescent.

A chill lingered in the air, reminding me that winter wasn't far away. As much as I wanted to appreciate autumn, I just couldn't. It was nothing more than the death of summer and I mourned it as though it were a close relative in hospice.

Autumn wasn't the only thing that was bothering me.

"I probably made a huge mistake," I said to my dog Fugly, who sat beside me on the passenger's seat.

Fugly tossed me a glance and looked back out his window, probably searching for squirrels. He was one of those dogs who was so ugly, he was almost cute, with a heavy emphasis on *almost*.

Truth be told, I was nervous about my new job. I had been hired to scout out locations for a popular paranormal television show. The job came with full benefits, decent pay and the opportunity to move out of my mother's basement, something that was becoming more important as the days progressed.

I wasn't sure why I even applied for it. I didn't have any experience with the paranormal, besides a few strange happenings in my childhood. Part of me worried that I got the job because the producer found me attractive.

I tucked a stray auburn curl behind my ear and sighed, thinking about the location. There was no hesitation there. It freaked me out more than a little bit.

The Parkesburg Sanatorium was an old insane asylum that was built in the mid 1800's. People were sent there for a multitude of disabilities, many of them treatable by today's standards. It was the kind of place where people were dumped because no one knew what to do with them. The conditions were horrid. Patients were left in their rooms for days on end with little care, many of them chained to beds.

In the 1930s it was used as a tuberculosis hospital and was later transformed into a nursing home before it was shut down by the state in the early 1970s. Since then, it sat vacant on fifty acres of fenced-off property. The only people who had visited it in the past forty years were the caretakers and the handful of trespassers who ventured onto the property. It was slated for demolition and a complete razing of the property, after which a condominium complex and office park would be built on the site. This was the paranormal show's only chance to investigate before it would be torn down.

My instructions were fairly clear. I needed to walk through the property, all fifty-thousand square feet of it, to determine the layout. Then, I needed to interview everyone who had ever had a paranormal experience at the location. After that, I would dig into the research, the part I really anticipated.

There was just something so alluring about walking into a library and being surrounded by all those books. My friends thought I was crazy, but I preferred the smell of an old book over any designer cologne. I've always been that way. Give me a thread of tantalizing information to pull and I'll make it my goal to unravel the entire ball of yarn. There was nothing I loved more than a good mystery.

While the research intrigued me, I wasn't sure what to make of the TV show itself. Prior to the interview, I forced myself to watch a few episodes of Paranormal Warriors to get a grasp of the format and found myself instantly hating everything about it, from the stupid name to the lead investigator.

Brock Daltry was the kind of guy that made my eyes roll back into my head. He was tall with spiky light-brown hair and more muscles and tattoos than were meant to grace a human body. Every time I saw him on TV, making sultry eyes at the camera, I had the overwhelming urge to throw something at my screen. Unfortunately, I was now part of his world.

I was told to make sure some of the candidates lined up for interviews with him were young attractive females. Beezer, the creepy producer, said it was good for the show's ratings, but I was fairly certain I was just screening Brock's next bedmates. I wondered if he and Beezer traded them back and forth. The thought made me grip my steering wheel tightly. Maybe I'd do a little extra screening and make sure at least one of them also had a highly contagious STD as well.

"That'll teach him to keep his pants on," I mumbled to myself.

Fugly barked, as if in agreement.

As we pulled onto the highway that led from southern Indiana to Kentucky, I began to settle into the ride. After twenty miles on the same road, I felt my mind relax, like it normally did on long car rides. I didn't hold much faith in things like yoga and meditation, but something about a long drive allowed me a chance to really dig deep.

Life was often filled with mysteries that could never be solved. Sometimes, one thing just led to another, leading me where I was supposed to go. I often followed this nudge with blind faith that I would eventually end up where I was intended but it didn't always work out for the best.

My last job wasn't a dream job. I didn't have a corner office with a view of the park and I rarely found myself above the fold on the daily newspaper, but I was happy. I had my street beat and I dug up interesting stories about the history and people of our town. They weren't the kind of articles that drew attention, not like the street shootings and murder stories you saw in bigger papers. They were slice-of-life pieces, a way of memorializing normal everyday people. You might see the stories when you flipped through the newspaper and then return to them after you've gorged yourself on flashy violence and anxiety-provoking political articles. They were the kind of stories you read on the toilet after everything else had been digested quickly and painfully.

When people stopped reading the newspaper and began getting their news online, budgets were cut and my efforts were the first to be snipped from the fray, telling me something that made me worry about humanity. People didn't want to hear the good news. They wanted the gore and the destruction.

I went through a short period where I pretty much hated everyone. I lost my cute apartment and sold off all my belongings before moving back in with my mother. This job was the first good thing that had happened to me in years. I only hoped it would turn out to be something meaningful.

I heard a thumping coming from the passenger seat and realized Fugly was watching me, wagging his tail. It was as though he read my thoughts and was telling me everything was going to be okay. Sometimes you needed that in your life, even if it came from someone who couldn't tell you the words aloud.

"Thanks, bud," I told him and ruffled his head.

He wasn't always a bad boy; sometimes he was my lifeline. He was there when I came home after losing my job, dropping my purse to the floor and finding my way to the couch. He was there through every bad breakup, every fight with my mother, and every other moment in my life when I desperately needed someone. He seemed to tune into me when I was feeling down. I wasn't sure if he was picking up on my body language or if he was feeling a vibe I emitted. Either way, it was useful. It made me wonder what else he was intuiting.

There were many times when he appeared to be watching something I couldn't see. The first time he did it, I assumed he was tracking a bug. When he continued to do it, I started looking for the bug and was a tad bit weirded out when I couldn't find one.

"Do you see ghosties?" I asked him, watching his eyes for a reaction. He just stared at me, giving nothing away.

If I subjected him to haunted locations, was he going to start reacting to every ghost we encountered? I wasn't sure how I was going to handle it. All I wanted to do was to go into the location, find the best places for the guys to set up their cameras and then hunker down at the local library to do research. I didn't want to deal with the ghosts themselves. The TV show could handle it.

The thought made my chest tighten a bit and it grew stronger over the course of the next five hours. By the time I pulled up to the long tangled driveway of the asylum, I was wound so tightly, I could have powered half the town with my anxiety-laden energy reserves.

A chain was looped over the driveway, so I coasted to a stop, my heart racing madly.

The gravel road ahead of me was nearly consumed by an overgrowth of trees and bushes. It reminded me of the kind of road you see in horror movies. Bad things happened on roads like that. People could jump out of the bushes at you or monsters could slither beneath the undercarriage of your car, latching on tightly until you stopped and opened your door.

My hand found its way to the gear lever and was in the process of putting it back in reverse when something pretty startling happened.

Someone pounded on my window.

Chapter 2

I turned so quickly, I nearly broke my neck. Standing beside my door was the scariest human being I've ever laid eyes on.

He was mammothly tall and broad; a mountain of flesh carved into the shape of a man. Wiry brown hair seemed to explode from his head, hanging to his shoulders in a tangle, merging together with his equally long beard in one enormous mass. All I could see of his face were two bright blue eyes piercing out of the bramble, pinning me to my seat with their intensity. He wore camel-colored coveralls that were streaked with dirt. For all the world, he looked as though he crawled out of the woods to eat me.

He reached into his pocket and extracted something long and dangly. For a second, I thought it was a snake and he was going to throw it through the four-inch gap on my window, but then I realized it was a lanyard with a name badge connected to it.

He slapped the badge to my window and gave me three seconds to see the photo and match the bright blue eyes to the face of the man who was glowering at me. Everything else about the picture was completely different. The bush of mane that hid most of his features was missing, replaced with a clean cut, smiling version of him. He looked like the kind of man who would open doors for people and help turtles cross the road. The man standing three feet from me looked like his polar opposite. If it weren't for the matching blue eyes, I would swear he butchered the person in the photo and stole his badge.

"Follow me," he grumbled and turned away from the window faster than I imagined him capable of moving. I swear I felt the ground tremble as he strode with purposeful steps towards the chain barrier.

He unhooked it and disappeared into the trees. Seconds later, I heard the roar of an engine, followed by a bright red four-wheeler emerging from the undergrowth. Without a glance behind him, he gunned the engine and took off down the gravel road ahead of him.

I had a handful of seconds to determine my fate. Do I follow the scary man into the depths of the haunted forest where he very well might carve me up into tiny pieces, or do I turn around and go back to my mother's house for a hunk of double-chocolate brownies?

Fugly growled beside me, his eyes pinned on the road ahead.

I had my hand on the gear shifter, ready to throw it into reverse when reality raised its ugly head. Double-chocolate brownies came with a steep price. I put my Jeep in drive and followed the quickly disappearing red taillights ahead of me.

As soon as I crossed through the entrance, it was as though I became swallowed alive by the woods. Daylight cut out as though a light switch had been thrown. All I could see was the blur of tall trees and dark green foliage zipping past my window. It made me wonder if the thick woods served as a deterrent for curiosity seekers. I didn't know too many people who would willingly step into that forest, even if there was a delicious mystery on the other side. You just didn't do some things, not even on a double-dog dare, and this was one of them.

Thankfully, the forest ended after several minutes of white-knuckled driving and we emerged into an open grassy field. The brightness of the daylight assaulted my eyes, making me blink furiously, wanting badly to reach for my wrap-around sunglasses, the ones my mother said made me look like a thug, but I didn't. I didn't want to miss one second of the scene ahead of me.

It was something out of a fairy tale, the dark and scary kind where children are shoved into ovens and dragons roast people like marshmallows. The grassy field continued for the length of a football field before ending at the base of an equally green grassy hill. It was so abrupt and unnatural; it looked as though a giant had taken a huge ice-cream scoop of earth and plopped it down in the middle of the field. I didn't spend much time looking at the hill though. What was on top of it was enough to give me goosebumps for a month.

The asylum was everything you'd ever wish for in a nightmare. It was long and sprawling with a crumbling stone façade covered with dead vines. The main body of the building had a castle-like appearance, with twin turrets at each corner of the imposing structure, making it look like it had horns. Four-story wings stretched out another hundred feet at each end. With a little imagination, it looked like a horned demon doing the splits.

The road looped around behind the building, winding up the hill at an angle. The pitch was steep, forcing me to keep my eyes on the road, but it was difficult to ignore the building I was approaching. The closer I got, the tighter my stomach grew.

The bushy-haired giant stopped his four-wheeler at the front of the building and cut the engine. I pulled up behind him and did the same. Silence washed over me like a tidal wave, filling the space once consumed by engines with a nothingness that felt alarming.

I stepped out of my Jeep, my feet crunching against the dead leaves that had blown up against the front of the building. I stopped for a second, acknowledging the otherwise absolute silence. There were no crickets chirping from the bushes and no birds singing from the trees. Even the wind was still, as though it was also holding its breath. I felt my pulse quicken, as I questioned why every living being in the area was keeping its distance. It also made me wonder why I wasn't following suit.

Fugly leapt out of the Jeep and promptly began sniffing around.

"No dogs!" the giant rumbled very abruptly from behind me. I hadn't heard him approach and his sudden appearance nearly made me wet my pants.

"He's part of my team. He's a spirit dog."

Fugly, doing his part, looked up at the man and wagged his tail. It was as close to charming as my dog could get and I silently thanked him for the contribution, because it seemed to work.

"Just keep him on a leash," he said and started towards the front door.

"Of course." I pulled Fugly's leash out and snapped it to his collar. Fugly wasn't fond of being leashed, but he took it like a champ and trotted towards the front door to follow the giant into the haunted asylum.

The sidewalk leading to the front steps was old and buckled, with patches of grass nearly covering the crumbling sandstone. Fugly stopped a few times to sniff at the cracks, while I gave them a wide berth, fearful of being pulled underground by zombie arms. As we reached the base of the steps, the giant turned back.

"I hope you brought a flashlight," he said.

I smiled tightly and pulled a penlight from my jacket pocket. I was quite proud of it. It hung on a lanyard I could put around my neck, leaving my hands free. He scoffed at me.

"That's not gonna work in here." He brushed past me and returned to his four-wheeler, where he pulled a long Maglite from the back compartment. It was nearly the length of my arm and weighed more than I was comfortable carrying, but I took it and thanked him.

"You're gonna need it in here. No electricity. Hasn't been for almost thirty years."

This was news to me and something the paranormal show wasn't going to be happy about. It meant they would have to use generators for the duration of the investigation. It also meant the inside of the building would be as dark as a crypt. I swallowed hard and followed him into the pits of hell.

As the door swung shut behind us, the blackout was complete. It was as though I had fallen into a void where sunlight had never penetrated. I struggled to find the switch on the Maglite as my inner voices shrieked at me. I finally gave up on it and turned on the mini-flashlight hanging from my neck and used it to figure out the Maglite.

"It screws on and off," the giant said from somewhere ahead of me. He hadn't turned on his light yet, which gave me serious doubts about his overall sanity.

After some more frustrated finagling, I finally figured out the flashlight. The beam came on with blinding intensity, but only cut a swatch into the penetrating abyss. I swept it ahead of me, finding the giant standing there, silently watching me. I gasped when I saw him, my mind returning to fun houses from my youth, where the lights catch glimpses of monsters in the darkness before cutting out altogether.

I was beginning to wonder if I'd made a grave mistake. Even though the man appeared to be the person on the badge, that didn't mean the badge was real. He could have glued his own photo on top of someone else's. I could be walking into a haunted asylum with a mass murderer, for all I knew.

"Ummm...you aren't, like, a serial killer or anything, are you?" I asked.

He chuckled somewhere in the black void ahead of me. I tried to find him with the light, but he had moved.

"I'd say it's a little late to be asking that question, isn't it? Follow me if you want a tour of the asylum. If you're too chicken-shit, the door is right behind you."

I took a deep breath for courage and followed the giant deeper into the foreboding darkness.

Chapter 3

I've been accused of a lot of things in my lifetime, but being brave isn't one of them.

I'm not a coward, or anything. I just have a tendency to always err on the side of caution. If there's a possibility I might get maimed or murdered, it makes no sense to take unnecessary risks.

Like most women of my era, I always parked under street lights when it was dark outside and I was always aware of my surroundings. I didn't wear earbuds when I went for walks so I would know if someone tried to walk up behind me. I was also a compulsive door-locker, making sure every door and window was sealed up tight before I could relax. If something horrible ever happened to me, it wouldn't be because I was oblivious to the danger. It would be because someone found a way around my internal burglar alarm.

These thoughts washed through my mind as I stood there watching the giant's flashlight beam grow smaller and smaller. There was still time to back out. I could just turn around and walk out the door. Of course, the decision came with some steep consequences. I'd also be quitting a job that promised to pay me a pretty decent salary and came with a huge bonus at the end of the first location. The bonus would be enough for a deposit on an apartment, as well as the first month's rent.

Fugly nudged me, as though encouraging me to push on.

"Alright buddy, but if something jumps out and tries to eat us, I'm pushing you out in front of me," I told him, even though we both knew my words didn't hold water. If I had to count the times I've already put my life on the line for my dog, I'd definitely run out of fingers.

The room I was in appeared to be a lobby of sorts, although time and the elements had withered it down. I beamed the light around the room, taking in the cracked marble tiles and white crumbling walls. The ceiling was over fifteen feet high with a huge wrought iron chandelier that had probably once been lit with gas lamps. Water damage had caused a large portion of the ceiling to collapse, leaving a pile of debris on the floor beneath it. Paint peeled off the wall in chunks, making it look like the scales of a fish.

I pressed my finger to my nose, warding off a sneeze. The room had a musty smell to it, the kind that made you think of really bad things like black mold and asbestos. It was enough to make me wish I'd brought along a face mask. I made a mental note to tell the paranormal team about it.

From my initial research, I knew the asylum had once been considered one of Ohio's premier mental facilities. When it opened in 1848 as a lunatic asylum for the feeble minded, the reasons for admittance could include anything from mental excitement to masturbation. If a husband grew weary of his wife, he could admit her for ailments like "imaginary female problems" or hysteria. It made me thankful for having been born in a modern time period. There was no doubt in my mind someone would have locked me up if I'd lived back then.

The hospital was designed to house 250 people, but soon was accommodating triple that number. By the early 1900s, over 2,500 patients were packed into the facility and were subject to the barbaric treatments of the period, including icepick lobotomies, freezing cold water baths and complete isolation. When tuberculosis grew rampant in the area in the early 1900s, the mental patients were weeded out, with the remainder crowded into the west wing of the building. The foyer was reappointed with marble, to make it look deceptively lavish for the wealthy patients. Open-air verandas were built along the east side of the building where the tuberculosis patients were housed because they believed fresh air was good for them. In many cases, the extreme cold and heat caused more problems than they solved and patients perished at an alarming rate.

A cure for tuberculosis was discovered in the 1940s and the hospital returned to its asylum origins for several decades. It eventually transformed into a nursing home for the elderly before it closed its doors for good in the 1970s. It had been sitting empty ever since.

I couldn't help but consider all the lives that passed through those doors. Thousands of people once stood in the shadow of my footsteps, their lives torn into shambles by what was on the other side of the double doors ahead of me. I could feel the anguish leaching out of the walls, rippling against the peeling paint. It was so real and tangible; I could easily imagine it lingering like a mist.

What were they thinking as they walked through the lobby? Were some of them hoping for a cure for tuberculosis, or did they know they were coming here to die? Were others led here by well-meaning relatives who had tired of caring for a mentally ill relative? Did they come back to visit them frequently in the beginning, the visits trickling down to nothing after a while? Did birthdays and holidays pass without acknowledgement as the minutes became more like years? I felt badly for all of them, but the ones I sympathized with the most were the ones who didn't belong here, the ones like me.

When I was five years old, I started talking to Sarah, a little girl who came to my room on rainy days. I can't really remember the first time she appeared to me, but she'd suddenly materialize, playing alongside me as I stacked blocks to build a fortress. She'd look up at me with big blue eyes and smile, then hand me the next block. After several months, she began to appear daily, sitting beside me at breakfast, dressed in a white pinafore dress, watching me eat my oatmeal, riding beside me in the car to the drug store with my mother, watching cartoons on the living room rug.

She never spoke, which annoyed me in the beginning. "Do you want the pink dress or the red dress?" I'd ask her as we sat playing with my dolls, and she'd point to the one she wanted.

"Why won't you talk?" I asked her, and she just smiled, and then covered her mouth with her hand.

"You can't talk?"

She shook her head.

My mother came into the room soon after, her eyebrows drawn closely together as she glanced anxiously around the room.

"Who are you talking to?"

I glanced at Sarah and sighed. "Nobody, Mom. Just my new friend, Sarah."

My mother knelt down beside me. "Is Sarah sitting here now?"

"Yeah, she's right there," I pointed to the edge of the rug beside my toy box where Sarah sat, frozen, watching my mother with fearful eyes.

"It's okay, Sarah. My mother won't hurt you. If she's mad at you, she won't let you have any dessert after dinner, but she won't hurt you."

My mother took a long look at the floor near the toy box, where she obviously didn't see a little girl, then retreated to her bedroom to look this up in her parenting book.

I eventually learned to communicate with Sarah in other ways. "Do you want one lump or two?" I'd ask her as we played tea party and sometimes she'd hold up two fingers and other times, I'd just know, the words coming to my mind, soft and delicate, forming in my mind like melted sugar. *Two please.*

After conferring with her parenting guide and talking the subject dry at her beauty parlor, my mother decided it was an imaginary friend. I'd always been somewhat of a loner, even as early as five, preferring to play quietly by myself than to be brawling with the neighborhood kids. She naturally assumed I was lonely and just needed more friends to play with. She began inviting children over for play dates, recruited from her patrons at the beauty salon, neighbors, and women at her church. I'd bring them to my room, hand them something to play with, and then go play with Sarah in the corner. After a while, the children stopped coming, begging their mothers not to make them play with the crazy girl who talked to herself. By the time I turned six, Sarah stopped coming as well.

Would I have ended up in a place like this had I been born in another era?

Over the years, I read about other people like me who sometimes heard voices. Some of them heard actual voices, while others heard music or tones similar to ear-ringing. There didn't seem to be a rhyme or reason for the phenomena. Sometimes, they were born with the ability, while other times it came on during middle-life. Many of them didn't initially realize what was going on and probably thought they were losing their minds. How many of those people had been locked up here, labeled as crazy?

Fugly nudged me again, making me realize I was still standing in the same spot while the giant was putting more and more distance between us.

"All right. Let's do this," I told him, and we headed towards the imposing double doors.

Chapter 4

The double doors were so heavy, I had to use both hands to tug one open. As it got to the halfway point, it let out a wail that sent cold chills down my spine. I pulled the digital recorder out of my pocket and turned it on.

"Double doors squeal like a banshee," I notated, then added, "The air smells musty. Remind the guys to bring face masks." I rolled my eyes at the last part. The guys might put their masks on initially, but as soon as the cameras started rolling, they'd whip them off for the sake of vanity. Brock Daltry and his teammate, Montgomery Snider, never showed up on camera with a hair out of place.

I hadn't met them yet, but I'd watched enough of their show to get a good idea of what they were about. If my convenient stereotyping was wrong, I'd eat my words later, but I just didn't see it happening. Anyone who made cheesy boy band posters of themselves were fair game for pigeonholing.

The doors eased shut behind me with another banshee wail and I found myself in the middle of a decrepit hallway.

The complete darkness gave me an instant sensation of claustrophobia. I turned in a circle, blasting away the shadows with my light to make sure something wasn't lurking behind me. My chest constricted and a vein began pulsing in my neck. The darkness felt carnal and palpable, as though I'd been dropped into a vat of tar. I didn't like it one bit. I wasn't sure where the giant had disappeared to, but he was long gone. I beamed the light to the end of the hallway but didn't see him. It made me more than a little uneasy to know I was standing there all alone. Wasn't he supposed to be leading me through?

I took a deep breath and tried to still my nerves.

"Nothing's going to get you, Shelby," I told myself and tried to focus on what was in front of me.

The hallway was long and wide with doorways on either side. It reminded me a lot of a hospital, providing you removed the gleaming white tiles and replaced them with something resembling the scum you found in your sink drain after washing dishes.

"Apparently, the marble floors are only in the lobby," I said to myself. Patients' families would see the pretty lobby and assume the rest of the facility was just as nice. The patients themselves would be in for a big surprise once those double doors wailed shut behind them. Gone was the carefully presented façade. In its place was something altogether different.

I directed my light into an open doorway. The window had been boarded up from the outside, preventing daylight from trespassing into the building. Even though it was only two o'clock in the afternoon, it was as black as midnight inside. I couldn't even see a crack of daylight around the edges of the boards.

I caught swatches of details as the light trailed over them. I saw a bare metal hospital bed pushed up against a wall. Piles of debris littered the floor. I recognized a few items, like a crusty metal bedpan and an old meal tray, but the rest was too broken and dirty to identify. I pointed the light upwards and could see portions of the ceiling missing. I fished out my recorder again.

"Tell the guys to be careful walking on the second floor," I said. If the ceiling on the first floor was crumbling, the floor above it was probably rotten too.

Fugly had been hanging close to my ankles but ventured further into the room to give the bedpan a quick sniff. I reeled him in before he could pee on it, his way of marking his territory.

"Nothing in here belongs to you. Get that straight now," I told him. If this place was haunted, the last thing I wanted to do was anger the ghosts by letting my dog urinate on one of their belongings.

Thoughts of the giant propelled me out of the room. For all I knew, he had given up on me and was relocking the front doors behind him. As I turned to leave, I heard a crash behind me. The sound rang out, piercing the silence. It sounded like something metal hitting a hard surface.

I jolted back around, swinging my flashlight out in front of me, a small scream ready to explode from my chest. The metal bedpan was now halfway across the room, sitting on a pile of soggy debris.

"Oh my God," I gasped, my heart thumping wildly.

Fugly strained against his leash, his nose going a mile a minute. A low growl rumbled in his chest.

What had moved the bedpan? I flashed the light all around the room to make sure some prankster wasn't hiding in the corner, but found the room to be as empty as it was before.

"Is somebody here?" I asked, my voice sounding small and frightened.

I looked around, inspecting the shadowed corners for movement, but nothing budged. Was something lurking there, invisible to my eyes? The thought was appropriately creepy. It was enough to make me break out in goosebumps. I could almost feel hostile eyes glaring at me, even though I couldn't see them. Something definitely didn't want me in its room.

I didn't waste any more time looking. I took it as a sign I needed to get out of there. I might not be brave, but it didn't mean I was stupid.

"Let's get out of here," I told Fugly, who seemed to agree. We hightailed it down the hallway in pursuit of the giant without even glancing into any of the other rooms. As we passed another room, something else clattered, making me wonder if bedpans were exploding in all the rooms in our wake.

The hallway seemed to go on forever. I turned and beamed the light behind us, seeing an equally long distance. By the time I made it to the end, I was thoroughly rattled. Small sounds seemed to emanate from the darkness around me. They were nothing more than little pops and ticks, possibly originating from mice or insects, but my mind couldn't make the connection. I kept thinking about the bedpan in the first room.

In between my hasty steps, I pulled the recorder out of my pocket again and noted the location of the room, in case the guys wanted to set a camera up there. Chances were strong it wouldn't happen again, especially on camera, but it was something they'd probably want to know about.

There was a stairway at the end of the hallway on the other side of another set of swinging doors. I let them fall shut behind us and stood quietly to see if I could hear the giant. More than likely, he went upstairs, but I couldn't be sure. If I went upstairs and he was downstairs, I might never find him.

I thought about calling out for him, but didn't know his name. I didn't think he'd take kindly to the nickname I'd given him. If I called out, "Yoo-hoo, Mr. Giant?" he might just leave me there to fend for myself. After several long seconds, where I was sure something was going to reach out and grab me, I heard a faint noise above me.

"Alright, let's go upstairs," I told my dog.

The staircase was industrial and metal, painted so many times it had a gummy texture. Black rubber treads covered the steps, worn down in places by thousands of footsteps. To the left was a metal handrail bolted into the wall, running the length of the stairs. I made sure to grasp onto it tightly, trying not to think of all the germs and diseases it had absorbed over the years. We took the stairs slowly, every step creaking and groaning as though it might break loose at any moment. The last thing I wanted to do was take an abrupt trip to the basement.

The first flight of stairs ended at a small landing. I had to make a U-turn to continue going up the next flight. It was the kind of staircase you could look down and see all the flights lined up beneath you. For the sake of curiosity, I leaned over the railing and directed my light through the crack. All I could see was a procession of rails leading to a bottomless pit of darkness. Just thinking about what was down there gave me a shiver. If the giant gave me a tour of the basement, I was going to hang onto his shirt-tail for the duration, no matter how bad he smelled.

As I started up the second flight, I could see daylight filtering through a door at the top of the stairs. I had forgotten that the second, third and fourth floors had open-air verandas. A sense of relief washed through me. I wasn't a fan of total darkness, to the point where I always slept with a nightlight. Being in a dark, haunted mental hospital sent my anxiety into overdrive.

The staircase opened up to another long hallway filled with doorways, similar to the first floor. Glorious daylight flooded through the windows, washing the debris-strewn floor with golden light. A rusty metal pipe ran the length of the ceiling, frequently interspaced with equally rusted sprinkler heads. Large portions of the plaster ceiling were missing, exposing rotten gray wood and dark spaces where the shadows bred freely.

Some of the doorways still sported brown metal doors with glass windows. As I looked down the line, I could only see one window that still retained its glass. The rest were broken out, some of the glass still littering the floor around them. The remaining doors balanced on precarious hinges, some of them sitting at odd angles with a hope and a prayer.

I pulled my cell phone out of my pocket and took a few pictures so the guys could see the layout. Beezer instructed me to always take a series of three pictures in a row. If I caught something paranormal in one of them, I'd have two other photos to compare it to. If the anomaly showed up in all three then it probably wasn't paranormal, but if it was only in one or two of the photos, it could be something they'd want to see.

I found myself instantly relaxing. Even though I knew I was probably surrounded by a crowd of ghosts, at least I wasn't doing it in total darkness. Instead of racing to the end of the hallway, I found myself slowing down a bit to inspect several of the rooms.

The first room I came to was similar to the one on the first floor with the exception of the veranda. I walked through the room, taking in the stark details. The room was void of furniture, but the floors were littered with the same amount of dirt and debris as the other room. Everything seemed to be cast in the same dingy color, a shade caught between off-white and grayish- brown. It was the color of neglect, created by dirt, rain and mildew over the course of several decades.

I looked around the room, not seeing any bedpans or dinner trays. All I could see were uncertain mounds of rotten wood and plaster. I picked my way around the piles and stepped out onto the veranda with Fugly glued to my side.

Warmth from the sunshine erased some of the goosebumps blossoming on my arms. I found myself drawn to the open windows along the brick veranda wall. It stretched from one end of the east wing to the other, with rooms opening onto it for easy access. I leaned against the waist high wall and rested my elbows on the nubby concrete ledge.

The view was breathtaking. Miles of trees surrounded the asylum, many of them awash in autumn finery. As I took in the kaleidoscope of red, yellow and orange foliage, I wondered what the patients would have thought of the view. Did it lift their spirits or was it a reminder of a life they left behind? I couldn't imagine being locked up in a place like this, surrounded by beauty you couldn't touch while death slithered around behind you, ready to strike at any moment.

I pried myself away from the window and walked down the veranda. I was no longer in any hurry since it was apparent the giant had gone off and left me. As I got closer to the end, a sense of sadness and longing came over me with a suddenness that left me breathless. The feeling was so profound, it brought tears to my eyes and I had to hold onto the window ledge for support.

What was happening to me?

I wasn't an overly emotional person and it took a lot more than a decrepit old hospital to bring me to tears, but here I was, crying like a baby. It felt as though a cloud of concentrated grief had descended upon me, covering me from head to toe with pure sorrow. I was unable to move, locked in the grips of the emotions. After a few moments, the sensation eased as though the cloud dissipated, leaving me gasping in its wake.

"What the hell was that?" I whispered.

I looked down at Fugly to see if he was also affected. He was staring intently down the veranda at something.

"What do you see, boy?"

He growled, low and deep.

I followed the line of his sight to the end of the veranda. The doorway leading back into the building was caught in the shadows but as my eyes adjusted, I could see something strange.

It was shaped like a man but was completely black.

As I stared, it turned and darted through the doorway.

With my heart pounding in my chest, I tugged on Fugly's leash. The last thing I wanted to do was to follow it, but I really had no choice.

Chapter 5

Adrenaline threaded through my body with spiked thorns, throwing my entire system into high alert. This was, hands down, the scariest thing I'd ever done.

The closest I'd ever been to this level of heightened terror was the time my car broke down at night in a rural area without cell service and I had to walk two miles to find the nearest phone. But even then, I was fearful of things I could actually see, like copperhead snakes or men with hatchets. This was a whole new level of terror.

It forced me to realize the world was a much scarier place than I had ever imagined. Not only were there angry human beings, natural disasters and dangerous animals with sharp teeth, there were also invisible beings out there with evil intentions.

I stopped in my tracks.

So, why was I following it?

It obviously was trying to get away from me, which should have been perfectly okay with me. I could just let it go and try to find the giant. As the thought ping-ponged through the passages of my brain, it must have clicked a switch.

"Good Lord, what am I doing?" I swore under my breath. Why was I pursuing something dark and scary? Was it curiosity? Was I simply attempting to uncover some hidden truth like I did when I was a reporter? I wasn't sure, but I put an immediate stop to it. I wasn't here to investigate the paranormal. I was here to see the layout of the asylum so other crazier people could put their lives on the line.

I turned on my heel and tugged Fugly back to the first doorway I found. We stepped over the threshold and picked our way through the dirt and rubble until we were back in the main hallway again.

I still didn't see hide nor hair of the giant, which was becoming stranger and stranger to me. He had an odd vibe to him, but why would he lead me into the asylum and then just disappear? I stopped again as a sobering thought came to me.

"What if he wasn't real?" I whispered. What if he was a ghost?

The concept began to gain momentum for about two seconds before I remembered the four-wheeler. I was open to a lot of strange notions, but I was pretty sure ghosts didn't operate motorized vehicles.

Or did they?

I closed my eyes and rubbed my hands down my face.

"You are absolutely losing your mind, Shelby Moore." The giant wasn't a ghost. He was a very strange and possibly deranged living human being. Something had changed him from a fresh faced young man into a feral version of himself. It would be easy for me to latch onto the easiest option and claim the asylum did it to him, but I didn't know anything about him besides what I saw on his employee ID. He could have gone through bankruptcy, divorce or any host of other tragedies. Life had a way of whittling people down, stripping away all the layers until you were left with nothing more than bare bones. Maybe this was what his rock bottom looked like.

When I allowed myself the luxury of a pity party, I often circled back to the overall brutality of life. As humans, we fought and clawed our way through adversity just to survive and find some semblance of happiness. All it took was one loose stone to send us back to the bottom of the heap. Maybe this had happened to the giant and he just decided to stay down there where it was safer. It was something I could appreciate. If my rock bottom didn't come with a nagging mother, I'd be tempted too.

I continued down the hallway, occasionally glancing into the rooms as I passed them. The bland uniformity made me sad. Every room was exactly the same. They were nothing more than square boxes with windows, and in the case of the rooms to my right, verandas.

The verandas were used for patients who still retained promise. Because they knew so little about tuberculosis, they thought the fresh air provided relief and possible treatment. Patients would be left outside, regardless of the weather. If it was cold, the patients were given heated blankets. If it was hot, they were provided with fans. Once their conditions deteriorated and it became clear they were on death's doorstep, they were moved across the hallway to the rooms without verandas.

I had to wonder how it must have felt to them. Did they go kicking and screaming, or were they already so weakened by their condition they didn't even notice?

I walked into one of the rooms on the left and looked around. It had been almost forty years since the last patient slept there, but the room had a certain feel to it. I imagined an old woman sitting in a rocking chair in the corner, working on cross-stitch while another patient down the hallway moaned. I could envision her so clearly in my mind's eye, I could see the pattern on the cloth in her lap. It was tiny lavender flowers in a bed of greenery. Home Sweet Home was printed on the fabric, but she hadn't gotten to it yet. She planned to fill it in with pink instead of blue, like the directions called for. Very suddenly, I caught a strong whiff of cheap perfume. It was so robust, it stung my nasal cavities.

The experience was so surreal and startling, I wanted to bolt. Was I actually feeling the presence of a ghost or was my imagination taking the wheel?

I pressed my eyes tightly shut, willing the smells and the images to dissolve. When I opened them again, I found myself looking at the empty room. There was no evidence a rocking chair had ever been in the corner, but I would have bet my life it had been there decades ago.

I looked down at Fugly to see what he was doing.

"See anything, boy?"

His nose was tipped upwards as he sniffed for something. After a few seconds, he looked up at me and whined.

"All right. Let's get out of here and go find the giant."

We walked out of the room and made our way to the end of the hallway. As my heartrate returned to some semblance of normal, I was able to look around and absorb some of the details. The walls were crumbling and faded, making it difficult to determine their original color. If someone put a gun to my head and forced me to pick one, I would have said, "white," because the paint was cheaper and easier to bleach. Oddly, I didn't see any graffiti.

From my online research, I knew the asylum was often frequented by trespassers. Kids who were looking for a thrill would sneak in at night and wander the hallways. I saw some of their photos posted online and most of them looked like the kind of punk kids who would bring cans full of spray paint to tag the walls. So far I hadn't seen even one mark.

If I hadn't seen their photos online, I would have thought the security at the asylum was keeping them out. So, what stopped them?

I looked around, feeling as though eyes were boring into the back of my head. Did trespassers feel the same sensation?

Several people reported seeing misty shapes and phantom shadows. It made sense to me. If enough light drifted through the verandas and painted the main hallway with moonlight, a moving shadow would be apparent. I certainly wasn't sticking around long enough to find out for myself, but the thought gave me a fresh dose of goosebumps.

Another thread talked about a crawler. According to the article, people would often see something crawling along the ceiling at the end of the hallway. It was shaped like a human, but maneuvered itself in ways a human was never intended to move. Its arms and legs moved in a crab-like manner, scurrying across the walls and ceilings like an oversized insect. Once you spotted it, it would fly towards you and drop to the ground directly in front of you. As you opened your mouth to scream, it would lunge right at you, disappearing the second it would have knocked you to the ground.

Some people wondered if the crawler was a demon, capable of possessing people and making them do unspeakable things. If it didn't sweep right through you, it might stay for a while and take up residency. One person reported being in the asylum with her boyfriend when the crawler appeared. After it ran towards them, her boyfriend began acting strangely, swinging his arms at anyone who attempted to lead him outside. It took them hours, but once they finally lured him outside, he had no recollection of the entire evening.

The thought made me glance upwards at the ceiling. If I ever witnessed one of those, it might be the last thing I ever saw. If I didn't have a heart attack and die on the spot, I would break land-speed records finding my way to the front door.

"You better hope we don't see the crawler because if we do, you're on your own," I told my dog.

He didn't even look up this time. His attention was fixated on the end of the hallway. He was ready to go and I didn't blame him. The asylum had four floors, but I wasn't willing to search the entire building for him. If we didn't find him on the third floor, then we were leaving. I'd go back to my hotel room and start writing notes about the layout and then make plans to visit the library and historical society the following day.

The hallway ended at another staircase similar to the last one. I stood for a moment and listened, but couldn't hear any tell-tale sounds from my missing tour guide.

A cold gust of wind blasted through the veranda, sending my long auburn curls into my face. I put my back to the wind and pulled my light denim jacket tightly around myself, wishing I'd lost those five pounds so I could actually button it. As soon as the wind died down, I turned back to face the hallway.

"All right, Fugs, let's check out the third floor," I told him, silently praying we wouldn't encounter any levitating bedpans or shadow people.

Fugly gave his tail a wag or two, letting me know he was supporting my decision but wasn't optimistic about the prospects. He was being abnormally submissive, allowing me to lead him around. Normally, he'd be straining at the end of the lead, trying to dictate the direction we were going to pursue. The fact that he was letting me make the decisions was appropriately telling. He didn't like this any more than I did.

We climbed the stairs to the third floor. The rooms were laid out similar to the other two floors, but stopped towards the end. The rest of the floor was open, as though to allow for large groups of people to congregate.

"I wonder if this was the dining hall." As I spoke the words, I could imagine people sitting at tables. Some were eating, while others were playing board games and hands of cards. Music played in the background, originating from an old piano in the corner where an older man grinned as he pounded out song after song. Before the images could fully form, I tugged on Fugly's leash and led him away.

I've always had an excellent imagination but these visions, or whatever they were, were starting to unnerve me. I needed a hot shower, a greasy cheeseburger and a bottle of wine. I didn't even care if they appeared out of order as long as the wine was still in the equation.

As we hurried down the hallway, we passed a room that was probably the old kitchen. All of the fixtures and equipment were long gone, but the walls were still lined with wooden cabinets, most of them missing their drawers. As I stood there staring, one of the cabinet doors opened.

The movement was so sudden, there was no way it happened by accident. My first inclination was to walk away and pretend it hadn't occurred, but my curiosity got the better of me. I pulled Fugly across the room for a closer look.

Inside the cabinet was a picture, lying face down.

I picked it up and looked at it, a gasp escaping my lips.

It was the woman I saw on the second floor. She was sitting in a rocking chair doing cross-stitch, smiling sweetly at the camera.

Chapter 6

If I were capable of formulating actual words, "Screw the fourth floor," would have come out of my mouth, but I was currently unable to speak. I stared down at the photo in my hand, my breath caught firmly in my chest. I couldn't breathe, I couldn't think, I couldn't talk. All I could do was stare.

The woman looked exactly like I saw her in my mind's eye.

She had short white hair with natural curls and sturdy black glasses. The glasses were too large for her face, making me wonder if someone gave them to her from the Lost and Found bin. Even though she was possibly a ghost, she wasn't frightening in the least. She looked like a sweet old lady who enjoyed her needlepoint. When she lived in her own house, she probably had several overfed cats and a wild bird feeder outside her kitchen window so she could watch the birds while she munched on her Corn Flakes every morning.

I caught the whiff of cheap perfume at the same time my ears began ringing, softly at first and then growing louder. It wasn't the normal tinnitus I sometimes got. This sounded more like static, the sound you hear between radio stations. It seemed to originate from a spot just to my right. I turned to look and saw what looked like a mist forming in the air.

I gasped as my eyes tried to make sense of what I was seeing.

What the hell was that?

The mist was a shade of dark gray that reminded me of storm clouds. It hovered several feet off the ground and blocked out some of the light from the window behind it.

I didn't have to wonder if I was losing my mind this time. Fugly saw it too. He let out a series of barks, hopping on his front legs as he filled the quiet space with his raucous voice. The barks seemed to echo against the walls, returning back with a bombardment of sound. I could almost feel them bounce around me, multiplying with every rebound until it sounded like a kennel full of dogs barking instead of just one.

As I watched, dumbstruck with fear, the mist began to condense tighter. It rolled in on itself, spinning and looping until it began to take the shape of a human being. A long torso separated at the sides, growing arms and then fingers. One of the arms reached out, as if to touch me, and I regained my ability to move.

With a scream lodged in my throat, I yanked Fugly backwards, nearly pulling him off his feet, and stumbled towards the kitchen doorway. By the time I crossed the threshold, the mist was almost gone. I wasn't going to wait and see what happened next. I gave it one more glance over my shoulder and raced down the hallway.

What was happening to me? Why was suddenly seeing so many ghosts? Was it the location or was it me? Thoughts rattled around inside my head like broken machinery.

The doorways swished by me in a blur. Fugly raced along beside me, barking gleefully. I probably should have taken comfort from his happiness because he wouldn't bark like that if he felt he was in danger. But it was impossible to alter my mental course halfway through the process of running for my life.

By the time I reached the staircase, the ringing sound was gone but my heart rate was still in the red zone. I paused at the staircase to catch my breath before I collapsed.

I pressed my back to the cold concrete wall and stared down the hallway. Daylight streamed through the veranda windows, painting bright stripes on the floor. Particles of dust floated through the air, twinkling like fairy dust as they passed through the fingers of light. I watched the hallway for a full minute, but nothing materialized in any of the doorways and the ceiling was void of crawlers.

What had I gotten myself into?

It was evident the building was crawling with ghosts. For all I knew, twenty of them were standing in a circle around me, dreaming up new and exciting ways to make me pee my pants. Why would someone willingly spend time here? All I could think about was getting out and never returning. The images already lodged into my brain would disrupt my sleep for months. Every time I closed my eyes the nightmares would assault me.

Was this what happened to the giant? Was he allured by the history and the hauntings? Was he curious about life after death? If he was interested in the paranormal, he'd have an entire asylum to explore. It wasn't something I'd ever do, but I could understand someone willingly diving through the rabbit hole. Was this what transformed him from a clean-shaven young man to a shaggy monster?

I wasn't sure about any of it, but one thing was for certain. I was ready to get the hell out of Dodge.

My breathing was still coming in long pulls, but the need to leave was becoming stronger than my desire to breathe.

"Let's get out of here," I told my dog, who sat looking up at me expectantly. Sometimes I thought he understood every word I spoke to him, but other times I think he was just waiting for the words "treaty-treats" to appear. Fugly would do anything for a dog biscuit.

"If you hurry, I think there's a treaty-treat in the Jeep for you," I said and he nearly pulled my arm off in his haste to get to the stairwell.

I cleared all three floors quickly without looking down the hallways once. I had seen more than enough and didn't want to witness anything else. Unlike the team of investigators who would soon explore the building, I had zero curiosity about what lurked in the dark corners and hallways of the asylum. If I never saw another ghost again for the rest of my life, that would be fine with me.

There were far easier ways to get my questions answered. I could read about them or interview paranormal investigators and psychic mediums. I didn't need to hang out in an insanely haunted asylum full of crazy dead people to get that information.

By the time I got back down to the first floor, my breathing was back under control and my heart rate was giving it a good effort. I still had the massive Maglite gripped in my hand, so I turned it on, allowing it to fill the dark landing with light.

I'd forgotten how pitch-black the first floor was. If I had to guess, I'd say they boarded up the first floor to prevent vandals from having easy access to the building. It certainly didn't do anything for the ambiance, unless creepy and spooky was the goal.

As soon as I stepped into the hallway, I felt as though I was being watched. The sensation was so powerful; it felt as though a group of people emerged from their rooms to glare at me. I pointed my light into the nearest doorway, but thankfully didn't see anything. I wasn't sure my heart could take another misty ghost.

"I'm leaving. Just let me pass," I told them, feeling foolish for talking to things I couldn't see.

As I walked, I beamed the light into the rooms I passed, just in case something was skulking in the shadows, getting ready to jump out and grab me. Most of the rooms were empty, with the exception of rubble and debris from decades of neglect. Old broken boards were wedged into mounds of dusty plaster. The smell of rot and dust assaulted my nose, giving me the urge to sneeze. I pressed a finger to my nose to ward off a sneeze and, once again, wished for a face mask. In one corner there was a pile of moldy fabric from bedsheets or curtains. I continued on, glancing into the rooms I passed. Occasionally, my light flickered on bits of reflective metal that could have been bedpans or mattress springs. Nothing moved or made any noises this time, which I took as a good sign.

It was hard to comprehend how the rooms must have once looked. There would have been hospital beds, which I did see in a few of the rooms, but they would have had other furniture as well. I lingered at one of the doorways a little longer than necessary, trying to mentally outfit the room. Surely there would have been an arm chair and some sort of table. I wasn't sure about the technology of the day, but there might have been an IV stand or some other sort of medical equipment.

Would they have hung pictures on the walls or put plants in the windowsills? It was so far removed from its early days, it was impossible to determine. What it was now had nothing to do with what it once was. A part of me was relieved they were tearing it down. Maybe it would release some of the memories and the ghosts that haunted it.

I wasn't certain how the paranormal world worked, but there must be layers to the haunting here. Were the ghosts of the asylum sitting side-by-side with the tuberculosis patients? And what about the nursing home ghosts? Several of the online articles suggested the nursing home patients weren't well cared for. The elderly were often left in soiled garments for days, provided with only the bare necessities to keep them alive. After a reporter snuck in with a camera, it ended fairly quickly. The nursing home closed, the windows were shuttered and the ghosts were left to their own devices. I couldn't imagine the horrors they must have lived through. I didn't blame them one bit for haunting the shit out of the place.

I pulled myself away from the doorway and headed back down the hallway. I had nearly forgotten about the giant during all the commotion.

Where the hell had he gone?

Unless he went up to the fourth floor and was up there waiting for me, he had vanished. As soon as I got outside, I was planning to call Beezer to complain. What he did wasn't cool. The building was dangerous and I could have suffered any number of tragedies inside of it. I could have really used his help in navigating through the dangers and understanding the layout of the rooms. As it was, I'd have to give the guys a fairly flimsy report.

I reached the end of the hall and was ready to push through the double doors when something caught my eye in the room to my right, where the bedpan had moved. If I could have short-circuited my natural reaction to look, I would have ignored it completely, but I couldn't help it. I stopped short and squinted into the room.

A flashlight sat in the middle of the floor with its bright beam of light pointing at the far wall. I directed my own light onto it and was shocked to see it was the same model I was using. It must be the giant's.

"What's that doing here?" I whispered to myself.

If I wasn't in a haunted asylum full of creepy, crazy happenings, I would have walked into the room for a better look, but I was apprehensive after my last experience. I wasn't sure if ghosts set traps for the living, but I wasn't taking any chances. I've watched way too many horror movies to know not to go into the scary room.

I stared at it for another fifteen seconds or so before I just shrugged my shoulders and started to turn away. At that precise moment, the flashlight did a slow spin.

It swiveled all the way around until it was pointing directly at me.

"Oh my God!" I gasped as Fugly went into a frenzy. He lunged forward on his leash, teeth bared and snapping, like he was trying to fend off something I couldn't see.

That was enough for me. I was about twenty steps away from the entrance. All I needed to do was to push through the double doors, bolt through the lobby and I was home free.

I yanked Fugly out of the room and hit the doors hard. They let out their banshee wail, but I hardly noticed it as I sprinted across the lobby with my flashlight bobbing at my side. Halfway across the room, I ran into something. It swayed as I collided with it.

My hands groped out in front of me, feeling something solid. The flashlight picked out details that didn't make sense. Worn work boots with leather laces, frayed cuffs on denim jeans. My God. It looked like a man…

I scrambled backwards and beamed my light upward.

Hanging from the grand chandelier on the ceiling was a rope. Hanging from the end of the rope was the giant.

Judging by the color of his face, he was long gone.

I did two things simultaneously: I screamed and I ran.

Chapter 7

I've never been good in emergencies. My mother was the complete opposite. She jumped into action, immediately making priority lists in her mind. Whether it was a car accident or a pot of spaghetti boiling over on the stove, she knew what to do and got to work, making it look far easier than it really was. I tended to just stand there and panic like a blubbering idiot.

I somehow managed to make it to the front door. Daylight stung my eyes as I stumbled out. It seemed brighter than normal, reminding me it was only mid-afternoon. An airplane painted a long contrail across the deep blue sky and in the distance, I could hear trucks rumbling on the highway, like it was just a normal day.

It felt wrong that everything else in the world was still functioning. Somewhere out there, children pushed each other on swing sets, while dogs hiked their legs on trees. People told jokes at the office as Canadian geese migrated to warmer climates overhead. It seemed like the world should have taken a moment to acknowledge what just happened. I felt my knees buckle as I came down the steps. I wanted to fall to the ground and scream "Stop!" so everyone would know.

My mind was on the brink of shutting down. All I could see was the giant's body swaying back and forth after I ran into it. My hands began shaking so hard, I nearly dropped Fugly's leash.

He was dead.

How the hell did that happen?

He was with me one minute and then gone the next.

I felt a sense of guilt wash over me. I'd been so angry he abandoned me. It never occurred to me something might have happened to him.

My mind spun with the implications. The ceiling was at least fifteen or twenty feet tall and there wasn't a ladder standing beside the body. It couldn't have been a suicide. I turned and stared at the doors to the asylum.

Was someone inside? Or did the ghosts do it?

The thought propelled me forward. Either way, I didn't want to be standing all by myself in front of the doors leading to his body.

I shoved my hand in my pocket and grabbed my keys.

Fugly was pulling on the leash, trying to drag me back to my Jeep, which was fine by me. I even fished my cell phone out of my pocket for good measure. There was nothing wrong with sitting in a running vehicle while I called 911.

As soon as I hung up with the police, I put a call into Beezer. His reaction wasn't what I had expected. If I had anticipated him being horrified and sympathetic, I was mistaken.

"Go back in there with your digital recorder, stand by his dead body and see if you can get an EVP," he instructed me.

I nearly came unglued. There was no way, absolutely zero chance, I was going back inside the building to stand next to a dead body and record the air, hoping for a ghost voice to be caught on my recorder.

"Not happening." I closed my eyes and rested my head on the headrest.

"That's what we pay you for…" he started, but I was quick to correct him.

"You pay me to scout out locations and do research. You don't pay me to disrupt a possible crime scene." My mind flashed to the visions I'd just witnessed. Someone or something lifted him up there. If his soul was somehow still lingering in the area, I wasn't going to disrespect it by trying to get it to talk to me.

"Fair enough, but at least go to the door and turn your recorder on. You don't even have to stand there. Just turn it on and leave it by the door," he told me.

I paused, still not convinced. It would take a lot to get me to leave the relative safety of my Jeep.

"Think of his family. If he comes through with a message for them, they'd want to know, right?" he said.

Ugh... I opened my eyes again and stared at the front of the building.

"Just run up, set your recorder on the ground and run back to your car. I'll wait while you do it."

Every horror movie I've ever watched ends badly when the heroine makes a shitty decision. I was certainly no one's idea of a heroine. I was barely a functioning human being. I would have gladly handed the reigns over to someone else, but I was all there was. Before I could think it through and talk myself out of it, I jumped out of my Jeep and ran back to the steps. I tossed my recorder onto the landing by the door and darted back to my vehicle.

"Done," I told him through gritted teeth.

"Good. Now, just run up and retrieve it again when you hear the police coming. You don't want them to see it," he said, completely sending me off the deep end.

"Beezer! They're going to be here any minute! You sent me back up there for nothing. What if someone is still inside there? What if they open the door and grab me when I get close?"

If he had a response, I didn't want to hear it. I hung up on him and then sat with my hands on my steering wheel and my eyes glued on the front doors in case something came busting out of them. If I saw the door budge even a fraction, I was out of there.

My phone vibrated and I glanced down to see I'd gotten a text message from Beezer.

The guys were coming early. They were catching the next flight out.

"Awesome." If I had it my way, I'd be on the road back home before they got here. The last thing I wanted was to hang out with Brock Daltry and his band of merry boneheads. I could just see them, running around with their paranormal equipment, trying to get a fresh EVP from a dead body, not thinking about the tragedy.

I wasn't necessarily a squeamish person, but my experience with dead bodies was fairly limited. I remember going to a funeral when I was a child, but the only true experience I'd had with death came after my father passed away seven years ago.

I'd always been close to my father. He always smelled like Aqua Velva and Juicy Fruit gum from the pack in his shirt pocket. He was tall and handsome with warm eyes and an easy smile. I always told him I was going to marry a man just like him when I grew up. I would hang out in his garage, handing him tools as he worked on his classic Shelby Cobra, the vehicle I was named after. We'd chat about everything and anything. Everyone loved him. People would show up at our door to talk with him and seek his opinion on anything automotive.

After I grew up and left home, I still came by to visit on occasion, but life tended to get in the way. My long hours at work left me drained. It was all I could do to fix myself dinner and camp out on the sofa until it was time to repeat the process all over again. It had been several weeks since I'd seen him, so I stopped by their house after work one day. As I came through the garage door, a flippant quip on my tongue, I found him collapsed on the floor, dead from a heart attack. His body was still warm, but there was no reviving him. I ran inside and got my mother, who jumped into action and called an ambulance.

The memory was a feast for my insomnia. I felt a tremendous deluge of guilt over his death. If I hadn't stopped for gas on the way over, I might have gotten there in time to save him. If I'd taken the CPR class down at the YMCA my mother told me about, I might have known what to do. Then, when I was finished examining those anxiety provoking thoughts, I worried I hadn't been a very good daughter. I didn't stop by to see him often enough, letting the gaps of time grow longer and longer until there weren't any opportunities left. Seeing the giant's dead body brought it all back.

I wiped away a stray tear, wondering if the grief belonged to my father or to a man I'd just met.

I heard a car on the gravel road, so I hopped out and retrieved my digital recorder before they could see it. Nothing happened to me as I snatched it off the stairs and I was back inside my Jeep before the first police car rounded the corner of the building. I tucked it in my pocket and swore at myself for being so damned compliant. One of these days, I needed to stand up to pushy people and just tell them no.

The policeman who came to my window was a cookie cutter image of every cop I'd ever met. He was young with a buzz cut, khaki uniform and serious eyes. I gave him a brief synopsis of what had happened to me and pointed at the door. There was no way I was going back in there.

He had his hand on his holstered gun as he opened the door to the asylum and disappeared inside. Minutes later, several other police cars pulled up and joined him inside. They came out several times to ask me questions, but I had no idea what they were doing and no desire to find out. All I wanted to do was hit the road and head back to my mother's house. She could nag me all she wanted. It seemed a small price to pay for security.

I was already making mental lists of the things I would do when I got home, starting with a huge glass of wine and ending with crawling into my bed in the basement with my dog snuggled up beside me, when one of the cops approached my window and completely blew my plans.

"We'll need you to come down to the station in the morning to make a formal statement," he said.

I sighed. It looked like I'd have at least one more night in hell.

Chapter 8

Beezer booked a room for me at the Happy Hollow Lodge not far from the asylum. As I pulled up in the circular driveway and got a good look at the 1960s-style motor lodge, I groaned. There was nothing happy about it and the only hollow I could see was the mud puddle in front of the office door.

The motor lodge consisted of a long wooden building with doors on it. Someone had attempted to give it a rustic appearance by nailing wooden planks along the front, but it didn't fool me for a second. I'd been in enough of those to know the interior layout and it didn't bode well with my current mental state. I needed more than a room with a bed and an attached bathroom. I needed space to pace back and forth and a nice view of something beautiful to soothe my soul. This definitely wasn't cutting it. I killed the engine and grabbed my purse off the floorboard.

"Stay here!" I told Fugly, who showed me several teeth.

Fugly hated being left in the car. "Be good and I'll give you a treat," I added for good measure. He lowered his lip ever so slightly and wagged the tip of his tail, which meant I could count on five minutes tops. Any longer than and I might come back to discover my steering wheel chewed to a stub.

I rolled both of the windows down to the halfway mark, to give him a little air, and found my way around the mud puddle to the office.

A blast of arctic air hit me as soon as I opened the door. Even though it was only in the mid-sixties outside, the little window air conditioner was chugging along at full steam. I pulled my jacket tighter around me as I walked up to the counter.

The room was covered in dark walnut paneling, the kind you often find in homes last modified in the 70s era. Cheap wildlife photos hung on the wall with a few taxidermy fish on boards thrown in to break up the monotony. The room smelled like floral carpet powder and moth balls for an added touch of nostalgia.

If I was expecting an elderly woman to part through the beaded curtain separating the office from the back room, I couldn't have been more surprised. The woman who greeted me looked like she stepped out of a gypsy limbo contest.

She had long dark hair and equally dark eyes flashing with mischief. She wore enough bangles and dangly jewelry to properly weigh her down if she ever decided to walk on the moon, complemented by a bright teal shirt and a tie-died hippy skirt that brushed her bare ankles. I would have bet money she also wore toe rings and an ankle bracelet, but I couldn't see that far down without leaning over the counter, which probably would have come off as rude.

"My name is Sonora," she said with a laugh, as though she were reading my thoughts. "How can I help you?"

Any harsh comments I might have had about the ambiance of the lodge disappeared as fast as a cat under a sprinkler. It was all I could do not to gawk at her. The reporter in me wanted to start pelting her with questions, starting with why someone like her was working at a place like this.

Before I could even open my mouth, she leaned around me and peered out the window.

"You should bring your doggy inside before he tears up your Jeep."

I swiveled around to see Fugly hanging from the window visor.

For other, more compliant dogs, all I would have to do is whistle out the door and they might jump from the open window and run to my side, but not Fugly. He demanded the full royal treatment.

With a groan, I walked outside and opened the door for him.

"You are being summoned inside, your majesty," I told him. He glared at me from under his scruffy fringe of hair and then hopped out, making sure to spray my front tire with another long stream of steaming urine. It was no wonder my Jeep always had a slightly funky smell to it. Between his flea-bitten hind-end on the passenger seat and his pee on my tires, it was a wonder it didn't reek to high heaven, making me question what I smelled like after sitting in it half the day.

"All right. Let's go," I told him and started walking towards the office door, hoping he was behind me. Usually, he was good and kept me within eyesight, but all bets were off if a random squirrel made an appearance.

Sonora opened the door for us, giving me full view of her bare ankles and feet, which were adorned with jewelry, as suspected. Fugly brushed past her and began an earnest inspection of the lobby.

"We are dog friendly, so he's more than welcome here. Are you checking in?"

I glanced out the window at the row of rooms. The grimace on my face must have been epic because she laughed.

"I can upgrade you. No worries. We have a cabin on the lake that just became available. Shall I transfer your reservation?"

Kinder words have never been spoken and they came at the perfect time. I was five seconds away from full combustion. Thoughts of a cabin on a lake was the perfect diffuser.

"Yes, please," I cooed. I slid my driver's license and credit card across the counter. Beezer would be taking care of my lodging, but a credit card was required for incidentals. Knowing my dog, I'd probably hit my credit limit fairly quickly. He's been known to eat an entire sofa in under an hour.

After she entered all the information into the computer, she handed me a key and then surprised me by coming around the corner. She knelt down and began giving Fugly a proper rub-down, one he relished thoroughly. He plopped down on the worn linoleum floor and rolled onto his back, giving her easy access to his belly. As she found his favorite spot, his back leg began thumping and his eyes rolled back into his head in delirium.

"If I were being polite, I'd tell you he's a sweet dog, but I think we'd both know I was lying. He most definitely has sweet moments, but his aura tells a different story. I believe he must have been royalty in a past life."

Before I could even react to what she said, she stood up and smiled at me.

"I'm off work now, so why don't I show you to your cabin? It's right beside mine." She flipped the sign on the door to the closed side and followed me out onto the sidewalk.

She stood with Fugly while I retrieved my bag from the Jeep. I snuck a glance in her direction, trying to figure her out. If she read auras, she definitely had Fugly's all wrong. His would be like Pigpen's from the Charlie Brown comics, with flies swarming around it in a cloud. The thought made me laugh and it felt good.

As I followed her, I realized I hadn't thought about my horrific experience at the asylum once in the past ten minutes. I wish I could have bottled her essence so I could huff it when life got all snarly.

She led me around the corner of the building to a slate footpath. It trailed around the back of the building to a set of concrete stairs that wound down a steep hill. Wildflowers and succulents covered the hill, with several stone angel statues peeking above the fading foliage. The contrast between the front of the building and the back were so dramatic, I felt as though I'd been transported to another realm.

"This is really pretty," I told her as she glided down the stairs ahead of me.

She turned to flash me a smile.

"Yes. I felt it needed a touch of serenity. It used to be nothing but weeds and briars. My uncle let me plant the flowers and add the angels. I wanted to put an alter at the bottom of the hill but he was afraid his guests wouldn't understand," she said.

I nearly tripped on the next stair. "Alter?"

My mind kicked into high gear, envisioning a stone slab where human sacrifices were offered to dark gods, when she stopped me short.

"I'm Wiccan. We have alters to honor the God and Goddess," she said with a smile in her voice. "I'm sure you've heard about us evil Wiccans before. Some people confuse our religion with darker witchcraft or even Satanism, but I can assure you nothing is further from the truth. We worship nature and all she provides. I have a book I can loan you, if you're interested."

Growing up in southern Indiana hadn't fully prepared me for the true diversity of the world outside our comfort zone. I lived in a world where country music and shopping malls were the norm; where fire pits were in nearly every back yard and drive-in movie theaters were still a thing. I grew up with summer Bible School and a lit porch light that was the signal to come inside at night. I had heard about Wicca but had tucked it into a category that also included flat-earthers, Bigfoot hunters and astrology freaks. Perhaps it was time to expand my comfort zone.

"Sure. I'd love to read it," I said as we got to the bottom of the hill. We stepped through an open gate flanked by tall hedges and I got my first look at the cabin and the lake beyond it.

The lake was bigger than I expected. I could barely see the other side of it. All along the banks, cabins were perched on stilts, keeping them high above the water. As I watched, a speed boat zoomed across the deep green surface with a water-skier in tow dressed in a tiny bikini, despite the chilliness of the day. She managed to wave as she saw us without falling on her face, which I took as a very good sign.

Sonora led me around the side of the cabin where a flight of wooden steps led to the living quarters. There was a shadowed porch beneath it, complete with a wooden porch swing and a table that could easily hold a beer. I was in heaven.

"I think you'll like this much more than the motor-lodge units. Hopefully, your boss doesn't protest over the extra expenses," she said, making me raise an eyebrow.

"How did you know my boss was paying for this?"

She gave me a secretive smile. "I know a lot about you, Shelby Moore. Your aura really gives you away," she said before turning to climb the stairs to my cabin.

I stared at the back of her retreating form, my mind spinning like a cow in a tornado. My life was just getting weirder and weirder.

Crazy Dead People

Chapter 9

The cabin was exactly what I needed. The door opened to reveal a casual living room with a kitchen on the other side. Behind it, on the back half of the house, was a roomy bathroom, flanked by two small bedrooms.

I walked to the wall of sliding glass doors on the front of the cabin and admired the view. There were comfortable lounging chairs and a round table on the deck, which would provide me with the perfect place to unwind and work, once I got to that point.

Fugly pressed his nose to the floor, sniffing every nook and cranny before he was ready to settle down. I had to wonder what he discovered during his investigations. Collie dog peed here? Small child with a dirty diaper sat here? Salad dressing spilled here? When he went into reconnaissance mode, I tended to watch where he spent the most time sniffing and made it a point not to sit there. Being the nasty dog he was, he tended to prefer the smelliest spots.

"I think you'll be comfortable here," Sonora said, her eyes gazing out the window at the picture perfect view of the lake.

"I'm sure I will." I sat my bag down beside the massive leather sofa and followed the line of her gaze out the window. I've always found water to be soothing and I needed an ocean full of it at the moment.

As though sensing my exhaustion, Sonora pulled herself away from the window and walked to the door.

"I'll leave you to rest. Perhaps you'll join me later for a glass of wine?"

I plopped down on the couch, feeling the weight of the world finally land soundly on my shoulders. Chatting with Sonora had been a nice diversion, but reality wasn't something you could hold off for long. It had a way of finding you, no matter how hard you tried to hide from it.

She opened the door but lingered in the entryway. "I can help you, Shelby. I know some of what you're going through. I'm very much like you because I see and hear things others aren't aware of," she said with a small sad smile. And with that, she walked through the door and closed it behind her, leaving me to my overwhelming thoughts.

I stared at the closed door, my mind spinning.

What had she meant? Was she somehow privy to information at the asylum or did it go much deeper?

Back home, there was an old woman in town who professed to speak with the dead. She lived in a rambling old house that was twenty years overdue for a paintjob, with dried herbs and animal pelts hanging from her porch. On her lawn was a wooden sign with an all-seeing eye on it. My mother told me she was a fortune teller.

Some of the women from my mom's beauty salon went to her for advice and remedies. My mother never went, but she often came home from work with stories about women who had utilized her services.

I'd never put much thought into psychic mediums and was fairly certain Althea Blake was a con artist, but I still kept my distance. The woman scared me more than a little bit. As kids, we would cross the street if we had to walk past her house and often held our breath for good measure, reciting prayers we learned at Bible school in our heads.

Was Sonora a psychic medium too?

I leaned my head back on the sofa, wanting to scream, cry and fall into a deep sleep all at once. My mind was so overburdened, I was nearing a meltdown.

What the hell happened?

I had so many unanswered questions. Who was Sonora and what could she help me with? What was going on at the asylum and why had the giant abandoned me so early on in the tour? If I had glued myself to him, would I have also ended up hanging from a chandelier?

The thought gave me head-to-toe chills.

Or would he be okay now? If I hadn't been so preoccupied by the ruination of the asylum, would he be home popping the top on a can of Pabst Blue Ribbon, watching an old rerun of *The Andy Griffith Show*? Or would he be watching the evening news? Or did he even have a television set? Maybe he would be sitting on his back porch, playing with his dog or whittling a piece of wood or dropping a line into a glass-topped lake, hoping for a bite.

I felt the brush of fur against my hand and realized Fugly had finished his explorations. He sat at my feet, looking up at me with sad eyes.

"Come on up," I told him.

He put his paws on the seat beside me and edged up slowly, knowing he really wasn't allowed on the furniture. I often came home and found rawhide bones and dog hair on my bed and couch, so I knew he wasn't always so compliant to my wishes, but he at least made an effort when I was there.

I ruffled his fur, my fingers finding the soft spot behind his ear that felt like satin.

"What did you see back there?" I asked him.

He trained his dark liquid eyes on me, as though he were attempting to transmit his thoughts directly into my brain. A part of me wished I could get inside his head and see the things he saw, but the other part of me was happy for the ignorance. Some things just couldn't be unseen.

I knew animals saw the world differently than we did. They saw a larger portion of the light spectrum which gave them an advantage in low-light situations. Their hearing was also far more advanced than ours, which was why silent dog whistles worked for them but not for us. This made me think about the digital recorder in my pocket.

I really didn't want to listen to it, but I really had no choice. If I was going to get to the bottom of it, I needed more information. Reluctantly, I pulled it out of my pocket and turned it on.

I listened to the last recording first and heard myself swearing as I tossed the recorder onto the steps. It was followed by the sound of my feet crunching in the gravel driveway and then the slam of my Jeep door. Five minutes later, the sounds were repeated as I ran to retrieve it. There was nothing in the middle.

I nearly threw the recorder across the room.

"Damn him!" Beezer was such an idiot. Why had I listened to him?

Fugly laid his head on my lap and looked up at me.

"I know. I need to be tougher. I need to learn how to say no to people." I sighed.

That was the story of my life. I've always been that person who says yes when she really wants to say no, feeling the tug of obligation overpower the need to protect my rights. When I was a girl, I helped a friend from school with her paper route, never asking for a penny in return, even though I ended up doing most of her route for her. As an adult, I became the one who handed out flyers for the local shops, the one who stayed late to work on projects for my boss, and the one who endured one bad relationship after another because I didn't know how to end it without hurting someone's feelings.

Exhaustion hit me with a sudden force, as though every ounce of energy had been drained from my body. I leaned back into the comfort of the couch and closed my eyes, riding the wave until I crashed into oblivion.

Just as I started to fall asleep, I became aware of a ringing sound, similar to what I heard in the asylum when I was in the old lady's room. I wasn't sure what I did with the picture I found of her in the kitchen cupboard. It was possible I dropped it on the floor. Regardless of what happened to it, I saw her very clearly in my mind as she followed me into my dreams.

I pursued her down a dimly lit hallway filled with doorways. I could hear the sound of people moaning in the distance, their voices combining to create a symphony of discontent. We came upon a man slumped over in a wheelchair in the hallway. As we passed him, I could smell a tang of urine radiating from him. He groaned and tried to reach for us, but his arm fell to the side, hanging there with a hopelessness I couldn't fathom.

She touched my arm and latched her long cold fingers around the crook of my elbow, leading me to where she wanted me to go. Although she didn't say a word, I knew she wanted to show me something.

We headed down the hallway. My head felt heavy and my stride was uncertain. All sense of balance had left me. I felt as though I'd aged sixty years in the time it took us to find the doorway she wanted to show me. As we passed the other doors, I caught glimpses of people lying in beds with small reading lamps on the table beside them. Most were sleeping, but several of them met my gaze, the sadness in their eyes needing no explanation.

Finally, we reached the doorway to her room. Instead of the rotten walls and filth covered floor, I saw the room as it had looked when she was a patient there.

The walls were a soft yellow. Framed photos hung unevenly on the walls as though tacked there with a shaky hand. I saw smiling faces in the pictures and wondered if they were her family.

"I don't see them often. I think they forgot about me," she told me.

What could I say? What could I say to make things better? There wasn't anything, so I offered her words of comfort instead.

"I'm sorry. I wouldn't have forgotten about you," I told her.

She released her grip on my arm and patted it.

"I know you wouldn't have, dear. Times were different then. This is what people did. It was how the world worked."

She led me to her bed and showed me a photo album. She flipped through it, smiling at the photos. The images were blurry for me, but I saw enough to know she was reliving memories through them. This was her life, or what was left of it.

"It's here, if you want to look at it," she told me and pointed to the spot beside her bed. "I'd like for you to have it."

She then led me out of the room and back down the hallway to show me other rooms. As I glanced in, I saw more evidence of neglect and abuse. Some patients were strapped to their beds, calling out for help that never came. Others were nearly comatose. As we neared the end of the hallway, I saw an orderly going into a room and we followed him to the doorway.

Inside the room was a dark-haired, disabled woman who appeared much younger than the other residents. She, too, was tied to the bed. She pulled against the straps when she saw him, trying desperately to get away, but it was useless.

"That's Janine," the woman told me. "She was here a long time before me. She had epilepsy, but they didn't understand it back then."

The orderly approached her bed and pulled up her nightgown, revealing her thin body. He reached for her and I turned away, unable to witness what I knew would come next.

"It's okay, dear. It's not something anyone wants to see."

She led me back out of the room to another room at the end of the hallway. The image wavered for a moment as though a transparent sheet were being laid over a projector. The vision of elderly people faded and was replaced with a vision of younger people. The hallways were filled with the sounds of coughing instead of moaning. Inside the room, a doctor in a white coat was leaning over a young woman with light-brown hair. In his hand was something resembling an ice pick. As he leaned over her, his intentions were clear and I'd had enough.

I jolted awake with a start.

"Icepick lobotomy," I whispered, aghast.

I'd read about them but didn't realize the patients were sometimes awake as they happened. What had the woman shown me?

I wasn't sure if it was just a dream or if the woman had actually come to me to give me a tour. I shook my head as if to erase the memories.

With a groan of frustration, I pulled myself up off the couch and found my way to the window. The sun was beginning its descent, nearly touching the water. The sky was the color of a ripe peach, streaked with broad dark paint strokes.

Thoughts of the giant returned to me. I hadn't known him, but it saddened me because he would never see this sunset. My stomach rumbled suddenly, reminding me I hadn't eaten since breakfast.

I glanced back at Fugly, who was eyeing me closely from the couch. He was probably hungry too.

"Let's go find some food," I told him, saying the magic words that propelled him from his resting place.

Chapter 10

As Fugly and I walked down the wooden stairs, I glanced over at the cabin next door. Sonora was sitting on her deck, a glass of burgundy wine in her hand. She looked so relaxed. I don't think I've ever felt so carefree. There were always thoughts to chase and problems to solve. I spent most of my life muddling through the sludge pot of emotions in my head.

She saw me and waved.

"We're going to go get dinner," I called to her.

While I desperately wanted a glass of wine, I knew I needed some food in my stomach first. I also needed to feed my dog, and his bucket of kibble was in the backseat of my Jeep.

"Come on over!" she called back. "I have a casserole coming out of the oven in a few minutes. Bring your dog too!"

It was a hard offer to turn down. If I went out in search of food, I'd be at least forty minutes away from shoveling something into my mouth. By going to Sonora's cabin, I could be eating within minutes. Plus, I might get some answers to some of my questions, starting with her evasive comment as she left.

I ran to my Jeep and grabbed Fugly's food. He wouldn't be happy with kibble when there were people-food smells in the air, but I tried to keep him on his diet. When I caved in to those pleading eyes and gave him some of my food, I was always rewarded later with doggy gas and nasty surprises I always managed to step in with bare feet.

"It's kibble for you, buddy. After the day I've had, I don't think I could handle your stink cloud all night."

He put his nose to the air, ignoring me.

We climbed the stairs to her cabin as a soft breeze blew the scent of dried autumn leaves and mossy lake water in our direction. I glanced off in the distance at the ring of cabins surrounding the tranquil waters of the lake, wondering why I lived where I did when I could live here instead.

Before I could knock, Sonora opened the door, unleashing the most heavenly scent I'd ever witnessed. Fugly wagged his tail in doggy nirvana.

"Come in," she said with a smile, moving back out of the doorway to give us room to pass.

Her cabin was laid out identical to mine with the exception that it had been properly decorated. While mine had the barebones of basic furniture and non-descript paintings on the walls, hers was decked out like a gypsy's dream.

Brightly-colored fringed pillows littered her leather sofa, coordinating with the random vases, lamps and knickknacks scattered around the room. Deep plum drapes hung from the windows and a multi-colored beaded curtain graced the doorway leading to the bedrooms. The paintings on the walls were abstract and colorful, picking up the blues, reds and yellows on the pillows.

An opened book and a teal blue afghan were on the couch, telling a tale of solitude. It reminded me a bit of the daydreams I often had about having my own place. She certainly had the beautiful view to go with it. My sense of wistfulness bloomed a little larger. Sometimes all it took was to see someone else's life to make your own life seem paltry by comparison.

She pulled the casserole from the oven and sat it on the counter.

"I hope you like tuna casserole," she said. "I don't cook much, but this is something my mother always made and it seemed appropriate tonight."

She scooped out massive servings onto dark magenta plates and added slices of garlic bread.

"Wine?" she asked with a knowing smile, already pouring me a glass.

"Like I'd ever say no to wine."

I wasn't typically a big drinker, but there were times when wine washed away the hard edges. This was definitely one of them.

I gave Fugly a bowl of his kibble and he completely ignored it as he continued to stare me down. Sometimes this routine worked and sometimes it didn't. He seemed to forget the failures and focused on the successes instead. I had to admire his optimism, even if it wasn't going to get him very far.

"Eat your food and I'll let you lick my plate afterwards," Sonora told him. Tail thumping, he dug into his bowl with zeal, as though he understood every word she said to him.

"He's a smart boy," she commented, forking a bite of the casserole into her mouth.

"Sometimes he's too smart." It was probably something everyone said about their dogs, but it was true with Fugly. He often felt more like a small person in a dog suit than a typical canine.

We ate in silence for a while. I savored every bite I shoved into my mouth, thankful for simple comfort food that came to the table without effort or planning. After our plates were half-empty, we began chatting about our lives. I learned she had grown up in Maryland but came to Ohio to help her uncle with the lodge five years ago. She fell in love with the area and never looked back. She was in her second year of college, studying art history, not because it would lead her to a job, but because she loved it. She seemed so content and happy with her life. I wasn't sure I'd ever met anyone like her.

After we finished our meals, she dutifully sat her plate on the floor for my dog to lick, even leaving several uneaten bites of casserole for him to devour. He licked the plate clean and then went to work on the floor around it, in case anything had fallen off. I mentally crossed my fingers he wouldn't have tummy issues later.

She refilled our wine glasses and we carried them out to the deck.

In the time it took to eat, the sun had almost completely disappeared below the horizon, sending shards of color up into the sky like angel fingers. A fish leapt from the still waters and landed with a deep plunk, creating rings on the surface that grew larger and larger until they finally disappeared.

I sunk down into a deck chair with a vibrant bright green cushion and felt the troubles of the day slough off me. I was so thankful I'd met her because I would have never known about the cabins and the lake as I sat in my small cramped room, watching mindless TV.

"This is nice," I told her.

"I'm glad you think so. I love it too."

Sonora had traded her teal top and bare feet for a knee-length navy sweater over faded blue jeans and calf boots. I pulled my denim jacket tighter around me, feeling the chill in the air. September was a fickle month that couldn't seem to decide on which side of the fence it should fall. During the day, it was as warm as summer but nighttime seemed to wash away all its aspirations.

"You've been to the asylum today?" she asked.

I nearly spewed a mouthful of wine. "How could you possibly know that?"

She laughed. "You have it all over you. It's like an oily coating." She took another sip of her wine and then sat the glass on a table beside her chair.

She reached out her hand. "Give me your hand."

The look on my face must have been priceless because she laughed. "Don't worry. I'm not going to bite you or read your fortune. I just want to feel your energy. Everyone and everything is made up of energy. Your energy field – your aura - includes everything you've experienced and all that you are. I can read your energy. It's nothing to be afraid of. It's just a gift I was born with."

Reluctantly, I gave her my hand. I felt an immediate tingle of warmth as she closed her hand around mine. I wasn't one of those people who always had cold hands either. Hers were warmer than normal.

"Now, close your eyes and just relax for a moment."

I'd like to say I felt a moment of revelation, that I could feel the transfer of energy between us as the stars and moon aligned, but I didn't. I just felt the warmth of her hands and the brush of wind from the lake on my face. After nearly a minute, she let go of my hand.

"Well...?" I asked, trying to pull information from the expression on her face and failing miserably. She didn't look any different than she had before.

"You have an interesting energy field. Turbulent on the outside, but smoother just below the surface. You make things difficult for yourself. You are hard on yourself...and unnecessarily. Do you often watch other people and try to emulate them because their lives look better than you think yours is?"

I had to break away from her intense gaze. I stared out at the water, admiring the last lingering brush of rose on the horizon. I wanted to buy into what she was saying, but a part of me resisted. It was like reading my daily horoscope. They were often so vague, they'd apply to anyone.

"Doesn't everybody feel that way?"

"Yes, to a certain degree. I think yours goes much deeper," she said.

Something about my demeanor must have given me away, because she stopped staring at me and reached for her glass of wine. "So tell me what happened at the asylum today."

I inhaled and let the air out slowly. While I really didn't want to talk about it and relive it through my memories, I felt like I needed to release it. I took another sip of my wine and then I told her everything. By the time I finished, it was fully dark.

She got up and lit a few candles on the deck, taking her time to position them so they filled the area with soft amber light.

"The giant's name is Benjamin Flood. From what I know, he moved here about twenty years ago with his wife and daughter. They had a house fire about ten years ago and he lost both of them. He hasn't been the same since. He always kept to himself. I saw him a few times around town but he would never make eye contact, so I couldn't even say hello to him," she said. Her dark eyes gleamed in the candle light, making me wonder if she was on the verge of crying.

"So, he doesn't have anyone?" I asked.

"Not to my knowledge."

I sunk back deeper into my chair. Knowing his history made me sad. I couldn't imagine losing everyone I loved in one fell swoop. It helped me understand why he became the person he was, how losing everything hollowed out his core.

I couldn't explain my connection to him. He had been rude and surly. Furthermore, he went off and left me all by myself. If nothing else, I should be angry at him, even if he was dead. I shouldn't be feeling so much remorse and sadness.

"I really want to know what happened to him. I can't explain why. I just feel a very strong need to know," I told her, frustration rising to the surface of my skin like a wild animal trying to escape.

Sonora gave me a knowing look. "It's because he wants you to. He's pulling you to do this."

"You mean, his ghost is trying to motivate me to find out what happened to him?" I asked, incredulously.

"Sort of. Remember how I told you how everything and everyone is made up of energy?" she waited for me to nod. "Well, the energy doesn't die with us. It lingers around on this side of the veil for a while, especially if the person's death was tragic or unexpected."

"So, now he's a ghost?"

"I've never been comfortable with that word because it brings to mind scary entities. But, yes. He is nothing more than energy now. Because he's newly dead, he won't be able to do more than possibly influence the living. He's probably not going to walk across your living room or tap on your windows. That seems to take them a lot longer to master. If you're feeling his energy, then it means you also have a gift. Have you had paranormal experiences before?" she asked.

I sighed. "Yeah and it's been happening more and more lately." I told her about my experiences as a child with my imaginary friend and she narrowed her eyes slightly, as if deep in thought.

"Many times, we're born with gifts but don't fully utilize them until we're older. This seems to be the case with you. You are starting to feel the energy like I do. It will probably grow stronger, especially if you begin paying attention to it." She held up her arm and flexed it until her bicep muscle enlarged. "It's like a muscle. The more you use it, the stronger it gets."

I wasn't sure what I thought about it. Frankly, it scared the hell out of me, but it also fascinated me too.

She stood up and retrieved our empty wine glasses from the table. "This is the most interesting thing that's happened to me all year. I'll help you, if you want me to."

"That sounds good, but I have no idea where to start and I'm certainly not going back to the asylum. Besides, it's probably crawling with cops by now. Where do we even begin?"

I followed her inside, where she put our glasses in the sink and grabbed her purse off the back of a chair.

"Have you had too much wine or can you drive?" she asked.

I felt like I just tripped and fell into a pit of confusion. I glanced down at my cell phone. It was already after seven. The library would be long closed, so we couldn't do research. I couldn't imagine where we could go to learn more information. "I'm fine, but where are we going?"

"Where else? To Benjamin's house," she said and headed out the door.

I followed behind her, knowing without knowing this was a very bad decision.

Crazy Dead People

Chapter 11

It doesn't take much to put me on edge. Once I believe danger is possibly lurking around the corner, I'm on high alert. It doesn't matter if the danger is real or imagined; I look under every bed and inside every closet. I carry my keys in my hands as I walk across dark parking lots and I always close my blinds at night in case someone is outside watching.

As I trekked across the gloomy lawn towards my Jeep, the fear was nearly palpable, growing at an alarming rate.

Sonora's words rattled around inside my head. I never thought I was different from other people. I just thought I frequently had strange experiences, but the more I thought about it, the more it made sense. Most people didn't see ghosts. Most people didn't even think about ghosts, but they were on my mind quite a bit, especially lately.

Was it possible I was born with an extra sense? Did I really have some sort of invisible antenna that helped me detect when a ghost was near? I thought about all the times in my life when I've felt as though someone was watching me, only to discover I was alone. I always attributed it to foolishness, but now I had to wonder.

We got into my Jeep and I plugged the address into my phone's GPS. I waited for Fugly to get comfortable in the backseat and for Sonora to get buckled in before I backed out of the parking lot.

As we drove, every tree seemed like a good place for a murderer to hide and every pile of leaves became an apparition. Truly, the last thing I needed was something new to be afraid of.

"Can you tell me more about this gift you think I have? I have to tell you, it really freaks me out," I said, turning onto the main road.

"I didn't mean to scare you. I guess I've lived with it for so long I've gotten used to it." She rolled down her window a few inches, allowing the sweet fragrance of the woods to fill the Jeep. "I think you are a sensitive. It means you are able to see and feel ghosts."

I swallowed hard. "How do I know if it's a ghost or just my imagination?"

"It's different for everybody. Some people might feel it as goosebumps, while someone else might feel his scalp crawl. Others hear voices or a sound that is similar to ear-ringing. Some people simply see them, sometimes with their eyes and other times inside their head.

"They call it the *clairs*. Clair means 'clear' in Latin," she said, holding up her hand. She began ticking them off on her fingers. "There's clairvoyant, which means clear seeing. Those people see ghosts either in their mind's eye or with their actual eyesight. There's clairsentient, which is clear feeling. Those people feel it physically, maybe with goosebumps or even headaches. There's claircognizant, which means clear knowing. Those people just know things they shouldn't know. And then there's clairaudient. They hear voices or sounds when a ghost is nearby," she said dropping her hand. "There are others, but they aren't as common, like Clairalience, where people smell phantom scents like perfume or cigar smoke."

I felt my stomach tighten. "I feel all of those sometimes. Does it mean I'm a full-blooded freak?"

She laughed. "You aren't a freak! You need to get that thought right out of your head. It's a gift. Just think about all you can do with it," she said, giving me a moment to digest the concept. If I was going to have a special gift, this wouldn't be one I would pick. I'd learn how to make myself invisible and walk around undetected or I'd learn to set things on fire with my mind, which could be very dangerous for the church ladies who often knocked on my door when I was napping.

Sonora continued, apparently not picking up on my inner turmoil. "As someone who pursues information, like you do, you have an inside track. You can actually communicate with the dead and learn their secrets."

I wasn't easily convinced. "I'd honestly rather learn it from more of a distance."

She reached over and patted my hand on the gear shifter. "It doesn't have to be scary. You have to learn how to protect yourself. That's all. And I can teach you. In fact, let's have our first lesson right now."

My blood pressure went through the roof. "While I'm driving?"

"Actually, this is the best time because you'll be able to focus on it easier since your body and mind is occupied. I often do my best meditations while driving or even going for walks. You just tap into your own energy easier because you have a diversion."

I wasn't easily convinced. "Driving into a tree is also a diversion."

"Oh Shelby. You are such a worry wart! Just keep your eyes open and focus on the road while you listen to my voice. It's really easy and safe. I promise!"

It sounded like the prelude to every bad decision I've ever made. Back in middle school, one of my friends used similar words by encouraging me to help her break into the school in the middle of the night. My mother wasn't amused when I returned home in the back of a police car.

"All right. Just tell me. We're only about six minutes away according to my GPS," I told her.

"It won't even take that long. We're going to start with grounding. Just take a deep breath and let it out. Imagine pure white light coming in through the crown of your head when you inhale. Pull it in and let it fill your body. When you exhale, imagine it pushing all the impurities out of your body through the soles of your feet."

I'm not one to latch onto every crazy notion thrown at me, but I did give it a try. On my first breath, I didn't feel any different, but by the time I had done it several times, I felt a bit lighter.

"Okay, that was good. I can do it," I told her.

"It's a way of purging out all the gunky energy we collect. Gifted people are often like sponges. We pull in energy from all around us and it tends to clog us up. Try it next time you're in a crowd or when you're around someone negative."

I imagined myself doing it the next time I went to Walmart and the thought took wings.

"Okay, the next step takes a little imagination, so hang in there with me," she told me. "Now, picture white light above your head expanding around your body like a bubble. Once it's fully in place, no other energy can penetrate it," she said.

"Not even ghosts?"

She laughed again, apparently amused by my fears. "Not even ghosts."

As I turned onto the road the giant lived on, I attempted to pull the bubble of white light down and around me. I wasn't sure if I had really accomplished anything, but it did make me feel a little better. I wasn't in the green zone yet, but I was swiftly edging away from full nuclear combustion, which was probably a good sign.

I was one of those people who needed to actually see something to believe it. I trusted Sonora though and was willing to give it a shot. If it worked, it would certainly make my life a lot easier. I'd put my shield on every day before I left the house and hopefully never have another paranormal experience.

According to my GPS, the giant's house was still a mile away. The closer we got, the less populated the area became. The spaces between the houses grew further and further apart until all there was left was a dark road surrounded by forest. Above us, the moon played peek-a-boo through the tops of the trees, appearing for a second before disappearing altogether.

The trees were just normal, everyday kind of trees, but in my mind, I saw them as hiding spots. Anything could be lurking behind them, watching us drive past. For all I knew, there was an army of ghosts and tree monsters waiting for us ahead.

"I don't like this," I said, my voice coming out with a tremble.

"It's not as bad during the daytime. It's actually quite lovely. I come down here to walk sometimes," Sonora said, looking out the window at the darkness.

From the backseat, Fugly let out a low growl, apparently siding with me on this one. If my dog didn't like it, I didn't like it either, unless it dealt with things like squirrels and cats. That was where we parted ways on opinions.

I watched the little arrow on my GPS grow closer until we were right in front of a long dirt driveway. If I hadn't known it was a driveway, I would have assumed it was an old game trail. It was rutted and muddy, tall weeds growing on either side of it, nearly obscuring it from view.

I didn't remember seeing another vehicle parked at the asylum, so I wasn't sure what the giant drove, but I was fairly certain it had four-wheel drive. A normal car wouldn't make it ten feet.

I shifted into four-wheel drive and made the turn, feeling as though I was in the process of making a monumental mistake. When it came to things like this, I was often divided. My curiosity would raise its big head and wonder where we were going while my fear tried to throttle it back down into place. This time, my curiosity won the battle. I needed to know what was at the end of the driveway, even if it killed me in the process.

The driveway seemed to go on forever, growing narrower and more overgrown the further we got.

"Are you sure this is the place?" I asked, driving over a large branch that had fallen across the road. I could hear it snap beneath my tires, making me wonder how long it had been since anyone had driven back here.

"I'm sure. There must be a back way in too. Maybe it's how he got in and out," she said, not sounding as certain as she had before.

As I was on the verge of giving up and looking for a wide spot to turn around, we came to an opening in the woods. Ahead of us was a small log cabin. It was nearly obscured by all the junked-out cars in the yard. My headlights reflected on several windshields and bumpers of vehicles being reclaimed by the earth. Vines and baby trees grew up and around them, using them as a foundation to cling onto. The front porch wasn't much better. An old washing machine sat next to a pile of broken machinery that could belong to anything.

I cut my engine but left the headlights on. Without taking my eyes off the front of the cabin, I reached into my glove compartment and pulled out my flashlight. It wasn't a huge Maglite, like the giant had loaned me, but it was bright enough to get me through the dangerous front lawn, if you could even call it a lawn. It looked like someone had built a house in the middle of a salvage yard.

As Sonora opened her door, Fugly pushed his nose into the space between the seat and the door, trying to wiggle his way out.

"Not a good idea, fur face. I don't want you stepping on something sharp in the weeds and end up at the vet's office tonight," I told him. He probably didn't understand a word I said, but he clearly understood the part about the vet. He slunk back into his seat and eyed me warily as if wondering if there was a random veterinarian hiding in the bushes.

I closed the door and joined Sonora by the front bumper.

My heart began hammering against the walls of my chest. This was a very bad idea.

Why did I feel the need to be here? What would I possibly find to help me put all the pieces into place?

Sonora started walking and I found myself following her, shining my flashlight all around me. The weeds were high, but there was a path cut through them where someone had once walked.

I turned around to look at my Jeep, knowing Fugly was watching me closely, even though I couldn't see anything except the bright headlights. I turned back to find Sonora ten feet ahead of me, so I hurried to catch up.

"Maybe we should just go back," I suggested as we reached the porch.

Before I could answer, we were nearly blinded by a bright light above the porch roof. I wasn't sure if it was automatically set off by motion or if someone was inside and threw the switch. My bladder didn't care about the difference though. I came very close to pissing myself and had to cross my legs to prevent it from continuing.

As we stood there, the light went back out.

"It's probably a motion-sensor light," Sonora told me, ever so helpfully. I started to say something I'd probably regret later, when something happened that made the pants-peeing episode seem like butterflies and daisies.

"What the fuck?" a voice screeched out from inside the house.

I didn't have to even consult with my curiosity to see if it was okay with my decision to bolt. My legs just took off on their own, helpfully tripping me halfway back to the Jeep.

Dear God, what had I gotten myself into?

Chapter 12

I scrambled to my feet, surprised to find Sonora still lingering near the porch.

"Wait just a second," she whispered to me, holding up her hand. Her face was pale in the moonlight, with wisps of her dark hair dancing against her cheek. She looked taut, ready to bolt, but was still holding her ground.

I watched her, admiring her bravery as I scrutinized her body language. If she so much as flinched, I would have been halfway back to the Jeep by the time she took her next breath.

"What the fuck? What the fuck?"

I jumped, but didn't run, still waiting for Sonora's cue. I had somehow assigned her the master of my reactions. If she bolted, I was going to bolt too. I felt completely disconnected from my own inclinations.

"What the fuck?" the voice said again, this time drawing out the last word and inlaying it with a slight warble. It sounded nasally and not entirely human. As my mind frantically searched through my database for something to compare it to, Sonora edged up onto the porch.

"I think I know what it is," she said, latching onto the doorknob.

I watched her, my mind filled with horror. She was going to go in there because she thought she knew what it was? My fears instantly detoured me into worst-case-scenario land. What if it wasn't what she thought it was? What if it was something presentencing to be something else to lure us into its trap? Before I could continue my mental list, she turned the doorknob.

The door opened with a squeal that was identical to the banshee door at the asylum. I felt the hairs on the back of my neck stand up as the memories returned.

I watched, confounded, as she disappeared through the doorway, her flashlight cutting a minuscule path in the darkness. She was certainly braver than I was. My natural proclivity in scary situations was to put as much distance between me and the scary thing as possible.

From my vantage point in the tall grass, I couldn't see any more than the dart of light from her flashlight. I pulled myself to my feet, feeling the adrenaline spike through my body, ready to skedaddle at the first scream. I wasn't sure about a lot of things, but if someone I barely knew made a stupid decision, I wasn't going to lay my life on the line and follow her into the lion's den. If it made me a coward, then so be it. I touched my cell phone in my pocket, wondering how long it would take the police to get her if I had to make a frantic call.

The silence was killing me. I imagined every possible horror unfolding inside the cabin. I held my breath, waiting for a scream to pierce through the stillness, but was stunned when I heard laughter instead. Moments later, she popped back through the doorway, still chuckling.

"Shelby, you have to come see this," she told me, ducking back into the house.

Relief nearly folded me in half, but my mind refused to latch onto her sudden change of emotions. Going from terrified to delighted wasn't something I did naturally or easily. It normally took me a moment to disentangle myself from my emotions, especially ones this extreme.

I approached the porch slowly, wondering about her mental state as well as mine. That little voice in the back of my mind reminded me I didn't know her very well. What if she was part of some sort of satanic cult and was luring me in for a sacrificial rite? What if she was simply blue goose crazy and I was foolishly following her inside for the slaughter?

My feet kept moving though, following an urge my mind wanted no part of.

As I reached the steps, Sonora must have turned the lights on because the interior went from a pitch-black pit to a hoarder's delight. I stopped short just inside in the doorway, trying to make sense of what I was seeing.

I temporarily forgot the voice that had called out to us as I mentally absorbed the colossal collection of junk squeezed into the tiny cabin. There were piles of papers and cardboard boxes stacked to the ceiling. If there was any furniture inside the room, it was buried beneath the mounds. Some of the boxes were leaning precariously, as though time and moisture had weakened their constitution. The room smelled like mold and mildew, instantly bringing my thoughts back to the asylum. Had he been collecting items from the asylum?

"What the fuck!" the voice said again, jolting me from my gawking.

I turned with a start to see Sonora laughing. Beside her was a massive cage. Inside the cage was a gray parrot.

"What the fuck!" the bird said again.

My knees wobbled uncertainly as my heart nearly jumped into my throat. Much more of this and I'd need a ride to the hospital.

"Oh my God! It's a parrot?" I said, pressing my hand to my chest.

The bird sat on a perch inside the cage, staring at us as though he was trying to figure us out too.

"One of my friends in high school had a bird like that and he was a real asshole," I told her. I'd never encountered anything like him before I came to her house one day. His vocabulary and intellect were astonishing. He recognized people and called to them by name and knew a dozen or more phrases that corresponded with his wants and needs. Every time my friend came home, he would say, "Who wants a banana?" which always struck me as funny. It was something they always said to him before giving him a banana, so he associated it with getting fed. She tried to retrain him to say, "I want a banana," but he stubbornly refused to change the phrase.

"What kind of bird is that?" I asked, unable to retrieve the name in my current mental state.

"I think it's an African Gray. I didn't realize he still had that bird," she said turning to look around the room, taking in the mess. "It was his wife's bird, but I thought he died in the fire along with the rest of the family."

In my current state of confusion, I wanted to poke him to make sure he was real. I put my finger near the cage and he lunged at it, making him real enough for me.

"Frank's a pretty bird," he told me.

"That's good to know," I said back to him. "Does Frank bite fingers?"

"What the fuck!" he screamed and then cackled like a witch, sending a fresh new wave of chills down my spine.

"Who would want a pet that did that?" I said, edging away from the cage. He was like a demented psycho disguised as a bird. If he knew dozens of phrases, I didn't want to know the rest of them after hearing the first few.

What would be next? Who wants to be murdered in her sleep?

As if in response to my mental ramblings, he leaned closer to the bars of the cage and said in a very deep confidential sort of voice, "Who farted?"

Sonora started laughing again. "Well, it goes to show Benjamin had a sense of humor at one point." It took me a few seconds to realize who she was even talking about until I remembered the giant's real name was Benjamin.

"Let's look around a bit. I'm pretty sure we're going to find something that helps us make some sense of this," she said, pulling the lid off of the nearest box. Inside were green file folders with names on the tops.

"Are those patient records?" I leaned in, suddenly interested, as she flipped open a file. Inside the folder were yellowed papers with patient documentation for a woman named Benita Sharp. She was born August 13th, 1934 and died July 30th, 1964. Her cause of death was listed as cardiac arrest, even though she was only thirty years old.

We pulled the next file from the folder and saw a similar story. That patient died at the age of 39, also from cardiac arrest. I flipped through several other files, seeing similar stories.

"What the hell happened at that asylum?" I said, mostly to myself. It made me remember the dream I had about the old woman in the rocking chair, the one who showed me the photo album.

"I think it was shut down due to abuse. Mentally ill people weren't treated very well back then," Sonora said.

I looked around until I found a canvas bag hanging from a doorknob. It contained a handful of plastic shopping bags, so I shook them out on the floor and used the now empty bag to tuck several of the file folders into. I found another box with more patient records dating back to the 1970s and added a few of those to my bag, as well. I wanted to know more about the patients and what happened to them. If I had their names, I could research them and learn more about the horrors they suffered.

I navigated around the boxes to the back of the cabin and found the kitchen. If I expected to find a mound of dirty rotten dishes moldering in the sink, I was wrong. The sink was empty, with clean dishes sitting on a draining rack beside it.

I opened several cabinets to find boxes of pasta mix and cans of vegetables. My curiosity was getting the best of me. Benjamin's world was filled with a plethora of contradictions and I needed to know why.

How could a man who hoarded patient records have such a clean kitchen? The two concepts just didn't go together.

I closed the cabinet door and made my way around the maze of boxes. The giant had left himself nothing more than a two-foot-wide path around the cabin, leading to the places he needed to go. Several times, I had to turn sideways to fit though the openings and wondered how a man his size managed it.

I'd read enough about hoarders to know it was a mental condition. They simply couldn't part with their possessions and soon ran out of space to keep everything. My mother tended to do this with food. Her pantry was so overstocked with cans and boxes, they were stacked on the floor outside the door, but she still bought more every week at the store. I gave her a hard time about it every chance I got, but often wondered if it was something I should be concerned about.

I squeezed around another corner and discovered the giant's bed. He hadn't provided himself with much space to sleep. The bed was completely boxed in on all four sides. He'd left himself an opening to get into the bed, but no room on the sides. A rumpled navy blue flannel blanket was draped across the bed with a matching pillow lying sideways across it, telling tales of a restless night's sleep.

Had he gotten up that morning with thoughts of meeting me on his mind? Did he set an alarm to awaken or did he wake with the morning sun? I couldn't imagine how he'd even know the sun had risen with all the boxes surrounding him. I looked around and couldn't even find a single window. If there was one, the boxes was covering it up.

I could hear Sonora rattling around in the kitchen, so I made my way back to the source of the sounds. She had a bag of parrot food in her hand and was looking through the cabinets for something else. On the floor beside her was a smaller parrot cage.

"You aren't seriously thinking about bringing that bird with you, are you?"

She gave up on her search and grabbed the parrot cage.

"Benjamin doesn't have any relatives or friends that I know of. If we don't take him, the bird will just sit there and starve to death."

"Oh," was all I could think of to say.

I couldn't handle the thought of any animal starving to death inside a cage, but I wasn't certain what we were going to do with a foul-mouthed parrot with a bloodthirst. I certainly wasn't going to take him home with me.

The smell of mildew was starting to get to me. I could feel my sinus passages swelling up as the urge to sneeze came over me. Before I could take measures to repress it, I sneezed three or four times, feeling like I was never going to stop.

"God bless you!" came from the other room. This voice sounded feminine, but still had the nasally tone as the rest of his phrases.

Sonora laughed. "At least he has some manners."

This was followed by another, "Who farted?" sending us both into hysterics.

As our laughter died out, it was apparent we were both done with the cabin. The sadness and clutter were just too much to handle. It made me think about the life this man had led, surrounded by boxes from the dead. I wondered if he ever interacted with the bird or if he just ignored it. The fact that he held onto his wife's pet made me even sadder. It must have been a constant reminder, hearing her voice being repeated over and over again even though she was long gone.

I followed Sonora back to the parrot cage and watched apprehensively as she opened the cage.

I fully expected the bird to explode from the cage in a flurry of feathers and angry beak, but I was sorely mistaken. The bird stepped up onto her outstretched arm and climbed up to her shoulder and began lovingly grooming her long hair.

"Does Frank want to go for a car ride?" she cooed at him.

He fluffed his feathers and his eyes dilated, making them go from black to red and back again.

"That's so freaky," I whispered.

Frank leaned towards me and opened his beak in a motion that could only be taken as aggressive.

"He doesn't like you very much. Maybe you should be nicer to him," Sonora helpfully suggested.

"Frank would make a good stew," I said, eyeing him in case he made a sudden move to pluck out my eyeballs.

I couldn't even imagine what Fugly was going to think about him when we put him in the backseat next to him. I might be driving back with a dog on my lap.

She opened the door on the smaller cage and the bird compliantly walked down her arm and climbed in. It was almost as though he knew what was happening and seemed happy for the rescue.

I grabbed the bag of bird food from her hand and stuffed it inside the canvas bag filled with file folders. As we got closer to the front door, I became aware of a flashing blue light coming from outside. I felt my breath catch in my throat.

"What the fuck!" Frank said helpfully as Sonora and I stopped in our tracks.

"Great," I whispered under my breath. This was all we needed.

Crazy Dead People

Chapter 13

Thankfully, my experience with law enforcement has been limited to the occasional speeding ticket, but it didn't mean my heart wasn't pounding like gangbusters. Getting caught trespassing inside a house of a recently deceased man probably wouldn't bode well for us. As we came out onto the porch, we were pinned with a bright light.

I held my breath for several seconds, waiting for someone to tell us to put our hands on our heads, but nothing happened. Sonora shielded her eyes with her hand, squinting into the light.

"Jimmy Bob, is that you?" she called out and the light was extinguished.

"Hey, Sonora! What are you doing out here?" the man said, his voice ripe with a southern accent.

I nearly collapsed into a people-shaped puddle of goo. I couldn't remember the last time I'd felt so many extreme emotions back-to-back. It would be a major miracle if I didn't develop a nervous tic by the time we were finished.

He met us in front of the porch, grinning from ear to ear. He was tall and handsome in a boyish kind of way, with light brown hair and dark eyes that reminded me of a puppy dog. He looked like the kind of guy who still helped his mama with the shopping and went to church every Sunday in his best duds.

I was a bit relieved to see none of the normal cop persona reflected in his eyes. He must have been new on the force. As if reading my mind, Sonora sat the cage down so she could focus on the howdy-dos.

"How long have you been with the Sheriff's department? I thought you were still helping your dad at his shop?" she asked.

He blushed, apparently embarrassed by the reminder. "Oh, about six months or so. Sherriff Bustler said they needed someone, so I just went for it," he said. They continued for a few more minutes, exchanging pleasantries I had no interest in hearing. It was apparent he wasn't going to slap cuffs on either of us, so I was ready to leave.

"I heard about Benjamin, so I wanted to come out and get his bird. I don't think anyone else will be interested in him, but if you hear of anyone who wants him, can you let me know?" she said. For all the world, it sounded like she was flirting with him. I didn't know if she was just using her feminine wiles, as my mother called them, to get us out of a prickly situation or if she had a genuine interest in the country bumpkin, but my impatience was beginning to get the best of me.

"We should really be getting back now," I told her.

I craned my neck, trying to see what Fugly was doing, but couldn't see my Jeep around the police car.

"That's probably a good idea," she said. "Well, we'll see you later, Jimmy Bob! Good luck with the new job!" she sang out as though he'd just picked up a job as a Walmart door greeter instead of one of Parkesburg's' finest.

After the polite goodbyes were exchanged, something I had very little patience for on a good day, we rounded the police car and picked our way through the tall grass to my Jeep. Fugly was sitting in the driver's seat, watching us intently. From my vantage point, it looked like the Jeep was still intact, which I took as a good sign. He was probably so worried about our safety, he didn't have time to rip it apart.

The thought gave me a chuckle. Fugly loved me. There was no doubt about it, but I'm fairly certain my safety wasn't high on his priority list. Like any other dog, he just wanted to be near me and was irritated to miss out on the opportunity to pee on something.

Sonora put the bird in the backseat and wrapped a seat belt around him, which Frank immediately began gnawing on through the bars of the cage.

"Bad bird!" she scolded him, as she removed the seat belt.

"What the fuck!" he said a bit too loud for the confines of my Jeep.

This captured Fugly's attention. He turned and looked at the bird as though a monster had sprouted from the upholstery. He growled, keeping the bird squarely in his sites.

"It's a bird, Fugly. Kind of like the chickens grandma cooks only still with feathers," I told him. He didn't take his eyes off the bird.

I tried again. "I'm not sure how well this is going to work, but you need to get in the backseat." I opened the back door and then shooed him out of my seat. He sniffed the tall grass for a second and then suddenly remembered the monster in the backseat.

He hopped up onto the back seat and pressed his nose to the side of the case for a good sniff. The bird reacted exactly like I thought he would. He lunged at the cage, attempting to separate Fugly's nose from his face.

All hell pretty much broke loose at that point. Fugly started barking at the bird, which caused the bird to begin screaming at the dog. I was fairly sure the amount of noise they were generating was comparable to a rock concert, but there wasn't much I could do about it.

Before he could jump back out again, I slammed the door behind him and climbed into the driver's seat. I was three seconds away from self-combustion when Sonora solved the problem. She put her fingers in her mouth and let loose a whistle that could halt a stampede. The animals stopped in mid-roar and looked at her with wide eyes.

"Thank you. Now settle down and be quiet," she told them.

I closed my eyes for a second, thanking my lucky stars for the silence. My nerves were already frayed and the noise nearly sent me over the edge. My hair wasn't as red as my mother's, but it didn't mean I didn't have her hairpin-trigger temper.

I backed up and did a nerve-wracking U-turn in the tall weeds, hoping I wouldn't run over anything sharp. A flat tire would have sent me into an abyss I might never find my way out of. By the time we made it to the road, the animals were still quiet, and my nerves were leisurely following suit.

I did have one question for Sonora, though.

"Jimmy Bob?"

She laughed, which was apparently something she did fairly often because it was her usual go-to response. "His name is really James Robert Rogers, but everybody calls him Jimmy Bob. I met him shortly after I moved here. He asked me out a few times and I always said no, but he's relatively harmless," she said which made me snicker inside. Those weren't exactly words you normally used to describe your local law enforcement members. Hopefully, he at least knew how to use his gun. She followed this with something that made me feel pretty worthless.

"His mother died a few years ago of cervical cancer. The entire town rallied around her with fundraisers for her treatment and prayer groups for the family. Jimmy Bob was taking classes down at the community college to become an accountant, but he dropped out after his mother died to help his dad with their hardware store. He's a good guy. He's more than a little green, but at least he didn't arrest us."

"Thank God for small miracles," I said, blowing a sigh through the front of my bangs.

We made it back to the cabins quickly. While I let Fugly out, Sonora unloaded the bird cage.

"I hate to tell you this, but Frank is going to have to stay with you. I'm allergic to birds," she said, making me narrow my eyes.

"How can you be allergic? You haven't sneezed once."

She gave me one of her winning smiles, the kind she's probably been using as effective leverage most of her life. "I break out in hives." She began scratching her arm. "As a matter of fact, I can already feel them coming on. I'll help you get him inside though."

I felt as though I'd been properly conned. If she knew she was allergic to birds, then why did she bring him with us to begin with? And what happened if nobody wanted him? There was no way in hell I was bringing that bird home with me. I could say "What the fuck?" just fine on my own. I didn't need to hear it from a smarty-pants pigeon a thousand times a day.

I managed to keep my mouth shut though. If I pissed off Sonora, I'd risk losing my comfy cabin and possibly assistance later with my research. She seemed to know a lot of people in town, which might help open some doors for me. Plus that, I liked her, which put her in a very rare category.

I sat Frank's cage on the kitchen table and made sure his food and water dishes were full. Fugly parked himself on the floor in front of the cage, staring intently at the bird while licking his lips just enough to make me nervous. There was no doubt in my mind if Frank ever got out of his cage, parrot hunting would soon be in season.

"Be good," I told both of them as I carried the bag full of files to the couch.

I had taken a dozen files from the house and every one of them painted a sad story. Almost all of the patients died young, with the exception of the four files I pulled from a different box. Those were files from when the asylum was used as a nursing home. A few of those files came with photos attached to help the nursing home staff match faces with names. As I flipped through them, I came to the last one and gasped.

The woman in the rocking chair stared back at me. The picture was identical to the one I'd found in the asylum kitchen.

"There's no way that happened by accident," I said, feeling trepidation fill my body. I stared at the photo for an eternity, feeling as though I'd been plunked down in a *Twilight Zone* episode. Her smiling face stared back at me, as though finding me through the impossible passages of time.

Fingers trembling, I continued scouring through the file. The woman's name was Bertha Simmons. She was eighty-four years old when she moved into the nursing home and died six years later at the age of ninety. She was diabetic and required daily insulin injections and had a hip replacement when she was seventy-seven.

I didn't understand a lot of the notations in her file and couldn't read some of the chicken scratch the doctors and nurses had penned, but one thing caught my attention fairly quickly.

On June 18th, 1971, Bertha began exhibiting early signs of schizophrenia. The notation said she was experiencing hallucinations and was growing agitated because there was a man in her room, crawling across her ceiling.

I gasped, dropping the file into my lap as though it was molten lava.

Did she see the crawler? "Oh my God," I whispered.

I stared into the air, my mind whirling as I tried to imagine what the poor woman went through. She wasn't mentally ill. She was seeing the crawler walk across the ceiling in her room and no one believed her. I stared down at the file, almost afraid to pick it up and read more. Ignorance might be bliss, but it was powerless against the rush of curiosity that overcame me. I picked it up again and opened it to the page I'd been reading.

They prescribed her some serious anti-psychotic medications, increasing the dosage every few months until she died a year later.

"That poor woman," I whispered.

At that precise moment, I caught the whiff of cheap perfume as my ears began ringing and knew I was no longer alone.

Bertha was here.

Crazy Dead People

Chapter 14

I held my breath, waiting for the air to begin prickling with a mist like it had at the asylum. Panic rolled through me, hot and wild, as I scanned the dimly lit room.

The living room was awash with shadows and dark contrasts. The gaps in the gleaming hardwood floors painted black lines against the shiny planks, trailing off into darkened corners. The light above the kitchen sink cast an amber glow in the kitchen area, showing me clean Formica countertops and polished appliances, but faded away into a murky chasm until the floor lamp near the front door took over.

I snapped on the tabletop lamp beside me and felt some of my anxiety dissipate with the sanctity of light. Its glow surrounded me like a bubble of protection, even though I knew the sense of safety was fallible.

I found myself suspiciously eyeing the shadowy corners. At first I thought I saw something, and then realized it was just my eyes adjusting to the light. What started off as an imp hunkered down behind the arm chair became a pillow on the floor. The apparition peeking out from behind the drapes became the white sheers hanging behind them.

"Get a grip, Shelby." I closed my eyes and took a few breaths, trying to stop myself from wigging out over nothing. The perfume smell was gone. Maybe the ear ringing was just tinnitus. The only problem with the explanation were the parts I didn't want to consider. The sound was clearly moving around the room.

At first, it was beside me and then it shifted directly in front of me. I moved my head, trying to determine the location. I finally came to realize it wasn't simple ear ringing. I was actually hearing something I couldn't see.

The thought made my mouth go dry. Just the concept alone was terrifying. An invisible person was standing directly in front of me, watching me trying to find her. It was like having a homeless person walk into my house and take up residence while I was completely unaware.

A part of me truly wanted to lose my shit and run out of the cabin, but I held onto my very last nerve. It was too easy to go to my internal data banks and pull up frightening images of ghosts from movies I've watched and books I've read. Ghosts were scary because they were unknown. If you could catch one and study it, some of the fear might dissipate, but ghosts can't be caught. What was standing in front of me could be a serial killer, or it could be a harmless old lady who needed help. How could I possibly tell the difference?

"Bertha? Is that you?" I whispered, drawing the attention of both animals. Fugly temporarily left his post by the bird cage to climb onto the couch with me. He parked himself beside me and began staring into the air as though he were watching something.

"God bless you!" Frank called out, his voice loud and abrupt. After I got past the initial shock, the aftertaste filled my mind with suspicion. Did Frank hear someone sneeze?

After a few minutes, nothing materialized, but I could still hear the high-pitched tone.

I felt myself calm down, ever so slightly. The tension in my shoulders eased as I allowed them to relax back into their normal position. Nothing bad had happened, so maybe it was Bertha. Was she just standing there, waiting for me to see her?

"Did you follow me home?" I asked, the thought sending a brand new wave of chills down my spine. Could ghosts follow people home? Had she been with me the entire day? I had a mental image of her buckled up in the backseat beside the squawking bird and shook my head, as if to erase it.

It couldn't be that simple. Sonora said we were all made up of energy. If there wasn't a physical body to hold the energy into place, could it take any form it wanted? The thought grew hairy legs.

What if it wasn't Bertha? What if it was the crawler?

I felt my pulse quicken as I looked around the room. After a few minutes, the sound faded away. I looked at Fugly for his reaction, but he was busy licking his privates.

"Have some pride, bud!" I gave him a nudge with my elbow and he looked up at me with adoring eyes. "And keep that tongue on your side of the couch!" He often tried to lick me after he was finished cleaning himself. I wasn't sure if he was trying to get the bad taste out of his mouth or if he enjoyed torturing me. Either way, I was having none of it. I pushed him off the couch for good measure.

After a few minutes, the ear-ringing sound ended. It felt as though it drifted away, growing softer and softer until I couldn't hear it any longer. I took it as a good sign. Maybe it was gone. I glanced down at my phone. It was already after ten and I was tired. The events of the day had worn me ragged.

I found a blanket in the closet and covered the bird cage, not wanting to be serenaded at all hours of the night by Frank. I'd already had enough of him to last a lifetime.

Tomorrow was going to be a back-breaking, nerve-wracking, ball-busting day. I didn't even want to think about meeting the paranormal team. If I allowed my mind to go there, I'd be up all night fingering through all the anxieties, alphabetizing them and ranking them accordingly.

"Let's go to bed, Fugs," I told my dog. I slipped my shoes off by the couch, grabbed my canvas travel bag and walked in stocking feet to the bedroom.

I turned on the light to the bedroom and just stood there, taking it in.

There was nothing inspiring about the accommodations. The two bedrooms were mirrors of each other, with double beds covered with beige nubby bedspreads that were several months overdue for a wash. There was a worn wooden nightstand on one side and a matching dresser on the wall beside the door. The prints on the wall were instantly forgettable, depicting fields of flowers and covered bridges.

I plopped my bag on top of the dresser and dug out my favorite sleep shirt with Bite Me scrawled on the front of it. The shirt alone probably explained my long-term single status but also justified my need to be alone. Anyone who interfered with my sleep was fair game for a good bite and I wasn't above giving it.

I pinched the bedspread gingerly between two fingers and pulled it to the end of the bed where the cooties couldn't reach me and was pleasantly surprised to see starched white sheets beneath it. Despite the clean appearance, I wasn't above checking the mattress for bedbugs before I climbed in. There was no sense in being totally crazy. Bedbugs were serious business and not something I wanted to add to my list of Bad Things that Happened to Me Today.

I leaned over to turn the light off when I realized my mistake. As soon as I clicked the light, I'd be plunging myself into complete darkness. I left all the lights on in the living room, which created a nice view from the bed, but I wasn't thrilled to be observing it from a dark pit.

I pulled myself out of bed and fished through my bag until my fingers latched onto my nightlight. I'd nearly forgotten it as I packed my bag and had actually had to run back into the house to get it before I left. It was as important to me as remembering my toothbrush.

Once it was plugged into a receptacle beside the door, I felt an immediate sense of relief. It was amusing how having light made me feel safer, when in fact, all it did was show me what I was afraid of. If something materialized in my room, I'd be far better off sleeping unaware in the darkness. It was a difficult habit to break.

Something about the darkness was both mesmerizing and terrifying at the same moment. There were times when I loved sitting on my mother's front porch swing with the sounds of nighttime enveloping me. I'd linger there for long moments, unable to see my hand on the rail, the only light coming from the dusk to dawn light at the end of the block. Not once did I ever feel afraid. Maybe it was because nothing bad had ever happened to me there, so I felt a sense of security in my surroundings. For some reason, the same sense of sanctity didn't follow me to my bedroom. Even though nothing bad had ever happened there, I still couldn't sleep without a light. A part of me wondered if it was the act of surrender. When I finally gave in and closed my eyes, no one was there to protect me, to watch my back as I slept, making me reexamine all the reasons why I chose to live alone.

I rolled over, ready to finally give into the yawning, when I remembered I hadn't plugged my cell phone in. This required another trip to my bag and another fishing expedition until I snagged the long cord.

Plugging it in required a little work, but soon I was climbing back into bed, hoping the third time was the charm. I was on the verge of mentally inspecting this old adage when I felt a tug on the end of the bed, followed by the sound of a whine.

I scrambled up, nearly knocking my pillows off the bed in my panic, only to see Fugly forlornly gazing at me from the side of the bed. He had a look on his scruffy little face that was impossible to resist. It was a mixture of pure love and loneliness, as if his entire world would shatter into a thousand pieces if he wasn't allowed on the bed with me. Maybe I had someone to watch my back after all.

I stared him down for a minute, trying to find a good reason to deny him and failed miserably. Maybe having him with me would help us both get a good night's sleep.

"All right. Come on up," I told him.

He backed up and took a running leap, landing in the middle of the bed with a thump that made my head goggle.

"No barking or bed hogging though!" I told him. "And stay down there on the nasty bedspread!" I pointed to the end of the bed and he followed the line of my finger. He gave it a good sniff and decided it would make a great place to sleep. After four or five turns, he plopped down with a sigh and eyed me through the fringe of his long bangs.

I hated to admit it, but having him there was a comfort. I wasn't certain what he would do if something dark and scary tried to eat me, but I was confident he'd at least let me know. He wasn't my knight in shining armor, but he'd do.

Much to my surprise, sleep found me swiftly, but it wouldn't last for long.

I awoke to the sound of Fugly going ballistic at the foot of the bed.

Crazy Dead People

Chapter 15

I couldn't believe what I was seeing.

A giant bat was flying around the room. It looked like the kind of monstrosity you see on the Creature Double Features from my youth. Its wingspan must have been two feet wide as it coasted near the ceiling. Something about it wasn't quite right though. It almost looked two-dimensional, like something cut from shadows.

I sat up in bed and blinked my eyes several times, trying to decide if I was still asleep or not, because this was definitely the fabric nightmares were made of.

The nightlight only provided a small amber fan of light, leaving the rest of the room lost in shadows. The edges of the room were especially dark, making it nearly impossible to see it when it coasted past the corners. It zoomed around the room again and Fugly went mental at the foot of the bed, bouncing on all fours like he does when a big dog comes into our yard.

The only experience I've ever had with bats was the time one got into my mother's house. It was a tiny thing, barely larger than a mouse with fluttery, paper-thin wings that whispered like the leaves on a tree as it flew. My mother grabbed a broom and chased it out of the open front door while I cowered in the kitchen, diving to the floor every time it came near.

This was completely different. The bat that swooped through my room was far larger and didn't make any of the same movements. Instead of bobbing around like a winged tennis ball, this one flew like it was on a wire. It stayed at the same level all the way around the room, never varying from its position.

As if reading my thoughts, it suddenly swooped down low as it passed over me during its next lap. I dove under the covers, terrified at the thought of it getting caught in my hair. If that happened, it would be all over for me. I'd need to be locked in a rubber room with extra rubber. I held on tight to the covers for several minutes, while my dog continued to guard the bed. After a while, Fugly quieted down, so I came back out for air.

I snaked my arm out and found the bedside lamp. As I jolted back around, I saw it sail through the doorway into the living room. I scrambled out of bed to see where it went. There was nothing worse than having something terrifying in your space and then have it disappear. I needed to know where it went.

Absolute horror filled my soul as I watched it fly into the wall and became a dark shadow. For several seconds, it was nothing more than a blob. If I'd walked into the room, unaware of it, I probably would have missed it altogether.

"What the hell is that?" I whispered.

I wanted to approach it to get a better look, but fear kept me stationary. If Fugly hadn't reacted to it too, I might have brushed it off as a dream, but it wasn't. It was as real as the shadow on the wall. Every muscle in my body was tensed, ready for action.

What was it going to do next? And furthermore, would I have time to run past it?

Thoughts blazed through my mind but none of them guaranteed my safety. Could it hurt me? Could it turn back into a bat at will? What was it?

I stared at it, absolutely transfixed, willing it to come out of the shadows.

After encountering the bat in my mother's kitchen, I did some research on them. I wasn't sure about Ohio, but the bats indigenous to Indiana were tiny, less than two inches long. They only come out at night, feeding on insects before returning to their home to hide during the daytime hours. In recent years, the overall population had significantly decreased due to a fungal disease called White-Nose Syndrome. It was wiping out the population dramatically all over the country. While I wasn't a huge fan of the creepy little critters, I was even less enamored with mosquitoes. It made me happy my mother had safely chased ours outdoors.

This one made me curious, because bats this large weren't normally found in our area. You'd have to travel to northeast Asia or Australia to find one this big. I wanted to get a closer look but my apprehension was far greater than my interest. If someone else was with me, I might have been braver and walked closer for a better look, but I didn't.

Fur brushed against my ankle and I jumped before realizing Fugly had joined me at the doorway. He was also keeping his distance.

As we both watched, the shadow suddenly began expanding. It was darker than a normal shadow, so dark it appeared to be a perfect void of light. It almost looked like an opening to another dimension. It grew from the size of a dinner plate to triple its size. Slowly, appendages emerged from the body, extending outwards until they formed into arms. Next came two legs.

It almost resembled a spider in its form. Both the legs and the arms stretched out to the sides in a manner no human could ever manage. I wrapped my arms around my body, suddenly chilled to the bone. Goosebumps peppered my skin as my breath puffed out in front of me.

The room had grown as cold as a freezer in a matter of seconds. I looked down at my feet on the cold bare floor, fully expecting to see frost on the wood beneath them.

I've never been so frightened in all my life. Nothing could have prepared me for this moment. It was all I could do to remember to breathe as I stared, spellbound and terrified at what might happen next.

Without warning, the shadow scrambled up to the ceiling.

Oh my God! It was the crawler!

I finally found my feet and took a step back, but became entangled with Fugly, who was also retreating from the living room. For several horrifying seconds, I thought I was going to fall and land on him, but I caught myself at the last moment. Fugly scurried to the side of the bed and I kept edging backwards, never taking my eyes off the monster on the ceiling. My legs soon impacted with the foot of the bed and I stopped short. There was nowhere else to go.

Thoughts raced through my mind like wildfire as I remembered some of the stories I read online about it.

It often appeared as a dark spot on the ceiling and raced towards people, dropping to the ground right in front of them before spearing through their bodies. One woman said it stalked her throughout the asylum one night when she and her friends broke in. She would see it at the end of the hallway and quickly move to another floor, only to find it waiting for her.

Another person said it followed him home one night after he and his friends broke into the asylum. He was almost asleep when he had the overwhelming sensation of being watched. When he opened his eyes, the entity was hovering on his ceiling directly above him. He doesn't remember what happened next because he lost consciousness. The following morning, he woke up to discover bloody claw marks on his chest.

I also remembered the story about the guy who became possessed and had to be forcibly removed from the asylum. My legs began trembling, barely supporting my body.

I wasn't certain what this monster was capable of, but I wasn't keen on finding out. It crouched on the ceiling, as if watching me. My heart nearly exploded from my body.

I glanced behind me at the window beside the bed. It was two stories above the ground and I began wondering about the fall. Would I break bones if I lunged out of the window? Would it be better than what I was about to encounter or worse?

Slowly, the shadow became three-dimensional, its body extending inch by inch until it was a fully formed mass. It was still as black as pitch, but now had substance. It lowered its head from the ceiling and I knew without knowing it was staring directly at me.

I edged around the bed to the nightstand where my phone was charging. As my fingers latched around it, I hesitated. Who would I call? Sonora?

I envisioned her coming through the door, worried about me and getting attacked herself. I couldn't let that happen. Everyone else I knew was hundreds of miles away. I grabbed my phone anyway. If something happened to me, I at least wanted someone to know what happened.

I've never been overly helpful in horrific situations, but I have always been able to think quickly on my feet. I turned on the video camera and pointed it at the doorway. The screen was too dark to see much, but I didn't have time to fiddle with it. I held it in front of me like a weapon, my legs shaking so badly, my knees began knocking together.

"I'm recording you so other people can see this," I warned it. I didn't know if it cared or even understood the words I was saying, but it was my only defense. Maybe it would go away if it didn't want to be recorded.

I glanced down at my phone to make sure I still had it in the frame when I noticed something strange. A white mist was appearing on the screen. I looked up from my phone and could see it with my own eyes. The swell of cheap perfume suddenly filled the room as my ears began ringing again, giving me the first glimmer of hope.

Bertha was here!

"Keep it away from me, Bertha," I pleaded, watching as the mist grew brighter and larger. It nearly covered the entire doorway to my bedroom, completely blocking out the black human-shaped mass on the ceiling.

Was she protecting me?

I wasn't even sure what she was capable of. Could she chase it away or would it just eat her as a snack before it got to me?

The mist grew brighter and brighter, as though it was lit from within by a blinding light. It swirled and rolled, like smoke mixed with glitter caught in a spotlight, growing so bright it hurt my eyes. Then, with a puff of mist, it disappeared altogether, taking the crawler with it.

I was frozen to the spot, the fear holding me hostage. It wasn't until Fugly edged out into the doorway before I could even lower the camera. I stared into the room, searching it for any signs of the shadow monster. I gave it five seconds longer and then I bolted from the room.

I didn't even bother to grab my shoes by the couch. I just hauled ass through the living room and out the door with Fugly close on my heels.

Crazy Dead People

Chapter 16

Sunlight streamed through the gauzy white curtains, filling the room with an earnest yellow glow. I lifted my head and looked around to find myself in a room similar to my bedroom at the cabin. It took me a minute to realize where I was.

A clanging sound emanated from the kitchen. Every muscle in my body protested as though I'd completed a triathlon the day before instead of surviving a paranormal encounter. I propped myself up on my elbows and caught a whiff of freshly brewed coffee and bacon, two of my favorite smells. I glanced down at the sides of my bed, surprised to not find Fugly sleeping beside me and then I remembered the bacon. There wasn't much my dog wouldn't do for a hunk of fried fatty pork.

I slipped out of bed and padded barefoot to the kitchen.

Sonora stood at the stove with a pan of sizzling bacon in front of her. Her hair was piled in a messy bun on the back of her head, but she was dressed for the day in cargo capris and a fuzzy burgundy sweater. Fugly was parked beside her, his ears tipped up at full attention. If she accidentally dropped anything, even something as non-edible as a kitchen sponge, he would have swallowed it before he even knew what he'd eaten.

Catching me out of the corner of her eye, she turned and grinned.

"You look like shit. Get any sleep?" she said, sweeping me with a long glance, taking in my Bite Me sleepshirt and my unruly hair that probably looked like a collie's hind end.

"A little," I said, nearly sleepwalking to the coffeepot. The truth was, I was awake until dawn, watching the corners of the room, fully expecting a repeat visit from the crawler. When I banged on Sonora's door after my experience, she had insisted on providing me with another glass of wine while I filled her in on all the night's events. After I finished, she poured herself a glass too.

We stayed up until the wee hours of the night, dissecting it and trying to make sense of it. We checked my phone, but the recording I'd made was nothing but fuzzy static. If I recorded the crawler, he somehow erased it.

Sonora was shocked by all of it. In all her years at the cabins, she'd never had anything like that happen before. It was obvious the crawler had followed me from the asylum.

The thought alone made my stomach tighten. Until last night, I was completely unaware that ghosts and creepy crawlers could actually leave their haunted house and follow people. In my ignorant mind, I imagined them being trapped there without the ability to travel. It brought forth all sorts of questions, starting with the location. Why haunt a creepy old insane asylum when you could be on Fiji? If I were a ghost, I'd haunt the hell out of a Tiki bar next to aquamarine waters. I came out of my internal musings to find Sonora watching me.

"I forgot to ask you something. How did Frank handle it?" she asked.

Realization hit me like a punch in the face. I hadn't thought about Frank once during the entire encounter. I slid off my chair.

"I'll be right back."

The sunlight was brighter than I was prepared for. It felt like someone pinned me with a spot light. I squinted into the sun, feeling a stab behind my eyes. I couldn't believe I'd forgotten about Frank. He hadn't made a single peep the entire time the crawler was taunting me. Had something happened to him?

I got my answer as I stepped gingerly across the cold wet grass between the cabins and grabbed onto the stair rail. Someone was singing *Somewhere over the Rainbow* in a very off key. The voice was nasally and could only come from a parrot.

"Somewheeeere....over the rainbow. Blue birds fly. Birds fly over the rainbow. Why then, oh why, can't I?" he wailed.

The steps were slippery from the morning dew, but I made it up without falling, which was a major feat for someone with my knack for clumsiness. I've not only tripped going up a set of stairs, I've done it so many times people often warn me to be careful before I start up them.

I opened the door but stood outside for a moment, making sure the cabin wasn't full of crawlers. The room looked exactly as it had when I'd left it. I took it as a good sign.

The bird cage was still parked on the kitchen table, covered with the beige blanket I'd thrown over it the evening before. Orange eyeballs stared at me from the bottom of the cage. It took me a second to comprehend what I was seeing. Frank must have found a gap in the blanket.

"Does Frank want out?" he called.

This made me chuckle, remembering my friend's bird. I pulled the cover off and eyed the bird.

He didn't look any worse for the wear. In fact, he looked exactly as he did the previous day. Apparently, the crawler hadn't been interested in him.

I filled his food and water dishes and then took the opportunity to shower. Everything felt so normal, I forgot about the crawler until I was halfway finished. My eyes immediately turned towards the ceiling, relieved to find it empty.

How long would it take me to get past this? Would I spend the rest of my life staring at ceilings in fear? It seemed like a living nightmare.

I finished quickly and hurried into my bedroom to get dressed. Rumbling through my bag, I was dismayed at all the inappropriate clothing I packed for myself. I guess I didn't know what to expect because I packed a lot of button-up blouses and dressy slacks. Thankfully, there was one pair of jeans and a long-sleeved navy-blue t-shirt.

I pulled it on and was happy enough with the way it looked. Blue was always a good color with my auburn hair and fair skin. It gave me a bit of color and brought out the green in my eyes.

I've never been a girly-girl and don't spend more time than I have to on my appearance. I'm not someone who layers on jewelry and makeup. A dab of mascara and a pair of silver earrings and I'm good to go.

As I was leaning up to the mirror applying my mascara, I heard a noise that stopped me mid-stroke.

It sounded like a squeaky door opening.

With trembling fingers, I sat the mascara wand down and moved to the bathroom doorway. I heard it again, clearer this time. My heart nearly stopped. It sounded exactly like the banshee door at the asylum.

I edged out of the bathroom and did a quick visual sweep of the room. Nothing appeared out of place. I checked the corners and the ceilings, but they were clear of both prowlers and crawlers.

The screen door was still closed and latched. A soft morning breeze drifted in, smelling strongly of lake water and dry leaves. I walked to the door and looked out.

No one was on the porch or stairs and the yard below was also empty. A breeze blew down the hill, sending a tumble of dry leaves in its wake. Somewhere in the distance, a crow cawed, loud and stark. If someone had been there, they evaporated on the spot.

I was on the brink of just bolting without worrying about applying mascara to my other eye when I heard it again. This time, it came from directly behind me.

Whirling around, I tracked the sound to the bird cage. Frank sat on his perch, eying me. As I watched, he made the sound again, nearly sending me to an early grave.

"Oh my God, you damn bird!" I yelled at him. African Gray parrots were apparently excellent mimickers because he had that particular sound down pat. It was a perfect imitation of the noise the giant's door made when it opened, which coincidentally – or maybe not coincidentally – sounded exactly like the door at the asylum.

I wasn't sure how much more I could take. If my hair wasn't stark white by the end of the week, I'd consider myself lucky.

I ran back to the bathroom and finished getting ready and then made tracks back to Sonora's cabin, where a plate of food was waiting for me on the table.

"It might be a bit on the cold side. I wasn't expecting you to be gone so long, but nice improvement," she said, refilling my coffee mug.

"Thanks. This looks amazing." I looked down at the plateful of scrambled eggs and bacon and nearly died and went to Heaven. The only thing stopping me was the prospects of not getting to meet the paranormal team later. That might be worth remaining earthbound for a bit longer.

Even though I initially dreaded meeting them, my curiosity rose above the aversion. I certainly wasn't a fan of the show but I had to admit the concept intrigued me. Two men and a film crew went into haunted locations and poked at the dead. Sometimes the dead poked back, which always made for good TV. Last season, Brock ended up in the hospital for nearly a month after falling through an unstable floor. After that, the production team decided to hire a location scout to go in ahead of them and make sure it didn't happen again. If anyone was going to fall through a rotten floor, it would be me instead.

I checked the time and realized I needed to leave.

"Come on, Fugly!" I called, but he didn't even glance back at me. He was still staring at Sonora who was lifting a piece of bacon to her mouth.

"He can stay with me. I'm home all day. I have some homework to do, but I'm sure he doesn't mind," she told me, reaching down to ruffle his head. If I ever thought my dog couldn't live without me, this was a defining moment. All it took was a piece of bacon to sway his affections.

"All right, then. Bye, Fugly! Be a good boy!" I sang out, but he still didn't budge from his begging spot. I shook my head and gave Sonora a weary smile. "Thanks for breakfast."

"You're very welcome. Good luck today. If you decide to bring something home today, make sure it's Brock Daltry and not another crawler," she said.

"Don't count on it." It would be a cold day in hell before I brought Brock Daltry home. I'd almost – with a big emphasis on the word *almost* – rather bring home the crawler.

My Jeep was sitting a bit side-goggled in the driveway from our nighttime foray to the giant's cabin. It seemed like something that had happened a week ago or even a month ago. So much had happened since then; it felt strange how only a few hours had passed.

By no means was I an adrenaline junky, but the events of the past day felt like getting off a rollercoaster. I was wired, but I was also tired, cranky and edgy, three qualities that didn't put me in a good frame of mind for meeting the paranormal team.

I drove to the asylum, barely noticing the backdrop of beautiful autumn trees and the drifts of leaves at the edge of the roads. My mind was preoccupied with the events of the previous night. They replayed through my head, making less sense with every reiteration.

Was Bertha really there, trying to help me?

I didn't actually see her, but I knew without any doubt it was her. How was that possible? And why would she willingly stay in a place where a crawler roamed? Why didn't she go to Heaven to be with her family? I had more questions than I had answers for. As much as I hated to admit it, I was hoping the paranormal team could answer some of them for me.

It wasn't until I got to the gates before I really thought about where I was going.

I stopped at the entrance to the woods, where the giant had removed the chain and led me through the haunted forest.

I was back at the asylum. Back at the crawler's home base

Crazy Dead People

Chapter 17

As I rounded the side of the massive stone building, I felt as though I'd driven onto a movie set. The small gravel driveway was filled with vehicles. Most of them consisted of black vans and matching black SUVs. If it weren't for the Paranormal Warriors logo plastered all over the vehicles, I might have thought the secret service had come to support our efforts.

Men with black shirts and big cameras stood in the driveway, their cameras pointed at the building. Others were bent over equipment boxes, rooting through coils of cords. A beige canopy had been set up across the driveway from the doorway with a table beneath it filled with computer monitors and boxy recording equipment. From watching the show, I knew this was going to be the command center. Someone would sit there for the duration of the investigation and keep tabs on the investigators.

A news van was parked amid the black trucks. The reporter was filming an interview out front, turning the tragedy into entertainment.

I was immediately thankful I didn't have Fugly with me. Knowing him, he would have latched onto an ankle in two seconds flat.

The transformation was jarring. I just sat in my Jeep for a moment, trying to wrap my mind around what I was seeing. The previous day, the asylum had a forgotten aura surrounding it. It felt lost and forlorn, sitting on the hill all by itself. Now, it was crawling with people, all of whom had a specific agenda. It felt like two completely different places.

A gas-fired generator sat beside the door with cables snaking out of it and trailing into the doorway of the asylum. I was fairly certain the interior would be lit up like the inside of a dentist's office. I was surprised the police were giving them full access to the building, considering what had transpired there less than a day ago.

I finally got out of my Jeep and approached the nearest black shirt with a clip board. "Isn't this a crime scene?"

"The coroner ruled it a suicide, so we have the green light," he told me and then went back to his clipboard.

"A suicide?" I said, apparently to myself because the black shirt had already moved away from me. How could they rule it a suicide? There was no way the giant could have hung himself without the benefit of a ladder or some way to get up to the chandelier.

The thought of him hanging there brought back an immediate memory. I relived the moment when I bumped into his body and caused it to sway. If I were Catholic, I would have crossed myself. Instead, I hugged my arms around my body as if warding off a chill.

Everything about this struck me as wrong. A man had just died here the day before. It seemed appropriate to give his memory some space instead of just pretending it didn't happen for the sake of a stupid television show. On my way there, I had envisioned myself finding the spot where the giant had died and saying a prayer for him, while the crickets chirped in the distance and the silence resounded all around me. That was no longer possible.

In its place were people who wanted to take advantage of his devastation. They were people who saw this as an opportunity to monopolize instead of a life that needed to be mourned. You could almost feel the excitement buzzing around them. It was like Christmas morning, instead of the moment of silence it should have been.

I walked to the doorway, not sure I wanted to be anywhere near the interior of the building. Actually, I was one-hundred percent certain I didn't want to be inside the building, but that probably wasn't going to be an option for me unless I wanted to quit my job on the spot and head back home to my mother's house. The conflict speared around inside of me, my ethics battling against my own needs. I felt horrible to be a part of this. Even when I told myself I didn't have a choice, I knew I was kidding myself. I did have a choice and I was no better by looking the other way instead of getting back in my Jeep and leaving a spray of gravel in my wake.

I heard a very distinct cackle from inside the foyer that could only come from one person.

One of the black shirts was walking inside, so I asked him to go get Beezer for me. Moments later, the cackling stopped and the little dweeb showed up at the door. I hated him just as much as I had the first time I met him.

We'd met briefly for a job interview and I had despised him on site.

Paranormal Warriors was the most popular paranormal show on television. Critics often blasted the show for fabricating supernatural encounters for the sake of ratings and people had mixed feelings about its stars. They either loved them or hated them. There wasn't much gray area to speak of. What everyone did agree on was that Beezer Harp was a scumbag who couldn't be trusted around women.

There were quite a few articles about his misconduct with female employees and witnesses at the locations. He didn't seem to be very picky either. Complaints came from women all over the spectrum, including age, weight, race and height. The only thing he apparently cared about was that they were female. He was accused of groping, attempting to solicit sexual favors for air time and overall poor behavior. The only reason I could see that he hadn't been fired was the fact that he was one of the executive producers and had financial control over the show. I planned to keep him at arm's length. If he tried anything, he was getting a size eight boot in a soft spot of my choosing.

"Hey Shelby!" he said as he came bursting through the door. He looked like an overgrown kid who just hit the winning homerun at his little league game.

He was short in stature with a halo of frizzy brown curls and a closely trimmed beard. His bright blue eyes were by far his best feature, but it was hard to stay focused on them due to the shirt he was wearing.

"I pooped today!" it read.

I looked up from the shirt to his face, hoping he'd make some sort of apologetic acknowledgement for wearing it to a crime scene, but he seemed oblivious. It was the kind of t-shirt I might find amusing at a backyard barbeque but it lost all of its charm in a supposedly professional environment. If I was going to give him some leeway for all the articles of misconduct I'd read online, hoping some of it was untrue, it all went away in the blink of an eye.

"I hear you had some excitement yesterday! Of course, I want all the details, but I'll grab the guys so they can hear it too."

Before I could protest, he turned and shouted into the doorway. "Brock! Montgomery! Shelby's here!"

A man with a sprout of black chin hair and an overload of facial piercings popped his head out of the door. I recognized him from the show as the man named

Montgomery. He was always the voice of reason to Brock's outlandish theories, the one who stopped Brock from going overboard. He didn't seem to have any of those qualities at the moment though.

"Oh hello," he said, tipping his ridiculous-looking trucker hat as he saw me. "We're in the middle of an EVP session. Bring her in here. Maybe the caretaker will talk to her."

Beezer clapped his hands together, in obvious delight. "Oh wonderful idea!" He put his hand on my back and sort of pushed me up the stairs to the doorway.

I crossed the threshold, not needing to allow my eyes to adjust. It was nearly as bright inside as it was outside. Massive floor lamps on tripods were positioned around the room. Someone had drawn an X with white tape on the floor where the giant had died. Surrounding it were a group of men with handheld equipment.

As they saw me, they turned to take me in, and I got my first look at Brock Daltry.

Much to my dismay, he was just as handsome in real life as he was on television. Secretly, I hoped he was at least afflicted with acne blemishes that needed to be covered up with a thick layer of paste, but it wasn't the case.

Some people have a vibe about them you can't repel. It's as though they emit an invisible pheromone that reaches out and snares you by the throat. There's no resisting it. You might feel it and know exactly what's going on, but you can't seem to break its hold.

I found myself drifting towards him with a goofy smile plastered on my face.

"Shelby! It's so nice to finally meet you! Beezer told us all about you," Brock said, exposing a glimmer of white teeth. His eyes were a light shade of blue that reminded me of Caribbean waters and when he smiled, they reflected the emotion, crinkling softly at the edges. He had a square jaw peppered with stubble and short brownish hair that looked like he'd finger-combed in in favor of spending hours with a stylist.

Instead of offering me his hand to shake, he opened his arms. "Sorry, but I'm a hugger," he said, pulling me into a hearty embrace that came with the knowledge of his firm body and tantalizing cologne.

As he pulled away, he gave me a thousand-watt smile. "I know it's strange to hug someone you just met, but I think of it as an energy exchange. It allows our energy to intermingle."

Montgomery bumped him aside and crowded into the intimate space he'd created. Instead of pulling me into a hug as well, he stuck out his hand.

"Don't listen to any of his mumbo-jumbo bullshit. He's just trying to cop a squeeze," he said, shaking my hand. He bumped Brock playfully with his shoulder. "I've noticed he's only a hugger with the ladies, never with the dudes. Now, why is that Brocky boy?"

For his part, Brock's face flushed and he ducked his head away.

As if on cue, the three of us moved backwards, expanding the circle. Beezer wasted no time slipping into our ring. He squeezed between the two men and clasped his hands over their shoulders, pulling them into an awkward position. They looked like they were lined up, ready for a photo. It made me wonder if Beezer often felt left out by their fame.

"These are my boys! What do you think of them?" he said enthusiastically, claiming them in a way that obviously made them both uncomfortable. They shifted away fairly quickly, making it clear they weren't thrilled with Beezer any more than I was.

As his smile faded, Brock took on a serious tone. "I understand you had a pretty terrifying experience yesterday?" he said, turning the statement into a question.

Before I could answer, Beezer butted in. "Oh yes, she did. Shelby, tell them about how you came through here and ran right into the caretaker. Didn't you say his body swung when you bumped into it?"

I happened to be looking at Brock when Beezer was talking and caught the flare of anger wash across his face. He erased it quickly and looked at me.

"Shelby, why don't the three of us walk the asylum and you can show us the places where we need to focus. Beezer can stay here and watch the monitors in case anything happens while we're walking around," he said. It was clearly a move to separate us from the obnoxious producer, something I was immensely grateful for.

"That sounds like a great idea," I said.

Without further ado, he turned and walked to the banshee door. As he pulled it open, the door rang out as though announcing our entrance into the depths of hell.

With all my heart, I didn't want to go back into the asylum, but I pushed my fears aside for the sake of doing the job I was hired to do.

I hoped I wouldn't live to regret it.

Chapter 18

The banshee door slammed with a thud behind us, plunging us into total darkness. I felt the asylum close in on me in an instant. Images of taunting dead people filled my mind as the ghosts separated from the stained walls, peeling themselves off in layers.

I could almost see translucent fingers swiping in front of my face, missing my nose by an inch. They crowded in by the dozens, pressing closer together until the spaces between them vanished. Arms and bodies became merged together, creating a woven blanket of souls. It grew thicker and thicker until it filled the entire hallway, pushing out all the air and leaving me breathless.

Without meaning to, I edged closer to the person beside me, which just happened to be Brock, and grabbed onto his arm.

"Don't you have a flashlight or something?" I hissed.

"What's the matter, Shelby? Don't you like the darkness?" Montgomery chuckled from my other side.

The arm I was latched onto moved and I let go of it long enough for him to dig in his pocket. If I was expecting a blinding Maglite like the giant had, I was sadly mistaken. He clicked his light on and the hallway was illuminated with a red glow.

"There. Is that better?" he said.

I looked over to where his voice was coming from and could only make out his general shape.

"Don't you have something brighter?" I glanced behind me to make sure the ghosts weren't creeping up on me before I turned back around, on the knife-edge of completely losing my shit.

Something touched my hair and I came unglued, batting at it with ninja skills I didn't know I possessed. Montgomery stilled me with a strong hand on my arm and then picked something out of my hair.

"It's just a cobweb," he said, dryly.

Brock laughed, his voice sounding strangely eerie in the darkness. I wasn't a big fan of this funhouse effect where voices manifested in the darkness and dead people surrounded us. I squinted at his shape to make sure it was him and not a ghost who slipped into his spot.

"Red light is better for investigations because it doesn't destroy your night vision. Once your eyes get adapted to the darkness, you can see better and won't need the light," he told me and then clicked the light back off. "Unless you'd rather have no light?"

I latched onto his arm again. "Turn it back on!"

This generated another chuckle before the light was switched back on. I wasn't sure if he was truly demonstrating the advantages of the red light or if he was messing with me, but I didn't like it. I let go of his arm and shifted until I bumped into the wall.

"I could do this, if it makes you more comfortable," he said, placing the red light beneath his chin and allowing it to beam up his face, turning him into an instant monster. It was such a childish gesture, something we did as kids. I couldn't help but feel slightly amused.

"Knock it off or I'm leaving!"

"Then you'd have to hang out with Beezer," Montgomery said from behind us. His voice startled me. I'd lost track of where he was.

Brock nudged my arm to get my attention. "I'd like to say Beezer means well, but he probably doesn't," he said, his voice losing its playful tone. "I shouldn't tell you this, and I pray it doesn't get back to him, but always watch him. Make sure someone else is with you when you're with him. We've had problems with him, as you're probably well aware of."

Before I could respond, Montgomery jumped into the conversation.

"Don't scare the poor woman, Brock!" he said and touched my shoulder, nearly causing me to have an out-of-body moment. "Just keep your head on straight and you'll be fine." He clapped me on the back, ending the discussion.

From watching several episodes of the show, I knew Montgomery often monitored the discussions, turning them in a different direction when he felt Brock was veering into controversial waters. On television, it was almost charming. In real life, it was something altogether different.

In many ways, it was dismissive and more than a bit rude. It reminded me of a relationship I was in years ago. Every time I tried to talk, I was corrected or shut down for being overly sensitive. My fiery red-headed side reared up briefly.

"Thank you for telling me that," I said to Brock. "He's already made me feel uncomfortable several times. I appreciate the warning."

"You're very welcome," he said with a smile in his voice again. "Shall we continue?"

He didn't wait for an answer. The red flashlight was redirected down the hallway, bringing my anxiety level back up to eye- twitching mode.

Something about the red light made the hallway even creepier. It seemed to enhance the drips trailing down from the ceiling and made the cracks in the plaster look like a place where fingers might suddenly appear from.

I wanted to tell them about my experience with the crawler, but certainly didn't want to have the conversation in the dark hallway where I might inadvertently invoke him. I'd save it for the second floor where there was natural daylight streaming through the windows.

We came to the room where the bedpan moved. The memories came back to me in a flash and I found myself backing up until I bumped into Montgomery.

"Hey, hey! No walking through walls here unless you're a ghost!" he said, shifting back out of my way.

I pressed my back to the slightly damp wall for a moment until the smell of mold and mildew made me take a step forward. I pulled my shirt away from my back and fanned it, not wanting any of the slimy residue touching my skin. When I got back to the cabin, I was boiling myself in the hottest shower I could manage.

"I'm sorry, but I had a weird experience in this room," I said and then went on to describe how the bedpan moved. Both men stepped into the room with an eagerness I couldn't fathom. I stood outside the doorway and watched them as the shadows behind me crowded in closer. I fumbled around in my pocket until I found my small flashlight. It wasn't bright enough to chase the shadows very far, but it at least gave me a sense of the space directly surrounding me.

The two men had some discussions about setting up a night vision camera in the room later in the day as Brock walked around, inspecting every inch of the room with his red flashlight. Finally satisfied, he pulled a digital recorder out of his pocket and sat it on the metal bed frame.

"We'll just leave this here in case anybody wants to talk to us while we're gone," he said, and we moved back down the hallway.

I hung close to the two men until we got to the stairs. Knowing there was light at the top gave me the energy to race up them, not stopping until I reached the second floor landing. I could hear the two men laughing at me from the bottom of the stairs, but I didn't care. Getting into the daylight was far more important to me than staying with the group, especially considering the group I was with. They were all about finding the scariest places and I was all about avoiding them.

Daylight pushed against the cracks of the doors, giving an immeasurable sense of relief. I pulled it open and didn't bother to stand there and hold it open for the guys. If they felt like poking around on the stairs, they could also open the door themselves.

I made a beeline through the first open room and found the veranda. The sunshine was warm on my skin. I closed my eyes and turned my face towards the sun, reveling in the sensation. I wanted to soak in as much of it as possible before I had to go back down to the darkness. There was an analogy in there somewhere, but I didn't have the fortitude to dwell on it.

As soon as the guys came through the door, I met them in the hall.

"I had two strange experiences on this floor," I told them, my sense of confidence returning now I could actually see where I was. I told them about the little old lady in the rocking chair and then led them to her room. I fully expected them to scoff at the vision I saw in my mind's eye of her sitting in her rocking chair, working on needlepoint, but they didn't. They had probably heard far stranger stories. When you make the paranormal your life, it probably takes a whole lot of weird before it begins to sound crazy.

I walked into her room, taking in the faded walls and lumps of debris on the floor.

"Her bed would have been here," I said, pointing to the wall on my left. "And this was where she sat in her rocking chair," I pointed to the space at the foot of her bed where I saw her.

I suddenly remembered the dream I had about her. She told me her photo album was still on the floor in her room, so I found the spot on the floor and began moving boards and gunky stuff I hoped was rotten plaster.

"What are you doing?" Montgomery asked from behind me.

"This is where she told me her photo album was," I said rather matter-of-factly. I was so confident I was going to find it; I really wasn't very surprised when I pulled up a board and saw it sitting there.

"I'll be damned," Montgomery said, while Brock knelt down beside me to get a closer look. It took everything I had to ignore the sensation of our thighs touching, but I pushed aside my hormonal impulses and cracked the book open.

It was filled with photos. Some of them were of her family, but others were of the asylum from when it was a nursing home. Dour-faced nurses with trays walked down the hallways, passing by patients sitting in wheelchairs. I wasn't sure how she managed to get the photos developed, but I was glad she had.

"Do you mind if we bring it back and look it over?" Brock asked.

I felt a roar building up inside of me. After everything I went through to get it, there was no way they were getting their hands on it until I was finished with it. I tamped down on the anger and took a deep breath.

"I want to research it a bit first," I said instead of something nasty that truly wanted to escape from my lips. The surge of emotions was strange to me. The last time I was here, I felt utter sadness and now I felt anger. It was as though I no longer had any control of my feelings. I stood up and dusted myself off as best as possible with one hand. Brock offered to take the photo album but I declined, trying to force my frown into a passable smile. He was only trying to help me. He wasn't trying to steal the album.

Good Lord! What was wrong with me?

I stepped back in the hallway and caught my breath.

The hallway stretched out for an eternity, striped with light from the veranda windows. As I stared down it, something dark separated from the shadows. My heart nearly stopped in an instant.

It was the crawler.

Chapter 19

"You said two things happened to you," Brock said from inside the room. "What was the second thing?"

I was incapable of speech. I just stood and stared gape-jawed at the black shape that was staring back at me from the end of the hallway. It was tall and profoundly solid, looking very much like a man dipped in tar. The shape was crisp but devoid of any shadowing that would give it a three-dimensional form. As I watched, it crossed its arms and seemingly leaned against a doorframe. The photo album slipped from my fingers and landed on the ground beside me with a plop.

"Shelby?" Montgomery asked.

They must have noticed my expression, because they came out of the room and stood beside me. I lifted my hand and pointed down the hallway.

There was a moment of stunned silence, followed by absolute chaos.

The two men tore off down the hallway.

"Is your camera on?" Brock yelled as they ran further away from me.

"Yeah. It should be," he said, fumbling with something on his shoulder. "Yeah. It's on."

I stood stock-still, watching them run. My legs were frozen to the spot as trembles overtook my body. For several long seconds, my mind disconnected from my body as the shock of the situation overloaded my senses.

The crawler held its ground until the two men were less than twenty feet away. It just stood there, daring them to come closer. At the last minute, it stepped into a doorway and disappeared from my line of sight.

The men reached the doorway and bolted through it, leaving me completely alone in the hallway. It was enough to break my paralysis. I took a step forward, not sure what to do. I certainly didn't want to join their chase, but I didn't want to be left alone in the hallway either. All imaginary notions about daylight being safer were now ashes and dust. If the crawler could appear in full daylight, there was no safe place.

I started walking down the hallway, uncertain of where I was going. The men's voices trailed off until I couldn't hear them at all. I had no idea where they went and no clue how to find them. A part of me wanted to just leave the asylum and go back to the cabin where Sonora and Fugly waited for me, but in order to do that, I'd have to walk through the pitch-black first floor.

I drifted towards the light at the veranda. The first thing they tell you about getting lost in the woods is to stay where you are so people can find you. Hopefully, once Brock and Montgomery finished their fruitless chase, they'd remember to come back and look for me.

I leaned against the concrete railing and tried to force my mind on happier thoughts. I found myself thinking about my father. He was the strongest man I knew. He took every situation seriously, pondering it over until he came to a conclusion. Then he'd work feverously until the issue was resolved. He did this with broken cars and with distraught people alike.

My father was also the smartest person I've ever known. I didn't have to ask myself what he would do in this situation because his words came to me, like they always did.

"Make it right, Shelby," I whispered.

My connection to my father wasn't built on metaphysics or psychic impressions. Even though I've heard of other people receiving signs from their loved ones who'd passed away, I wasn't certain I had ever felt my father near me. He wasn't the kind of person to send me butterflies and rainbows because he knew I'd logically break it down and label it happenstance. He would come to me with the words he taught me.

I'd make it right.

I wasn't sure how I'd accomplish the task, but I wasn't beyond trying. First though, I would have to find a way to push away my fears. It seemed like an impossibly tall mountain to climb, especially considering I was inexperienced and metaphysically challenged.

It was highly unlikely I was going to conquer the asylum monster with my bare hands, chasing it down the hallway like my investigator friends were currently doing. It was doubtful they were going to accomplish anything either, unless simply capturing its image on camera was enough for them.

I didn't care what it looked like or what it wanted. I just wanted it gone. It seemed to have a hold on the building, pushing everything else to the corners while it held court. I thought about all those lost souls in the asylum and wondered if it had something to do with it.

Was it holding them hostage, forcing them to remain there?

The thought was mind numbing. I leaned back against the railing and tipped my head so the sunshine could warm my face. I wasn't sure how to even start, but I knew I needed to focus on my strengths instead of attempting something new. My strength was my ability to dislodge information. I was a damn good researcher which was where I would start.

The photo album was still lying in the hallway where I dropped it. I craned my neck, trying to see it, but it was out of my range of sight. I stared at the wall that was preventing me from seeing the photo album, praying there wasn't something hiding behind it.

If there was one asylum monster, there could be a whole mess of them. They could all be lurking on the other side of that wall, just waiting for me to fall into their trap. I felt my stomach tighten with the thought and then I heard my father's words inside my head.

"Anything worth doing is worth the risk of failure," he told me repetitively. Usually, his advice was centered on real world issues, such as a class project or graduating from college, making it far easier to follow. It never hinged on a life or death situation, which brought to mind another equally jarring thought.

Could the crawler really hurt me?

It wasn't made of matter, only energy. Was it capable of manipulating its environment to produce physical effects? How could something made of air harm someone? Did it simply use the power of fear to motivate me? Maybe it was nothing more than a soft-bodied bully, the kind that uses intimidation as a weapon with no real means to back it up.

It wasn't much and I wasn't fully convinced of its accuracy, but it was enough to propel me away from the railing.

The door to the patient room was long gone, so all I had to do was step through the concrete doorway and walk across the room to the other open doorway.

I stopped at the threshold and peered out. The hallway was empty. All I could see were long, striped shadows trailing off to the end. I studied the doorways, especially the darker ones on the other side of the hallway.

Did those rooms absorb some of the sadness and despair, creating a template for the others who followed? I didn't know a lot about paranormal energy, but I had been to places that felt oddly disquieting.

While I was writing an article on unemployment, I once visited a house that was the site of a triple murder. There, I found an able-bodied woman who couldn't get up from her couch. She suffered from social anxiety and extreme depression, two things she hadn't experienced prior to moving there. I later learned her life turned around dramatically after she was evicted.

I always wondered if the house had something to do with it. While I was there, my head began pounding with an excruciating migraine. As soon as I left, it went away on its own. Could the bad energy from the triple murder create a black cloud around the house? If that was the case, I couldn't imagine what it did to the asylum where triple-murders were committed every morning.

So many ill-fated patients suffered from the medical incompetence of the era. Ice pick lobotomies and electric-shock therapy were normal treatments. Tuberculosis patients often had several of their ribs removed because the doctors thought it would give them more room to breathe. I hated to think what happened when the asylum was a nursing home. All they had to do was ignore them and allow them to perish on their own.

The photo album was still lying in the middle of the hallway to my left. I hurried over and snatched it up, returning to the veranda where I felt safer. I wasn't sure why I felt safer because light didn't have any apparent effect on the crawler, but I liked the way it felt as it warmed my skin.

I slid down the concrete wall and sat cross-legged with the album on my lap, trying not to think about the cobwebs and grime beneath me. I brushed my hand across the album cover, removing the top level of dust. It might have once been baby blue, but only a few spots of original shade remained. The rest was the color of the asylum: of death, despair and a hundred years of neglect.

Something rattled near the far end of the veranda. I jumped as though I were goosed. I peered down the hallway, not seeing anything that could have made the noise. It almost sounded like a piece of paper flipping over in the wind, even though the air was deathly still.

"Hello?" I called, hoping the guys were on their way back, but there wasn't a response. I stared for another thirty seconds before returning my attention back to the photo album.

I cracked it open, flipping slowly through the photos. The first several pages were filled with pictures from the fifties and sixties. A woman sat on a dun-colored sofa with a baby on her lap. In consecutive photos, the baby grew into a blond-haired girl. There was a photo of her sitting on a pony, followed by another photo of her with Santa Claus. It was apparent she meant the world to Bertha.

As I moved through the pages, I watched her daughter grow into a young woman. The family images stopped with a wedding photo of her next to a handsome young man. Then, the photos of the woman ended and were replaced with images from the nursing home.

The first few were of smiling residents, but as I flipped through the pages, the smiles faded and were replaced with a sense of sadness. I could almost feel the neglect and loneliness radiate from the photos.

One photo caught my attention. In it, a stone-faced man stood in a doorway with a clipboard in his hand. The expression on his face was anything but friendly. He was tall and slim with dark slicked-back hair and cruel black eyes. If what they said about eyes being mirrors of the soul was true, his soul was pure evil. The longer I stared at his face, the more I became convinced he had something to do with the current haunting.

I could see a name embroidered on his white lab coat, but I couldn't make it out. I pulled my cell phone out of my pocket and snapped a photo of it, hoping I could enhance it on my computer when I got back and pull in more detail.

Voices murmured in the distance, becoming louder with every second.

The guys were back.

I pulled myself up to a standing position and dusted off my butt as much as possible. I started to reach down to grab the photo album when I heard the paper rattling sound again.

I squinted down the veranda hallway, trying to make it out. Something was moving towards me. The metal caught the sunlight as it got closer. I backed up a few steps, wishing the guys would hurry up. They couldn't see me because the patient rooms blocked their view.

"Hey guys?" I called out.

The sound of their voices trailed off as the patter of their footsteps increased. They reached the doorway to the veranda at the same time the moving item reached me.

It was a wheelchair.

Caught in the rungs of the wheel was a piece of paper.

With trembling fingers, I reached down and grabbed it, horrified at what I saw.

It was the first page of Bertha's hospital record.

Chapter 20

"What is that?" Brock asked, stepping out onto the veranda.

"It appears to be a wheelchair," Montgomery said with a perfect deadpan, earning him a smack.

"I know that! But what is it doing here? How did it get here? And what is that piece of paper?"

I handed him the page from Bertha's file and watched while he tried to make sense of it.

"It belongs to Bertha Simmons. She lived here when this place was a nursing home," I held out the photo album. "And this album I found...was hers."

I watched them for a moment while my mind did mental gymnastics. The sheet of paper with Bertha's information on it had been at my cabin the night before. Somehow, it was magically teleported from my cabin to the asylum. I tried to find a logical explanation for it, but failed miserably. I knew for a fact it was sitting on my couch last night.

The guys were still staring at me, waiting for an explanation, so I told them how Sonora and I had visited the giant's cabin the night before.

"Let me get this straight...you took several of the files from the boxes and this one just happened to be one of them?" Montgomery asked, waving the piece of paper.

"Yes. That's exactly right. I didn't look at any of the files. I just grabbed a handful."

"So, how did it end up back here, attached to the wheelchair?" Brock asked.

I shrugged my shoulders. "Either Bertha brought it back or the crawler did."

Both men looked at me with amusingly astonished expressions. If we weren't in the middle of an insanely haunted asylum, possibly being stalked by an evil crawler, I would have laughed. Instead, I decided to blow their minds a little further.

"And the thing you were chasing? The crawler? It was in my cabin last night." I told them the story about the bat that turned into the crawler. By the time I finished, their twin looks of bewilderment had transformed into near ecstasy.

"We have to get a camera in her cabin. Maybe it'll come back and we can get it on film...," Montgomery started to say but I cut him off.

"No way are you putting a camera in my cabin. There's more to this than just capturing evidence for a stupid television show. It's about what this thing is doing to the asylum," I said, plowing right through Montgomery's scowl as I called their show stupid. "I think this thing is keeping some of the souls trapped here."

Brock arched an eyebrow and then rubbed his eye with a knuckle. "You do know how crazy that sounds, right?"

This warranted him a full eye roll. "You think this is crazy?"

The two exchanged knowing glances. "Yeah, just a little bit," Montgomery told me. "Keep it up and somebody might lock you up in a place like this."

While I appreciated their attempt at humor, it nearly sent me over the deep end.

"Seriously! You guys chase shadows for a living. Give me a freaking break," I turned with the intention of walking to the stairs and heading to my Jeep, before I remembered the unlit first floor. It was extremely difficult to make a statement in a haunted asylum.

Thankfully, the guys had nearly forgotten all about me. "Let's go hook up your camera to the computer and see if we got anything," Brock suggested.

"I'm pretty sure we did. It was pointing right at it." He detached the tiny camera from his shoulder and looked at it. I wasn't sure about it, but it looked like one of those tiny cameras motorcycle racers attach to their helmets to record the race.

They started walking towards the door, when Montgomery turned, as if in afterthought to make sure I was still behind them. "Good job holding your ground back there when the wheelchair rolled towards you. I know a lot of big strong *handsome* guys who would have squealed and run like little schoolgirls if it had happened to them." He elbowed Brock, who turned his face away.

I stifled back a chuckle. Brock was supposed to be the fearless one, but he often went running when the shit got real. Someone had made a meme of him on social media, his face frozen in a scream with the words "Run! It's a demon!" below it.

There were a lot of discussions about the validity of the show. When they first started out, they chased ghosts and actually caught some fairly compelling evidence of their existence, but things had been going south for the past few years. Viewers, as it seemed, weren't as frightened by mere ghosts anymore, so the Paranormal Warriors now chased after demons. It was the next greatest thing and people began watching the show again, increasing the ratings. I wasn't sure how much of it was made up and how much of it was real. The only thing I was sure of was what I had personally experienced and it scared the piss out of me.

"That thing we saw. They call it the crawler, but what do you think it really is?" I asked. They kept walking for a few steps until Brock stopped and turned to look at me.

He looked tired. His eyes were red from the dust in the asylum and his hair was a little messier than normal. "It's a shadow person. We've encountered them several times over the years and they're never good. Personally, I think they come from another dimension, but Montgomery thinks they're demons." He held his hands up, palms up. "Who knows though? Nobody knows what they are for sure. It's why we study them, so we can learn more about them and what they want."

I was a bit confused. My research into the paranormal was still in its infancy. "What do you mean by another dimension?"

"Well, many people theorize our world, our dimension," he said, emphasizing it by holding up his hands as though he were holding an invisible world, "sits alongside other dimensions. They have their own world just like we have ours. Now imagine if someone from the other dimension was able to pop through into our dimension," he said, allowing the thought to sit there and gain momentum for a moment.

"That has to be the creepiest thing anyone has ever said to me." I tried to wrap my mind around what he said, but I just couldn't make it work. It all felt too much like science fiction to me. As much as I hated to admit it, I liked Montgomery's demon idea better. Demons were something I could come closer to understanding.

We made our way down the stairs to the first floor. I hung tight between the guys, latching onto both of their arms so firmly they probably lost feeling in their hands by the time we got to the banshee door.

I'd nearly forgotten about Beezer until I saw his ugly face staring expectantly at us. He clapped his hands together.

"You guys were gone for a long time. Anything happen?" he asked, taking a few steps to intercept the guys. They moved around him as though he was invisible and found their way outside to the command center.

Several laptops sat on top of the folding table. Both men hurried to the other side and sat down. Within seconds, Montgomery's camera was hooked up to the computer and images were fast forwarding across the screen.

"Please be there. Please be there," he chanted as we watched ourselves zip around on the screen like ants on a hot sidewalk. He slowed it down to normal speed as the camera panned to me, pointing down the hallway. Then it all turned to static.

For the next three minutes, the screen was full of snow.

We hadn't captured a single shot of the crawler.

"Oh my God. That's exactly what happened to my recording last night," I gasped, incredulously.

The men exchanged weary glances. "We've had it happen before. Some of the higher level entities know how to interfere with the equipment," Montgomery offered.

"Higher level?" I had no idea there was a hierarchy system for ghosts. The concept made my head hurt.

Brock flipped the laptop closed and sat down in the chair behind the table. "Some of them have been around a lot longer than others and they've learned things. Imagine how much you would know if you were two-hundred years old and locked in the same place all that time. Some of them pay attention and learn how to do things," he offered.

"That's where Brock and I disagree," Montgomery chimed in. "I think some of them are more powerful than others. If this crawler is a demon, it would have access to all the information in the underworld."

The two of them were confusing the hell out of me.

"So is it an interdimensional being or is it a demon? How do you explain this on your show when the two of you can't agree on what it is?"

"Maybe it's both," said a voice from directly behind me. I'd forgotten about Beezer and nearly jumped out of my skin when his voice boomed in my ear. I swiveled around to find him within elbow range. Even though I was itching to plant mine directly in his solar plexus, I was intrigued by his line of thinking. I shifted to the end of the table.

"What do you mean?" I asked.

He favored me with a conspiratory smile. "What if Hell is another dimension?" He let the words hang there for a moment before he continued. "As a culture, we've always thought of Hell being beneath us and Heaven above us, but what if that's wrong? What if Heaven and Hell are nothing more than alternate dimensions sitting alongside our dimension?"

I wasn't sure what to make of what he was saying. The concept of alternate dimensions was something I just couldn't grasp. I had a hard enough time balancing my checkbook. The truth was: I didn't care what it was and I doubted anyone would ever know for certain. You could study it all you wanted but it would block you at every turn because it didn't want to be figured out. While their hypotheses were somewhat intriguing, and more than a little bit confusing, I wasn't interested in them. I just wanted them removed from the building.

It was obvious we had differing opinions. They wanted to study the entity and learn more about it for the sake of good ratings on their television show. If they captured footage of a crawler and were able to broadcast it to the world, they'd be celebrated worldwide. People would flock to them and call them revolutionaries and maybe even heroes. They'd have their pictures on the front of major newspapers and magazines. Every news program in existence would hound them for an interview.

My agenda was a little simpler. I didn't want all the fame and fortune. I just wanted to make things right and I'd do whatever it took to make it happen.

I snatched Bertha's paperwork off the table and dug in my pocket for my keys.

"I've had enough for the day," I told them and turned on my heels and left.

As I walked to my Jeep, I entertained the thought of never returning to the asylum again, but I knew it was just a fantasy. If I was going to help those souls, I'd definitely have to return.

The thought sent a shiver down my spine, but I pushed it away.

Before any of that happened, I needed to be armed with more information.

I started my Jeep, my thoughts turning to happier places like government buildings and libraries where the books didn't try to eat you.

Crazy Dead People

Chapter 21

I've always considered myself an open-minded person, someone who often gives the benefit of doubt before making harsh judgements, but this was taking it a step too far. Any more of it and my head might explode.

As I drove down the road, heading back into the town of Parkesburg, I found myself zoning out. I missed most of the beautiful autumn scenery. Once in a while, an especially pretty tree would catch my eye and I'd emerge from deep inside my head to appreciate it, but most of the ride to town was spent in deep, contemplative thought.

I went into this job with a basic belief in ghosts. After having an experience as a child with a supposedly imaginary playmate, my vistas were broader than most. I was a prime candidate for a paranormal endeavor.

I could handle the concept of sharing our world with ghosts. In fact, I was fairly certain there were more of them milling around than most people were aware of. As I drove past an old gas station that had obviously been closed for decades, I could easily imagine a ghost man standing beside the place where the pump once stood, ready for his next customer. A house down the street with a broad Victorian porch and baskets of red geraniums hanging from the posts would be the perfect place for a woman with a fancy hat to loiter, remembering the old days.

As inconceivable as it was for most people, it was a plausible possibility to me. If I was honest with myself, which I seldom was, I would admit I've probably been feeling the presence of ghosts for most of my life. Most of them were so benign, they were like the prick of a mosquito bite, and were easy to ignore. Being thrust into such an insanely haunted environment like the asylum was like being subjected to a thousand mosquito bites at the same time. There was just no ignoring it at that level.

While I was okay with the prospect of ghosts in general, all the other stuff was hard to conceptualize. Why couldn't they just leave it at ghosts? Why add all the other strange theories like multiple universes and demonic realms? Did we really need all that? For me, it just made a very questionable theory even more concentrated, turning alphabet soup into a big bowl of quantum physics burgoo.

For most people, ghosts were scary. They were the invisible beings in horror movies springing up at people when their guards were down. They were the monsters under the bed and the demented clowns in the closet. They had evil intentions and made it their goal to scare the living daylights out of people. For me, it was different.

I thought of ghosts as the souls of living people. If my mother died and became a ghost, I would be no more afraid of her than I was when she was alive. I laughed as the thought came through my mind. Actually, I was afraid of my mother most of the time, but I wouldn't be more afraid of her as a ghost. Bad example.

A sign announcing the Parkesburg city limits came into view. Soon after it passed by my window, the spaces between the houses lessened and then thinned out until I found myself driving through a modest business district. The buildings were all one-story and showing age, with tenants ranging from tattoo parlors to Chinese restaurants to pawn shops. The trashcans were spilling out onto the sidewalks and graffiti graced many of the buildings.

I nudged my hand over to the lock button, feeling very little relief from the action. All it would take was someone with a gun at the next red light and I'd be toast. I know this because I have Netflix and have watched every episode of *Cops*. I'd like to say if someone came to my window with a gun, I'd just stomp on the gas, while simultaneously ducking down to avoid gunfire, when in reality, I'd probably just piss myself.

After three more blocks of similar offerings, I found the library. It was a two-story brick building tucked between a dog grooming parlor and a daycare. A group of youngsters were playing on colorful plastic playground toys behind a chain-link fence on one side. On the other side, a woman walked a fussy looking white dog on a rhinestone leash out to her Subaru while all the dogs inside the salon barked wildly. It probably made quiet time at the library a contradiction.

Twin concrete lions on brick posts guarded the steps leading up to the double doors. They almost felt too stoic and graceful for a neighborhood so full of regrets. I was surprised no one had pushed one of them over or decorated it with an orange mustache. I bounded up the stairs, eager to get inside.

In my opinion, there was no better smell than the aroma of a library. The perfume of old books filled my soul with a glee I hadn't felt in days, maybe weeks. I just stood there for a moment with closed eyes and breathed it in.

My revelry was cut short by quickly approaching footsteps. I looked up to see a young woman with unnaturally orange hair standing in front of me.

"Can I help you?" she asked. "Oh…and welcome to the Parkesburg Library!" she added.

I was temporarily incapable of speech as I took her in. Despite being a peculiar color, her bright orange hair was pulled into clips to make it stand up in odd plumes on her head. She obviously went to great lengths to obtain this specific appearance, although I felt someone should have told her how bad it looked. It made me wonder if she was an outcast because anyone with friends wouldn't show up like that in public. She had black, oversized glasses that slid down her nose. She pushed them back up with a finger sporting a Wonder Woman bandage and chipped blue fingernails.

"Hi. Yes, I could use some help," I finally managed to say.

"Awesome! I'm Kiki!" she said. "Kiki Dawes! I'm a volunteer here, but I'm hoping they'll hire me for a full-time position after winter break."

I was happy she repeated her name because I thought she said her name was Kooky, which actually fit better. I told her what I needed, and she went to work gathering material for me.

I situated myself at along table in one of the library's reading rooms and began sorting the material into stacks, according to subject. As I was cracking open the first book, I realized Kiki was still standing there, watching me expectantly.

"Are you researching the asylum?" she asked.

I had my mouth open to answer, but that apparently wasn't necessary because she kept on talking.

"I love that place. I broke in there with a few friends several times and we saw the strangest things. I know they talk about seeing a crawler running across the ceiling, but we didn't see it. We did see shadows moving down that long hallway until that big man with the beard chased us out. I know everything there is to know about the asylum.

Some people say I'm a walking, talking encyclopedia about it. Ask me anything! Go on!"

I marveled at her breath control because she spewed out her entire monologue in one breath. She really needed a built-in pause button or a Xanax. She was wound so tight, she could zip around the room like a popped balloon.

"Have a seat," I motioned towards the chair to my right. "I'm interested in the history of abuse when the asylum was a nursing home. Do you know anything about it?"

She plopped down and started twirling several colorful string bracelets on her wrist. "Oh yes! The Parkesburg Nursing Home opened back in 1953. Here's a book with pictures of it," she said and dug through the pile to show me a book with color photos.

I flipped through, barely recognizing the asylum. The photos were obviously promotional pictures, taken to encourage people to park their parents there. The long, scary hallway was painted stark white with gleaming white floor tiles. The patient rooms had wreaths on their doors, signifying the timeline as Christmas. In another photo, a group of elderly people sat on long sofas in a common room. The walls were paneled in dark walnut and lined with bookcases. In one corner, two gentlemen played a game of checkers. An old-fashioned television set was situated on a low table. In another photo, a group of old women sat at long white tables making holiday wreaths. There weren't any photos of the patient rooms, but I could use my imagination on what they had looked like.

"This isn't how it always looked. Their government funding was cut in the late sixties and everything got pretty run down. Jobs were cut and there were fewer people there to look after the patients. They didn't take any pictures of that," she told me, eyeing me over the top of the large black glasses.

Even though I already knew the answer, I had to ask. "Were the patients abused?"

"Oh Lordy, were they!" she said, pushing the glasses back up, making her brown eyes look magnified. "People were left in their beds for days on end until their bedsores got infected. Some of them were even tied to their wheelchairs and left in the hallways for hours at a time. Some reporter snuck in there with a camera in 1973. You might have seen it. It was on one of those news shows." She gave her bracelet another twirl. "Anyways, the hospital was shut down the next year and it's been sitting there as haunted as all get-out ever since."

I remembered the picture of the man in Bertha's photo album. I pulled my phone out of my pocket and showed it to her.

"Do you know who this guy is?"

"Oh definitely! That's Doctor Crask. He was an evil man...pure evil! He used to do experiments on some of the patients. He was studying dementia and would put them through some purely awful tests. He'd put them in these big horse troughs full of ice until their fingers turned blue and would shock their brains with probes. I think he died of a heart attack at the asylum just before it shut down," she said, stopping to take a breath. Her eyes widened. "You don't think he's there, do you...haunting the place?"

I wasn't sure, but it seemed like a good place to start. "Can I bring these home with me?"

"Oh sure! Just don't tell anybody I gave them to you. They're supposed to stay in the building, but as long as you bring them back, nobody will mind. Nobody ever looks at those."

While she was a wealth of information, I knew the only way I was going to be able to actually read the documents myself was by removing myself from her presence. I'd bring them to the cabin where it was nice and quiet.

I didn't alert her to the reasons for my questions. I knew she'd make a perfect candidate for the interview list Beezer had asked for, but I wasn't sure I wanted to turn her over to the scumbag. She was just a tad too eager and green for comfort. She seemed like the sort who would compromise her ethics for the sake of being on television and I didn't want it on my conscious. Maybe I'd tell Brock and Montgomery about her and see if they would interview her at the library without Beezer present.

I took her phone number, which she eagerly scrawled out on the back of a Walmart receipt, collected my books and was halfway back down the concrete stairs when my phone rang.

The number was from Los Angeles, California. It wasn't Beezer because I already had his number in my phone. It could only mean one thing.

I answered it, bracing myself for what came next.

Chapter 22

"Hey...Shelby!" the voice on the other end of the line purred. The sound of his voice was nearly musical and hit me on a primal level, his pheromones reaching through the phone lines like caressing fingers.

My instant reaction was to respond in kind, returning his purr with one of my own, but I stopped myself short, not wanting to fall victim to pheromones. Pretty boys like him were like chocolate. The first bite was always delicious but if you ate too much, you'd make yourself sick. It was better to just resist the temptation altogether.

"Hey, Brock. What's up?" I said instead, mentally congratulating myself.

There was a pause as he collected himself. After a lifetime of women fawning all over him, my abrupt greeting probably knocked him off his game. It forced him to come up with something else to say instead of "it's good to hear your voice too."

"Montgomery and I found something we want you to listen to," he said finally, the purr gone from his voice. "Do you remember the digital voice recorder we left in the room where the bedpan moved?"

I reached my car and began fumbling with my car keys, trying to find the right key with my trembling fingers. The mere mention of it made my gut clench.

"Yeah, I remember it."

"Well, we caught something you really need to hear. Can you meet with us?"

After the day I'd had, the last thing I wanted to do was to spend more time talking about the asylum. I wanted to curl up on the couch with my dog and watch some mindless

TV and drink gallons of wine until my head was nothing more than mush.

He properly interpreted my lengthy pause. "We can come to your place, if you want," he suggested.

I mentally removed the mindless TV, but kept the dog and the wine and inserted Brock and Montgomery into the equation and then pondered it.

"I'd invite you to our place, but we got in so early this morning the only place with a vacancy was an old motel just off the highway. Our room is less than stellar," he said, nearly making me laugh. He was probably at the same motel as I was, and had checked in after I scored the last cabin.

"No, that's fine. I'm at the Parkesburg Motor Lodge in one of the cabins on the lake. I'm heading there now. I can meet you in the parking lot," I told him.

I heard a slight intake of breath, but if he said anything else, I missed it as I disconnected the call.

I finally got control of my keys and stabbed one into the lock. Ten minutes later, I was pulling into the parking lot of the motel, my mind a weary, muddy mess.

I wasn't sure if I was up for more paranormal discussions. Unlike Brock and Montgomery, I didn't live on an exclusive ghostly diet. I needed a buffer in between encounters.

"Just get through it," I murmured to myself.

I stopped in the lot and waited until I saw a door open further down the row of rooms. Brock and Montgomery emerged, carrying a black backpack. It was only two in the afternoon, but the shadows were already lengthening, providing harsh contrasts as the sinking orange sun eyed us steadily. I rolled down my window and allowed the fresh air to fill the car while I waited for them to cross the parking lot. Somewhere in the distance, I could hear the hum of a leaf blower, followed by the brash caw of a crow. I took a deep breath, willing myself to endure what was about to come next.

Before the men could reach me, a car with a Domino's topper on the roof pulled into the lot. The men intercepted the driver before he could drive around aimlessly looking for the wrong room. By the time they made it to my door, there was a large pizza in Brock's hands and a smile on his face.

"I figured you probably haven't had lunch yet, so we ordered a pizza," he said.

I wasn't so easily swayed. Domino's typically takes longer than ten minutes. More than likely, they'd already ordered the pizza before calling me, so the chivalry of the moment was lost on me. However, it was pizza. There wasn't too much I wouldn't do for a thick slice of heaven.

"It's down there," I said, pointing in the general direction of the cabin. "Follow me," I said and put my Jeep in gear. I probably should have been nice and invited them to climb in for the short drive down the hill to the cabin, but I wasn't feeling especially generous at the moment.

It wasn't Brock's fault I was mistrustful of most men, but he was an easy target to cast the blame on. By the time I parked my Jeep, I began feeling the first pangs of guilt and made a mental note to be a bit nicer to him, at least until we'd cracked the lid on the pizza box.

The wind caught my hair as I climbed down out of my Jeep, sending my errant curls across my face. My hair was often weather intolerant, going from curls to frizz with the first hint of humidity. I couldn't imagine what it looked like, but I also didn't care. I swept it out of my face to find Brock watching me with hooded eyes.

I stared back for the duration of several heartbeats until my mind snapped into place.

Resist! Resist! Resist!

With a hearty push, I slammed the Jeep door and nearly dropped the pile of books and papers in the process, completely ruining the moment. Brock immediately came to my aid.

"Here, let me help you with those," he said, handing off the pizza box to Montgomery and taking half of the books before I could protest.

I was saved from further conversation by the sudden appearance of a barking ball of gray fur.

We all turned at once, as if controlled by marionette strings, as Fugly came bounding up the hill. Sonora wasn't far behind them, waving apologetically.

"Sorry!" she called. "He heard you and took off before I could catch him."

I watched as both men's eyes moved from the barking dog to the beautiful woman. It was almost enough to make me laugh. She picked her way up the hill slowly; fully aware she had an audience. I studied her, taking note of the way she gracefully tucked her long dark hair behind one ear as the wind caught it. She had changed clothes since I saw her earlier that morning. Instead of the fuzzy sweater and capris, she was back to a long flowing gypsy skirt and a navy form-fitting shirt. Her sense of femininity was wrapped around her like a second skin, making her seem helpless and impossibly resilient at the same time. She was the kind of woman men would fight over and hope to claim as their own.

As Fugly finally found me, jumping up on my leg to give me a happy-dog greeting, I glanced at the guys, not surprised to see them nearly drooling in Sonora's direction. They would be sadly mistaken if they mistook her for a damsel in distress. She'd eat them for breakfast and then use their bones to make a dreamcatcher.

"Hey fur face," I said, nuzzling Fugly's head.

He responded with a half-hearted lick on my hand before he smelled the pizza. He abandoned me quickly and ran over to suck up to Montgomery. It didn't escape me that my dog's reaction to the pizza was very similar to the guys' reaction to Sonora.

I didn't blame them completely about Sonora. She was exotic in a way you didn't expect, like finding a secret decoder ring in the bottom of your cereal box when you were expecting a temporary tattoo sticker. All eyes were on her as she stopped in front of us and graced us with an easy smile.

"Sonora, this is Brock and Montgomery from Paranormal Warriors," I said.

She flicked a playful smile at each of them and then reached down to nuzzle Fugly, who had shamelessly returned to her side.

"I'm sorry I wasn't there when you checked in this morning, but it's very nice to meet both of you."

My attention faded as they all fawned over each other for a moment. A part of me was green with envy at the way she effortlessly flirted with the two men. Ten more minutes of this, and they'd be offering to wash her car. It was like watching aliens communicate. I was so far removed from Sonora's world; I might as well have been an alien myself.

Flirting was an effort for me and I did it so poorly, it always came off as goofy and awkward. I'd finally had enough.

"We'd better get inside before the pizza gets cold," I said, pulling them out of their bubble of mutual adoration.

We carried the pizza into my cabin and wasted no time devouring it, crumbs and all. For his part, Fugly was privy to several of Sonora's crusts and he made it his point to hang close to her in case another bite magically appeared. She also gave a piece to Frank, who sat in his cage and methodically picked at it, dropping most of it onto the floor of his bird cage.

"What the fuck?" he said a few times as the bits hit the bottom of his cage.

I carried the box to the trash and sat it on the lid, having no patience to attempt to fold it up into a small enough square to fit inside the can. I was regretting having no beverages to offer my impromptu guests, when Montgomery pulled a six-pack from his backpack and began passing them out.

He spent an inordinate amount of time popping the top off of Sonora's beer before someone remembered I didn't have one yet.

"Beer?" he asked, tossing me one before I was prepared to catch it. Any feelings of solidarity I might have been secretly harboring quickly took a flush down the toilet. I managed to catch the beer before it landed on the floor and popped my own damn top.

"You have something you want me to listen to?" I said in a tone that left very little to the imagination.

Brock came out of his Sonora daze and looked at me, long and hard. It was as if he'd forgotten I was there until I spoke. I held his gaze a bit longer than was comfortable, feeling the same transfer of energy I always felt when I was around him. He was the kind of guy I could fall for and then live to regret it later.

"Yeah, as a matter of fact we do, Shelby," he said, drawing out my name, making it sound like lyrics in a song. He finally broke eye contact to glance back at Montgomery, who still had his gaze locked on Sonora. "Montgomery?"

I rolled my eyes. If this went on any longer, I'd have to ask Sonora to leave. She was obviously distracting my two testosterone-laden companions.

For his part, Montgomery recovered rather quickly. He pulled a laptop from the backpack and sat it on the coffee table in front of us. He moved to a spot directly beside me and began fiddling with the computer until he found what he was looking for.

"Do you remember how Brock left his recorder in the bedpan room?" he asked and waited for my nod. "Well, we captured something I don't think you're going to like," he said. He clicked the play button.

We all leaned in, our eyes watching the computer screen.

"We'll just leave this here in case anybody wants to talk to us while we're gone," Brock's voice said over the computer, bringing me right back to the moment when we left the room and headed down the hall.

I could hear the faint sound of our footsteps as we retreated further away.

Montgomery leaned over and began fiddling with the computer. "There's about two minutes of total silence. Let me skip over it and get to the good part," he said. After he finished doing his thing, the computer sprang to life again. We heard a rustling noise that was followed by a harsh scrape. It sounded like the bedpan grating against the concrete floor. Montgomery held up his hand and then pointed to the computer.

"Right here. Listen to this," he said.

The grating sound happened again, but this time it somehow morphed into a voice.

"I need help...Shelby, come back!" it said, throwing us all into stunned silence.

"What the hell..." I said, feeling goosebumps pop up on my arms.

We all stared at one another wide-eyed and astonished. No one said a word for several long seconds as we processed what we heard. A ghost said my name. That meant he knew who I was...and he was asking for my help.

"What the fuck?" Frank added loudly, causing us all to jump as though we'd been electrocuted.

I fell back into the couch, my mind a literal mess.

If I was on the fence about helping them, I fell onto one side.

I'd do whatever I could at that point, moving bedpan or not.

Chapter 23

Sonora was the first to react.

"That's so sad. I don't know what to say about it." She turned to Brock. "Please tell me you try to help them when you can."

Brock looked a little embarrassed by her question. "We do what we can, but we are really just there to research and document the location."

She leaned forward, her eyebrows knitted together. "You don't cross them over into the light?"

She had certainly garnered my attention. "Can you explain how that works?" I'd heard something about it years ago, but never heard the intricate details. Having someone to explain it to me felt like a birthday present.

"Here's my theory about death," she said, taking a deep inhale as though preparing herself for a long story. "When people die, they see a white light. It's a doorway to the other side, something most of us call Heaven. Most people who die walk right into it and move onto the next phase in their existence, but some people balk. They won't walk through it."

I was confused. "Why wouldn't they walk through it?"

She let go of the frown and arched her eyebrows. "I'm sure there are as many reasons as there are people. Some of them don't cross over because they want to watch over their families or homes. A lot of them won't cross over because of guilt and fear," she said, glancing down at her hands in her lap before looking up again. "Imagine you've committed a horrendous crime while you were alive. Maybe you murdered someone or stole something. When you die, you might worry the bright light is going to bring you to Hell instead of Heaven. When that happens, they remain earthbound and become ghosts."

I was astounded by what she said. It resonated with me in a way I hadn't expected.

"So how do you cross over someone who chose to avoid the light in the first place?" I asked.

I looked over to find Brock listening intently. Montgomery was feeding Frank a piece of pizza crust and didn't appear to be following the conversation.

"Well, to begin with, you treat them like people. Even the nasty ones became negative for a reason. They might have started out nice enough, but then life handed them a curveball and they allowed the negativity to envelope them. If you run into one like that, you have to counsel him like you would with a living person. If he decides to cross over, you just envision a white light on the ceiling and encourage him to go through it," she said, making it sound far easier than it probably was.

"What happens if you can't envision a white light?" I asked, knowing I'd lose the image three seconds after I started.

"It's actually not even necessary. They have the free will to cross over at any time. But the encouragement and visualizations help them make the decision."

"That's fascinating," Brock finally said. "How do you know all this?"

Sonora flicked a small smile at him. "Oh, I was raised by a psychic medium mother. I picked up on a few things over the years with her. I saw how it impacted her though…long hours, always dealing with dead people…I decided not to pursue it myself."

It certainly gave me something to think about. I wasn't sure I was capable, but I'd surely try if given the chance, especially after hearing the message on the audio recorder.

Sonora stood up and carried her empty beer bottle to the kitchen. When she returned, she favored us with an apologetic smile.

"I have to take off and go to work now, but it was nice meeting you guys," she said, giving them a small wave. As she reached the door, she caught my eyes. "I'll talk to you later, okay?"

"Sure," I gave her an awkward wave back. I was so out of practice with the whole friendship thing. If this kept up, I'd need a Friendship for Dummies book.

As soon as she left, I came back to the couch and sat down with a heavy plop.

Daylight streamed weakly through the double sliding doors, providing the room with its only light. Even though it was only late afternoon, it felt much later. I reached beside me and snapped on the table lamp, feeling measurably better with another source of light in the room.

"I know you guys deal with this stuff all the time, but honestly..." I heaved a sigh that was loud enough for Frank to call out "God Bless You!" from the kitchen.

Brock exchanged his empty beer for a fresh one. "I remember the first time I heard my name on an EVP. We were investigating an old prison in Texas for the show. We'd been all over the building and hardly anything had happened, so we went home for the night," he said. Unlike many of the paranormal shows that did one-night investigations, the Paranormal Warriors spent upwards of a week at the locations, giving them the luxury of actually leaving for the night.

"What happened?" I asked.

"Well, we left a few recorders there overnight. When we came back the next day and listened to what we recorded, we found out the ghosts had been talking about us. One of the EVPs said, "Brock needs to die," and someone else said, "Let's do it." It freaked me out, to be honest."

His words gave me a chill, making me thankful these ghosts wanted help instead of a new playmate.

"So, what do we do about it?" I asked.

Brock gave me a level stare. "We do what we can to help them."

"Do you think we can cross them over?"

Montgomery snapped his fingers in the direction of the six-pack and Brock tossed him the last one. He obviously had something to say, so we waited until he'd popped the top and swigged a healthy gulp.

"We can try. Are you up for it? You can lead us through it."

I started to protest but Brock held his hand up. "You're the one they asked for. They must think you're capable of helping them."

I leaned my head against the back of the couch, wishing Montgomery hadn't drunk the last beer. I felt like I could use a six-pack of my own just to drown out all the craziness bouncing around inside my head.

How was I supposed to help an asylum full of ghosts? I nearly wet myself during my first visit there. Surely, there was someone out there with more resources. They'd be better off with pretty much anyone over me. We'd never learn what truly happened to the giant.

Thinking of the giant brought back another thought I'd moved to the back burner.

"How could the coroner have ruled the caretaker's death a suicide? There wasn't a ladder or anything he could have climbed on to get that high," I said, sitting back down beside Montgomery.

Brock scooted his chair closer to the coffee table. "We got there after they'd cut the body down and removed it from the building, but we had a long talk with the coroner. Apparently, the caretaker threw the rope up to the chandelier and then jumped up, grabbed the rope and put his head in the noose. His feet were only a few feet off the ground," he said, bringing back some horrific memories.

"Is that even possible?" I was flabbergasted anyone believed it.

"It must be because the coroner signed off on it," Montgomery said.

I must have not looked convinced because Brock leaned forward. "What do you think happened, Shelby?" The look in his eyes was intense and I had a difficult time maintaining eye contact with him for fear he'd short circuit my brain.

"I don't know, but he was really weird the entire time I was there. He basically took off and left me right from the beginning. When I came back down, he was hanging there, already dead." In my mind, I was imagining all the creepy crawlies from the asylum surrounding him and hanging him. As the thought drifted through my head, trying to find a landing place, there was a sudden knock on the door.

We all jumped and Fugly went absolutely bonkers. He rose from a near coma state to launch himself at the door, barking like he had half a chance against whatever was on the other side. Sometimes I think he forgets he was only forty pounds of flab.

"Who farted?" Frank said helpfully and then made the sound of the door squeaking open.

"That's friggin creepy!" Montgomery said with a laugh. "I think I need that bird."

"Oh, he's all yours if you want him. He belonged to Benjamin, the caretaker," I said, rising to see who nearly gave us a heart attack.

I grabbed Fugly by his collar and opened the door to find Deputy Jimmy Bob standing there. He had a sheepish look on his boyish face as he held his brown hat in his oversized hands. He looked like a teenager who'd been called to the principal's office instead of a sworn officer of the law.

"Afternoon, Ms. Moore. We didn't see you down at the station, so I thought I'd swing by and take your statement about what happened down at the asylum yesterday," he said.

"Sure. Come on in." I stood back and allowed him room to pass. He stepped into the room, obviously trying to maintain some sort of cop persona that seemed foreign to him. As soon as he caught sight of Brock and Montgomery sitting in my living room, it all fell away in an instant.

"Oh my gosh! I watch you guys on TV!" he said, turning into an instant pile of fanboy goo.

He rushed over to them, with all the grace of a newborn giraffe trying to walk for the first time. The guys stood and shook his hand as he fussed over them and told him all his favorite parts of their show. To their credit, they looked a bit embarrassed by the attention.

My formal statement became far less important than it had been twenty seconds earlier. Jimmy Bob pulled the paper out of his pocket and absently handed it to me, asking me to fill it out. I was pretty sure I was supposed to tell him my story and he was supposed to take notes, but I wasn't arguing with him. It would go a lot faster if I wrote it out.

Brock pulled a few publicity photos from the backpack, which was quickly becoming the magical backpack. It seemed like every time we needed something, Montgomery had it stashed away in there. As the two men signed them for Jimmy Bob, I filled out his report.

As soon as I finished, I handed it back to him and it went into his back pocket without a glance. I could have said Santa Claus and the Tooth Fairy murdered the giant and he'd be none the wiser.

I came back around to sit on the couch. Fugly followed me stiff-legged, giving the deputy a long, suspicious sniff on his way past.

"Come on up," I said, patting the couch between me and Montgomery, and he slunk up in slow motion, his eyes never leaving the deputy. He had a thing for men in uniform and it wasn't good. If dogs had belts, his would have multiple notches from the mailman and the UPS driver. After his last bite, we were no longer treated to mail delivery and had to pick everything up at the post office. It was almost worth it, getting to watch the mailman skedaddle past our house in full paranoia mode every afternoon.

Brock rose from his seat and went to the kitchen to drag over another chair.

"Have a seat, Deputy Rogers…" he started to say, but Jimmy Bob cut him off.

"Oh, go on! Call me Jimmy Bob. Everybody does!" he gushed.

I was beginning to feel like I'd been plunked down in Mayberry. Besides Sonora, who was obviously an anomaly, everyone I'd met so far, from the girl at the library to the deputy sheriff, was a bit on the looney-tunes side. If there was something in the water, I planned to stay far away from it. If I went back home with an "aw shucks!" twang, my mother would kick my butt so hard, I'd never be able to sit down again.

"Shelby is having a hard time making sense of the caretaker's death. Were you there when they cut the body down?" Brock asked him.

"Yes, sir. I was the second one on the scene. It was pretty bad. I'd never seen anything like it in my life. Of course, I've only been a deputy for a few months, so it's not like that happens every day here. It was really bad though."

"Did it look like something the caretaker could have done by himself?" Brock asked.

"Oh I don't know. I leave that stuff up to the coroner. It's his job." He trailed away and looked down at his hands. "I guess it could be possible though. If the coroner thought that was what happened, that's good enough for me," he said.

His words did little to convince me. His reaction was probably similar to the other cops. As I sat in my Jeep, they walked in, took a look and then came back out pretty quickly with green faces to visit the bushes. The coroner was the only one to spend any real time with the body.

I probably should have just dropped it. The giant hadn't been very kind to me and I didn't owe him anything. I should have been able to dismiss it as easily as everyone else had, but I couldn't. Something bothered me about it and I wasn't letting go of it until I knew what really happened.

The conversation died out, causing Jimmy Bob to rise from his seat. "Well, this has been a real treat, meeting you guys. Maybe I'll run into you again while you're in town and we can drink a beer or two," he said, which warranted him several half-hearted acknowledgements that would probably never become reality.

As soon as the door closed behind him, Brock stood up and looked at me expectantly.

"Are you ready?" he asked.

I looked at him, purely dumbfounded, wondering if I'd forgotten about something we were supposed to do. "Ready for what?"

He smirked at Montgomery, who was apparently privy to this plan. Montgomery grabbed his laptop and my recorder off the coffee table and stuffed it into the magic backpack.

"We're going back to the asylum, remember? We have some work to do," he said.

I think I might have groaned, but somehow found myself getting up from my chair.

"Come on Fugly. Let's go for a ride."

Crazy Dead People

Chapter 24

We were only a few days into October and on the right side of Daylight Savings, but the days were still getting shorter. Even though we only spent an hour inside my cabin, the sun hung even lower in the sky, piercing in its intensity. I pulled my visor down but was still blinded by the orange orb the entire drive.

Brock sat beside me in the passenger seat, while Montgomery and Fugly took the backseat. Fugly wasn't happy about relinquishing his seat, but he made the best of it by bugging Montgomery with unexpected, intermittent wet licks on the face.

"Knock it off!" Montgomery said for perhaps the fifth time. "Shelby, tell your dog to stop licking me!"

I looked in the rear-view mirror to see Fugly nearly grinning. His mouth was open and his tongue lolled out. Besides the bacon, this was probably the most fun he'd had all day.

"You must taste good to him. How can I stop that?" I asked, laughing as Fugly tried to lean in for another smooch. Montgomery wiped his arm across his face, nearly entangling his sleeve in the multiple facial piercings. For his sake, I hoped he never walked through a spider's web. It might take him days to get all the webbing out of the rings.

As we drove, my mind returned to the conversation we had with Sonora. I could see some of her words being helpful, but how in the world would you cross over a crawler? Somehow I didn't think he would be willing to listen to reason. It left me feeling a bit hopeless.

We stopped at a convenience store to pick up a few sodas and bottled waters for our trip to the asylum. As we were checking out, the clerk and a customer in the store recognized the guys and began chatting them up about everything paranormal.

It seemed a bit surreal to be casually hanging out with famous people. I've never been someone who is easily starstruck. I think if I actually encountered a famous person, present company excluded, I'd just leave them alone. I might take a second glance to compare it against what I'd seen on the media, but I'd never approach them. Other people didn't seem to have that sense of discretion. As soon as one person stopped chatting with them, another took his place.

Any mild wishes for fame were erased quickly after seeing the glance Brock and Montgomery exchanged after a ten minute conversation with a UFO enthusiast.

"Do you get that all the time?" I asked as we finally climbed into my Jeep.

Brock buckled himself in and gave me a weary smile, one that projected more information than his words ever could. "You have no idea, but it comes with the job."

Montgomery reached up and slapped him on the shoulder, grinning like a monkey. "And it comes with all the babes!"

Brock immediately shot me an apologetic glance. "Don't believe everything you hear. The babes come with a price too." He looked out the window as the scenery passed by. "I hate to complain because I worked really hard to get this job, but let's just say everything isn't as it seems. You quickly learn who your friends are."

I couldn't help but feel bad for him. I wasn't sure how far his fame with the paranormal show extended, but I'd read stories about celebrities who couldn't even go grocery shopping for fear of being mobbed. It would certainly put a quick end to my bedheaded, bra-less forays out to grab the Sunday paper.

"Everybody wants to be on TV," Montgomery mused from the backseat.

"Yeah. There's that too." Brock let his words trail off. It made me realize how much I hated to admit that I genuinely liked these guys. I was set to hate them on site, but here we were.

"I know you probably get asked this a lot, but how did you get involved in the paranormal?" I asked. It's not like you could go to a job placement office and selected paranormal investigator as a profession.

Brock rubbed his hand through his hair, making it stand up in dark spikes. "Mine started early," he said, favoring me with a quick glance. "When I was a kid, we lived in a house that was paranormally active. I'd wake up sometimes to find an old woman sitting on the side of my bed, watching me. Nobody believed me when I ran to my parent's room in the middle of the night until they started seeing her too. We finally moved out a few years later, but it stuck with me. I always wondered who she was and why she was there. I joined a paranormal group when I was a teen and started investigating." He turned to look at Montgomery. "And I kind of pulled poor Montgomery into it. We were friends in college. He was studying filmmaking and I knew he had a camera, so we started going out to dark, creepy places looking for spooks."

"Hey, but it has babes!" Montgomery chimed in, the tone in his voice dripping with sarcasm.

I could see Brock staring at me out of my peripheral vision. "Yes, it does. It certainly has babes."

I wasn't sure how to respond, so I just let it hang there.

With a mighty pull on the steering wheel, I turned off the two-lane highway onto the road to the asylum and the Jeep grew quiet. I wasn't sure what the other two were thinking about, but I began conjuring up visions of dark hallways and giants hanging from ropes. By the time we got to the gate, the small muscles in my fingers were trembling on the steering wheel.

If we had a game plan, the guys hadn't shared their information with me. My biggest hope, besides not getting murdered by demons, was that we wouldn't have to endure Beezer at the location. It was beginning to dawn on me he had a lot to do with the show's negative aura.

When he told me to make sure several of the witnesses were attractive women, I made the natural assumption they were for Brock and Montgomery to slather over. Now, I had second thoughts. Judging by the way he was with me, combined with his obnoxious t-shirts, the attractive witnesses were probably his idea. They might make for better TV, as he was fond of telling me, but he wasn't getting them from me. I'd make sure they could all qualify as linebackers so they could squish him like the slug he was. If nothing else, it was a good life lesson for me.

I was thankful when we pulled up and the parking area was empty.

"I'm not complaining or anything, but where did everybody go?" I asked.

Brock opened his door and Fugly bullied his way over Montgomery's lap to jump out first. He ran directly to his favorite pee spot and soaked my rear tire, then kicked his back legs like he was trying to bury it in asylum dirt.

Brock laughed. He held the seat forward for Montgomery to climb out. "They're all gone for the day. Our permits don't actually kick in for another week, so they're working to get the dates changed."

I felt my eyebrows rise. "So, we're not supposed to be here?"

The two exchanged knowing glances.

"Not technically. We just have to hope nobody notices we're here," Montgomery said, pulling his trucker cap a bit lower on his forehead to shield his eyes from the blinding sun.

I've never been a big fan of trespassing. I just didn't like the idea of being somewhere I wasn't supposed to be. A psychologist would probably have a field day with me.

I bit my tongue, swallowed my concerns and followed them in through the door. Montgomery switched on one of the stand lights and the room became eerily illuminated. The bright light was pointed directly towards the chandelier, sending long, dramatic shadows around the room. As I took in the details, I realized the rope the giant hung himself with was still attached to the light fixture.

"Is that...?" I couldn't even finish the sentence.

Brock followed the line of my stare. "Yeah, that's it, the rope he hung himself with," he said. The expression on my face must have turned sour. "I know. It's probably in bad taste to leave it up there while we investigate, but it might help us connect with him easier. We'll remove it before we start filming. Don't worry."

I wasn't sure how to respond. My feelings were definitely mixed. While I too wanted to know more about the giant's death, I didn't want to feel like I was taking advantage of a tragic situation. If it was indeed suicide, I didn't want to cause him any more trauma. I did want answers, though, in case it wasn't what it looked like.

Breaking away from the guys, I got closer to the rope. The wall was too far away for him to have used it for leverage. I tried to remember how far his feet were from the ground, but couldn't. Everything that happened in those horrifying seconds was pretty much a blur.

"How tall was the caretaker?" Brock asked, watching me.

"I don't know. Over six feet. I'm really bad with heights."

He sidled up next to me, a little too close for comfort. Judging by the slight smile on his face, he was aware of this fact.

"I'm six foot one. Was he taller than me?" he asked, moving so close I could feel his breath blow against my hair.

I instinctively took a quick step back. "I think taller," I said quickly, trying to cover my actions with words but it only garnered me a deeper smile. He was getting to me and he knew it.

I moved the other side of the room, putting more distance between us. "I just don't see anyone jumping up to grab a rope and then putting it around his neck. It just doesn't make sense to me. There are piles of wood and junk all over the place here. If he truly killed himself, why wouldn't he have used something to stand on? Why make it so difficult?"

Montgomery arched his eyebrows. "Let's see if we can find out."

He dug around in his backpack until he found a small black box connected to a speaker. He turned it on and the room echoed with a loud, choppy, electronic sound.

"This is a spirit box. It scans through the radio stations rapidly. Sometimes ghosts use the white noise to talk to us," he said, looking up at Brock. "You still have your digital recorder on you?"

Brock nodded and pulled it out of his pocket. "We always record our spirit box sessions because sometimes it's difficult to make out. If we record it, we can play it back and enhance it so we can understand what they're saying better."

Montgomery hit a button on the spirit box, causing it to start scanning through the stations. Fugly's ears perked up and he tilted his head sideways as the voices started pouring out.

"Hello!" a female voice said.

"What's up?" said another voice.

There was a three-second pause before the next voice chimed in. "Who's that?"

It was quickly followed by "What's he doing?"

I found myself staggering backwards, stunned by the voices. When I watched their show, they sometimes got lucky and got a response or two, but never anything this profound. The voices were coming in clear, one after another. I looked at the guys to see if they were as shocked as I was and was pleased to see surprise on both their faces.

"Grab a camera. We need to get this on film," Brock said, kneeling down in front of the spirit box.

Montgomery opened a shiny metal box near the door and pulled out a professional looking camera. I didn't know much about cameras, but it looked like ones they used on newscasts for those "men on the streets" interviews. He stood back and started rolling.

Instantly, I forgot about the job at hand and began worrying about my hair, my outfit, my posture. I ran a hand through my hair, trying to get a reading on the frizz factor.

"Is this going to end up on TV?" I asked in a near-panic. I certainly didn't want my fifteen minutes of fame to be of me looking like one of the asylum patients.

"You look fine. Just relax," he told me. When I leveled him with a look that should have set his hair on fire, he nodded at Montgomery. "Try to keep her out of the shots," he said, which brought my tension level back down a few notches.

"Thank you," I sighed. Telling a woman to relax when she was upset was never a good idea. It only made things worse.

Brock was still kneeling beside the box. It was hard not to notice the way his jeans rode low on his back. A slice of skin with a sliver of tattoo was exposed, making me wonder what the rest of the tattoo looked like. If I could have slapped myself and gotten away with it without anyone noticing, I would have. Instead, I moved back out of camera range and crossed my arms around my chest. Fugly nuzzled against my leg, watching the men as closely as I was.

"We come to you as friends. We just want to talk to you," Brock said, his voice low and nearly lyrical. "Can you tell us your name?" he asked and looked up at Montgomery.

There was no answer. All the voices seemed to have gone away as soon as the camera was turned on.

"Are you feeling shy with the camera running?" he asked. "We can turn it off and set it down over there, if it helps," he said and then winked at Montgomery.

Montgomery pulled the camera from his face and sat it down on the ground. The red light was still on, so I figured out their little ploy pretty fast. Apparently, the ghosts did too because we didn't get a single voice.

Something caught my attention near the banshee door. I pushed off from my hiding spot against the wall and approached the door. I couldn't see very well because my body was creating a shadow, so I pulled my cell phone out of my pocket. I clicked on the flashlight app and nearly dropped my phone.

Hundreds of tiny spiders were pouring out from beneath the door.

That was all it took to get me out of the asylum.

I'm not sure if I screamed, but I definitely ran.

Crazy Dead People

Chapter 25

"It's just spiders, Shelby," Brock told me as I sat firmly in my Jeep, my eyes glued on the front of the building in case they started pouring out of that doorway too.

"There's no such thing as *just* spiders. That's like saying, 'It's just an apocalypse, Shelby,'" I told him. They didn't understand the depths of my phobia. I've been terrified of spiders since I was nine years-old and walked through a web, catching an especially large, long-legged spider on my nose. I once avoided my kitchen for an entire week because a wolf spider skittered under my refrigerator.

Montgomery came out of the front door of the asylum, skipping down the stairs with a casualness I couldn't fathom. He had a can of hairspray in one hand.

He joined Brock at my window. "All clear now. I torched the little suckers!" He showed us the hairspray can and then held up a blue lighter in his other hand.

Brock's shock matched my own. "You didn't do what I think you did, did you?"

Montgomery ducked his head. "Don't worry. I didn't burn down the building. I just toasted me some baby spiders," he said. Before Brock could lay into him about the dangers of what he'd just done, he continued. "I think our lights created a warmer atmosphere inside the asylum, causing all those spider eggs to hatch. We'll just have to watch the lights going forward," he said.

Brock's face looked like it was made of stone. "We'll talk about this later, okay bud?"

Montgomery grinned and ducked his head, sheepishly. I understood Brock's concerns, but I was with Montgomery on this one. Burning the little suckers was a great idea. I would have slapped him a high-five if Brock hadn't been standing there, glaring at him.

Brock clapped his hands, ending the moment and starting a new one.

"Any chance we can get you to go back in there?" he asked, the corner of his lip pulled up in the slightest of smiles. I met his perfect blue eyes, knowing full well he was using his manly wiles to lure me back in. Unfortunately for him, he was dealing with a stubborn redhead.

"Nope. Not a chance. I'll need to see a shop-vac go in there first, followed by a day of absolutely zero spider sightings." I was firm on this and it must have shown on my face because Brock gave up quickly.

"Okay then…let's move onto Plan B," he said, pulling a piece of paper out of his back pocket. He unfolded it and handed it to me. It looked like a hand-drawn map of the asylum property.

He reached into my window, his arm brushing against my shoulder as he pointed to a spot on the map.

"Beezer gave me this earlier today. It's a map of the property. There's supposed to be a potter's field graveyard over here," he said, pointing to a spot on the map. "I know you haven't really had a chance to start your research yet, but maybe we could check it out?" he asked. His voice was so tentative and full of yearning, I found myself budging on my decision to stay in my Jeep.

I met his eyes and stared him down for a moment.

"I'll be on full spider alert! I promise," he said, nearly singing his words. There was such a sense of playfulness in his voice, I found myself rolling my eyes.

"Fine!" I opened my door and allowed Fugly to jump out first. "But if we see even one spider, I'm out of there!" I said.

"That sounds perfectly acceptable." He held out his hand to assist me out of my Jeep, which was taking things a bit too far. I couldn't come up with a quick enough reason to ignore it without completely alienating him, so I accepted the assistance and then let go of his hand as soon as my feet touched the ground.

I wasn't telling Brock this, but he pretty much made my day with his suggestion of a graveyard fieldtrip. I've always loved cemeteries. They were an absolute treasure-trove of history. In many cases, they were the only remembrances of people's lives. Once their family history became eroded by time, it was often the only mark they had left on this earth. When I was bored, I sometimes went to the cemetery near my mother's house and just meandered along the stones, reading what someone felt summed up another person's life.

It also made me more aware of my own mortality. It was a reminder that everything we did as living beings eventually ended. Nothing was forever. I know it's corny to say we should live each day as though it were our last, but I really took this to heart, especially after spending several hours with the dead. I'm sure they'd have a lot to say about regrets if they had the chance to speak.

Brock led us down the side of the hill. The grade was so steep, I nearly slipped several times, but I made it all the way down without embarrassing myself, which was a major feat in itself. Fugly raced down ahead of us, his nose to the ground. I prayed he didn't spook a rabbit hiding in the grass. He would probably make it all the way to Kentucky before I could catch him.

A thick thatch of forest surrounded the hill, like fringe on a bald man's head. I stopped and studied it for a moment, feeling my stomach tighten. We had no idea what we were walking into. The forest could be filled with all sorts of dangers, ranging from redneck hillbilly camps to roaming herds of sasquatches.

"You okay?" Brock asked, touching my elbow.

"Yeah, I'm okay." It was enough to prompt me back into motion.

We found a narrow dirt path leading into the overgrowth. It looked like a trail deer might use as they navigated through the densely growing trees. Once we entered into the forest, the temperature dropped nearly twenty degrees, making me wish I'd grabbed more than a light denim jacket before I left the cabin. I wrapped my arms around myself and peered up at the tall tower of trees that nearly blocked out the daylight.

The trail was narrow, forcing us to walk single file. We followed behind Brock as he continually checked the map. Somehow, I ended up at the back of the group, something that was beginning to give me anxiety. I kept thinking I heard footsteps behind me, but every time I turned, nothing was there.

Thoughts of the crawler slipped into my mind. After my experiences, it was difficult to push it very far from my thoughts. I imagined it lurking behind me everywhere I went, like an evil shadow. I wondered how long it would take to stop thinking about it. Would thoughts of it follow me back to my mother's house? Would I constantly be looking over my shoulder and watching shadows? I was already phobic about heights, spiders and darkness. Would I also be adding shadows to the mix? The thought was sobering. I needed to get a better grasp on things or I'd end up in a straightjacket. This jarred a thought loose from my head.

"Hey Brock?" I called and he stopped. Beads of sweat dotted his forehead and he wiped them away with the back of his hand.

"It just occurred to me that we've only seen half of the asylum. There's a whole other wing on the other side of the lobby, right?" I asked.

Montgomery took the opportunity to remove the backpack and set it on the ground. He dug around inside of it, coming out with three water bottles that he passed out to us.

I didn't realize how thirsty I was until I took my first drink. I didn't come up for air until I'd nearly drained the bottle. I poured the other half into my hand, dribble by dribble, and let Fugly have the rest.

"The other side is the part they used for the insane asylum. The owner of the property says it's in pretty rough condition and probably isn't safe for us to explore," he said, eyeing Montgomery with a sudden mischievous grin.

Montgomery looked at me, the same grin transferred to his face as though it were contagious. "We couldn't find the door, or we would have already been all over that side. But, we're not done looking. If nothing else, we can climb through one of the first floor windows."

The curiosity seeker in me reared her nosy head. Although I'm not a fan of trespassing, I am a big fan of uncovering secrets. If I ever suffer from a tragic death, it will be because I went somewhere I wasn't supposed to go to see something I wasn't supposed to see. It was deeply embedded in me, something I had absolutely no power over. If there was a mystery to solve, I was front and center, ready to explore it.

"Count me in," I said and they both shot me looks of surprise.

"Really?" Brock said. "What if there are spiders?"

I rolled my eyes at him. "We'll just have to make sure Montgomery has his spider torch with him and I'll be all set."

The guys took one more swig of water and then we continued down the trail again with Fugly taking the lead this time. Thoughts of the hidden wing haunted me, no pun intended. The idea of it was tantalizing and alluring, something that called to me deep in my mind. If the doorway had been sealed off, there must be a reason. I didn't buy the excuse that it was structurally dangerous. From the outside, it looked exactly like its twin on the other side. There must be another reason why they didn't want us in, which made it absolutely irresistible, providing we went during daylight hours, of course.

We walked for another five minutes before the forest opened up to a broad meadow. Even though it was clearly depicted on the map, it was still surprising to discover it.

The area consisted of about three acres, by my estimation. The forest grew tightly around it, making it feel like a sacred space. Birds called to one another from the edges of the trees, punctuated by the occasional outburst of an angry crow. Tall grass grew gracefully in the space, tipping over in places from long-gone summer breezes. I saw something in the grass and stepped around the guys to inspect it closer.

It appeared to be a stone monument. I knelt down and brushed the tall grass aside to read it.

"Parkesburg Asylum Cemetery," I read. Below the name was a brief description, molded in bronzed metal. "This cemetery was used from 1901 until 1974. Here, laid to rest, are 5,643 departed Parkesburg patients. May their souls rest in peace." As the words left my lips, a chill filled my body.

"I don't think they're at peace," Brock said, staring wistfully across the acres of unmarked graves.

"They didn't even get gravestones," I added.

As I stared, I could make out indentations in the soil, hinting to what was buried beneath it. I wanted to walk out into the meadow and get a better look, but something stopped me. It almost felt as though I wasn't supposed to walk on the graves. I gave both men sidelong glances and noticed they were both rooted in place, as well. Something here was speaking to all of us and we understood its language.

Dusk was beginning to settle. The bright orange sun had finally fallen below the tree line, casting the edges of the forest into shadows. I could easily imagine coming here during the summer at dawn, watching the mist burn off as the first rays of sunlight broke through the tree lines, making the dew on the long grass sparkle like diamonds.

Crickets began chirping, their cadence growing stronger as the minutes passed. The crow called out again, making me jump despite myself. Something about this place touched me in a way I had never felt before. It felt like hallowed ground, a place where the world held its breath. Time had no meaning here. It was caught in a moment that would never end. The seasons might change and the landscape would alter along with it, but the sense of hush was permanent, soaked into the ground like a second layer of soil.

"What's that?" Montgomery asked, pointing out across the meadow.

We followed the line of his finger to the other side of the meadow where the shadows had grown long and reaching. At first, I didn't see anything, but then something caught my eye. It looked like a tiny bubble of blue light.

"Grab your camera," Brock whispered. "Get this on film."

Montgomery slowly lowered the backpack to the ground and unzipped it quietly, his every movement geared towards silence. I watched him for a second, but found my gaze drawn back to the meadow. The light bobbed as it grazed the tops of the grass.

As we watched in breathless amazement, another light joined the first. This one appeared amber in color, lit from within like the blue orb. Soon, there was another and then another, until the field was filled with colorful, bobbing lights.

"They almost look like fairy lights," I whispered, watching them in absolute awe. It was a moment of true wonder, something that would be permanently tattooed in my brain until I took my last breath.

In a way, they almost looked like fireflies. They were all so far away; I couldn't see them as clearly as I wanted to. A part of me itched to walk out into the meadow and become surrounded by them, but a strong sensation held me back. I wasn't allowed.

Even Fugly seemed transfixed. He sat quietly beside me, panting softly with his tongue lolling out of the side of his mouth. Normally, this would be something he'd want to chase or at least get a closer sniff at, but he was as still as we were.

I glanced over at Brock and Montgomery, seeing the same looks of wonder on their faces that I too probably wore. They were investigators, people who often trespassed in places where they weren't welcome, but they weren't budging either. This was something we were supposed to witness but not participate in.

We watched them for about ten minutes, standing so still my legs became stiff and filled with pins and needles. Then, it was all over. The crow called out again, closer this time. His voice rang out across the meadow and extinguished every last light.

Montgomery lowered his camera and stared at us like a child on Christmas morning after seeing his pile of presents.

"Oh my God, man!" he whispered.

"Did you catch it on camera?" Brock asked, causing Montgomery to begin fiddling with his camera. I stepped closer to see the screen and was elated to see our experience playing out on his screen.

"I did, indeed."

It felt like a moment of celebration. We all stood there and stared at each other, the wonderment of what we'd just experienced together radiating off us like fireworks. If I had my way, I probably would have stood there all night in hopes of seeing it again, but I knew in my heart the moment had passed. What we had witnessed was a gift and I wasn't going to waste it.

Brock finally broke the silence.

"So…anybody up for a little adventure?" he asked.

I narrowed my eyes, confused. "Didn't we just have an adventure?"

"Yes, we did, but one adventure often leads to another one." He grinned, his face becoming lost in the shadows.

"What did you have in mind?" I asked.

"Let's go find the hidden side of the asylum," he said.

I might have been brave earlier, but it didn't mean my heart didn't start beating faster.

For all we knew, we were going into the crawler's den.

Chapter 26

We were all quiet as we picked our way out of the forest. The birds had grown silent as well. Even the crows were keeping their opinions to themselves. It was almost as though every last ounce of energy was drained from the area once the performance had ended.

I watched the trail beneath my feet, my mind a million miles away as I tried to process what I'd just experienced. It made me think long and hard about synchronicities.

There have been many times in my life where one thing has seemingly led me to another. I once went on a job interview and met a woman in the lobby who was also waiting for an interview. As we chatted, she told me she was leaving her current employer because she didn't like the work. I ended up leaving my interview and went to her workplace where I was hired on the spot. It was one of the best jobs I've ever had.

Another time, I was late leaving my house because I couldn't find my keys and then later learned about a fatal car accident on the road I normally took. There was no guarantee I would have been in the accident had I left on time, but then again, no one could prove it otherwise either.

Over time, I began to realize the more I noticed the synchronicities, the more often they occurred, and I began following them like breadcrumbs. I wasn't sure who was leaving them, but they always felt helpful. I've never been one to trust anyone or anything easily, so seeing proof was paramount to my belief system.

Everything about the evening felt as though it had planned. I mulled over it as I crunched through the dry leaves.

The trail wound around another turn and then spit us out at the base of the asylum hill. We paused as though guided by an unspoken agenda. Montgomery opened his pack and handed out three more bottles of water.

"So, what do you think those lights were?" I finally asked.

Brock took a long pull of his water before answering. "They kind of remind me of the Marfa Lights," he said. When I frowned, not knowing the story, he continued. "There's a little town in Texas, fifty miles from the Mexican border, where people often see lights like that at night. It seems to happen more during the winter than the summer, but they've been seeing them for over 150 years now. Nobody can explain them, and believe me, they've tried."

"So what do you think they are?" I asked again, not happy with his answer because he didn't really answer it to begin with.

"I don't know, to be honest," he said, scratching his head. "I want to say it's the souls of the people buried there, but that seems too easy. Maybe it's angels, visiting their graves? I have no idea."

"Maybe it's aliens," Montgomery chimed in, his voice drenched in sarcasm.

Brock flicked his trucker hat, causing it to sail to the ground. "You've been spending too much time talking to alien enthusiasts." He shook his head. "What do you think it is?" he asked me.

I took a deep breath and let it out in a sigh. "I don't think we will ever know for certain, but I do think we were meant to see it. Think about all the things that had to happen before we ended up there. We weren't going to go there tonight. We were going to check out the foyer. The only reason why we didn't stay there was the spiders. And what kind of weird coincidence was that? Why now? Those spiders have had all day with lights pouring on them. Why pick that moment to suddenly hatch and come visit us?" I watched them absorb my words. "Whatever it was, we were meant to see it."

A sparkle came into Brock's eyes. "Ahhh...synchronicities. Are you a believer?"

I hated being pinned down by my belief system. If I said yes, would he make fun of me?

"I don't think anything in this world happens by coincidence. I think everything has a reason," I said, not directly answering his question.

Montgomery almost buzzed with delight. "Just playing devil's advocate here, but what good could possibly come from something like the holocaust or a car crash that kills an entire family except for one child?"

"I didn't say something good came out of it. I said there was a reason. The holocaust was a really horrible period in history, but it taught us a lesson in humanity. People learned that looking the other way instead of protesting could lead to genocide. And as for the car crash, I don't know. Maybe the girl went on to become a valuable neurosurgeon after the experience so she could save thousands of other lives. We don't always get to see the reasons," I said, allowing the anger he sparked to burn itself off.

It was clear Montgomery had only gotten started. "But what about..."

"Enough!" Brock said, getting between us with outstretched referee arms. "Let's get up the hill and put our minds to work on finding the hidden doorway."

Montgomery tipped his hat at me, his eyes still sparkling with amusement. "This is a discussion we'll save for later, Miss Shelby."

I glared at him for a long second. I hate it when somebody pushes my buttons and then gloats over it.

Fugly led us up the hill, making better time than we did. By the time we made it all the way up, my legs were burning and my lungs were on fire. If I got any hotter, I might set the field on fire. I drank half my water and gave the rest to Fugly.

I'd completely forgotten about the spiders until we got to the front door.

"Big nope," I told them, stopping short of the stairs.

Brock's lips turned into a tight line as he studied the front of the building. "We've already been all over the lobby. If there was a door there, they walled it off decades ago. There has to be another way in." He took a few steps to the left of the doorway and tested one of the ground floor windows, but the board held firm. "Let's walk around to the back and see what we can find."

We stopped at every window to test the boards but none of them were even remotely loose.

"Do you know anything about the insane asylum wing?" I asked him, feeling guilty for not having the information. I probably should have done more research before I left home, but I had no way of knowing I'd be thrown into a situation like this.

"I don't know much. I just know they kept the people with the most severe mental illnesses on that side. I think they might have even taken several criminally insane patients."

I stopped, nearly causing Fugly to run into the back of my legs. "What kind of criminally insane patients? People who murdered other people?"

Brock pulled on another board with no luck. "I think so. There were some pretty dark characters locked up inside here at one point." He turned to me with an amused smile. "It makes them pretty nasty ghosties too." The thought gave me a chill. It was no wonder there were entities like the crawler inside there considering some of the people who died there.

We continued along the front of the building with both men testing all the windows every few feet. As we walked, I found myself staring up at the façade, taking in all the details.

The building was constructed with stone and concrete, giving it an imposing impression. While all the windows on the first floor were covered with boards, the second and third floor windows were open. Unlike the other side, there weren't any covered verandas. Instead, most of the windows had steel bars. If there had been glass in them at one time, it was long gone. I imagined kids with slingshots and strong throwing arms daring each other to knock out all the windows. The passage of time and the brutality of the elements had taken care of the rest.

Thick ivy climbed up the side of the building, growing in and around some of the windows. Several of the windows were so thick with greenery, I couldn't see inside. It was difficult to imagine people living here, some of whom hadn't committed any crimes beyond mental illness. What would it have been like for them to sit and stare out those windows at the world below, not knowing what normal life looked like any longer?

I wished I'd at least taken more time reading through the books Kiki found for me at the library. It would be a lot easier going in armed with knowledge. I hated being so ignorant when I was supposed to be the expert.

A crow cawed out suddenly, bringing my attention to a third-floor window.

The crow strutted along the stone windowsill, reminding me of the crow from the potter's field. I knew it couldn't be the same one, but I still watched him closely to make sure he was real.

Crows were once considered the harbingers of death. To see one meant someone would soon die. I wondered what they felt about the already-dead that roamed the hallways.

We finally came to the corner of the building. The grass was especially tall on this side, making me wonder how long it had been since anyone had touched it with a mower. I high stepped through it, trying to flatten it down with my feet as I walked, feeling the sense of neglect permeate through my soul.

The side of the building had a fire escape, but it was rusted in place and well out of our reach. I wasn't sure I would trust it anyway. It looked as though it was hanging onto the building with equally rusty bolts.

It was growing darker by the moment. The sun barely peeked over the trees, giving the sky a somber umber cast that caught the low- hanging clouds. As we crossed into the shadows of the backside of the building, it was even darker. If we were lucky, we'd have another hour before full darkness fell. I pulled my cell phone out of my pocket and turned on the flashlight app while Brock dug out his red flashlight.

Between the two, we could see very little, but it didn't stop us from continuing. Towards the middle of the building, we finally hit pay dirt.

Brock leaned down and moved away dried leaves and grass to discover a bulkhead door.

He pulled on the heavy metal door and it opened with a squeal, releasing the smell of dead, stale air.

My heart froze as I realized what I was looking at.

The asylum had a basement.

"Are you ready for this?" Brock asked.

There really wasn't a good answer to that question, but I bit back my fear and followed him down the dark, damp moss- covered stairs. I knew it wasn't a good idea, but I had no idea how bad it was until the bulkhead door slammed shut behind us.

We were in the dark in the basement of the haunted asylum. It didn't get any creepier than that.

Crazy Dead People

Chapter 27

The basement was my worst nightmare come to life. With our inadequate lighting, we could see no farther than ten to fifteen feet away and even then, we were limited. I spun in a circle, sending my light out in an arc just to make sure something wasn't sneaking up on me.

Sometimes, I allowed myself to get caught up in the moment and ended up in places where I didn't want to be. This was definitely one of those times.

Why had I followed them down into the basement? Was it peer pressure? Did I feel I had something to prove? Or had I just lost my freaking mind and forgotten how terrifying the asylum was?

"Nothing's going to hurt me," I chanted in my head. I'm not sure it helped.

I thought I heard a foot scrape against the concrete floor behind me and whirled around to beam my pathetic camera light at it. At this point, I'd have to chase things down just to get a better look at them.

"Don't you have a brighter flashlight in your magic backpack?" I hissed at Montgomery.

I turned to find him in the darkness, already digging through the pack. He came up with two small flashlights and tossed one to me. I didn't see it coming until it nearly bonked me in the nose. I swiped at it and knocked it to the ground instead of catching it. It hit the ground with a clunk and rolled inside a metal contraption on the floor behind me.

I pointed my cell phone light towards it and could see it sitting only several inches from the edge, wrapped in a thick wad of cobwebs. It took every ounce of courage in my body, but I reached inside and grabbed it, confirming the fact that my fear of darkness was greater than my fear of spiders.

I shook off the cobwebs, getting a serious case of the heebie-jeebies.

It was a smaller version of the flashlight the giant had loaned me. I rotated the end as though I was trying to twist a turkey's neck and was rewarded with a quarter-sized beam of light. It wasn't a whole lot better than my cell phone light, but it at least extended further into the darkness.

I took the opportunity to get a better look at the metal contraption it had rolled inside. The bars went all the way to the floor and were sunk into the concrete. There was a floor drain in the middle. My heart began thudding heavier as I realized it was probably an old holding cell. It came to about eye level on me, making it about five feet tall. If someone was locked up inside, they couldn't even stand up straight...unless it was made for children.

"Oh my God, guys! Have you seen this?" I called out. I turned and directed my flashlight in their general direction and the light bounced on more bars.

"The whole basement is full of them," Montgomery called back.

The thought was sobering. How many people were kept down here? Did they have to live in total darkness or did they have lighting? And why were they so short? Surely, they weren't for children. A glance over my shoulder showed me the guys had moved further away than what I was comfortable with. I'd also lost track of Fugly.

The sharp tang of urine brought me to his last location. It dripped down the bars and landed in a big yellow puddle on the concrete floor. Leave it to Fugly to mark his territory in a place like this.

"Fugly?" I called, but there was no answer. I mentally kicked myself for not slipping his leash on him before we got down there. It would be impossible to find him if he snuck away and didn't want to be interrupted in his sniffing excursion. Panic grew wings inside of me and flapped wildly through every vein as my worst nightmares marched through my mind.

"He's down here," Brock called back, pushing my anxiety back down into its hidey hole. I closed my eyes for a second and pulled in a deep breath of moldy air, trying to control the adrenaline rush.

"Nothing's going to hurt me," I tried again. "Nothing's going to hurt me."

I didn't like being so far away from the guys, making me a better candidate for the leash instead of my dog. I wasn't sure if safety in numbers applied in this particular situation, but it made me feel better. I high-tailed it towards them.

"What do you think those cages were used for?" I asked Brock once I caught up with him.

He shone his light down the row and I gasped at the amount. If I had to guess, I'd say there were at least fifty of them. Even one would have been a staggering sight. Fifty made my stomach twist.

"I don't know for sure, but I'd guess they were punishment cages. Back in the early 1900s they used to put patients in cages to punish them for bad behavior. Sometimes, they'd throw an armful of straw on the ground for them to sleep on and give them a piece of bread once or twice a day. I read a story about a woman who was kept in a cage like this for six years. She couldn't stand up and was dressed in rags. By the time they pulled her out, she was too weak to walk after having crouched down in a cage for so long."

I stared ahead at the darkness, the small muscles in my jaw beginning to twitch. "So, what would happen to someone like that after they died?" I was almost afraid to hear the answer.

Brock moved closer to me so I could almost see his face. "It would depend. If they died and crossed over to the other side, then they'd be okay. But a lot of people who die in tragic events and in situations like this don't cross over. They are too confused and angry. Sometimes, they don't even know they're dead."

"Oh," was all I could say. In my head, I was doing the math. Fifty cages times one-hundred and fifty years was a whole lot of angry, pissed off ghosts. And I was probably standing right in the middle of them.

"You should see this," Montgomery said from just ahead of us. He was filming with his camera. I could see the glowing screen floating in the darkness. Judging by the green cast, he was probably filming with a night vision camera.

We joined him and crowded around the small screen. If I looked at the doorway with my eyes, I could only see blackness, but the screen gave us a far better perspective. The cages ended at a cinderblock wall.

Fugly was standing beside Montgomery staring in the same direction, his ears pricked upwards. I took the opportunity to slip his leash from my pocket and hook it onto his collar before he could take off after whatever they were watching.

"What are you looking at?" I asked, not seeing anything interesting on the screen.

"Just watch," Montgomery whispered.

I stared at the screen for what seemed like an eternity. All I could see was the glint of light reflecting on the bars of the cages and the dirty cinderblock wall. Shards of debris littered the floor, but not as much as we saw upstairs in the other wing.

"There!" he whispered.

My heart nearly lunged out of my body as I saw the hazy shape of a woman cross in front of the wall. She disappeared into the shadows and was gone.

Before I could say anything, Brock grabbed the back of Montgomery's backpack and began unzipping it. "Is the thermal camera in here?"

"Yeah, I think so. It should be on the very bottom in a plastic case."

He pulled out a plastic box and extracted a device that resembled a grocery store price scanner

"What is that?" I asked, keeping my voice as low as possible. Beside me, Fugly began growling deep in his chest, a sure sign he was also seeing something.

"It's a thermal camera. It picks up on heat signatures. If I pointed it at you, you will show up red and yellow because you emit heat. If I shine it on a ghost, it will show up dark blue because they don't have any heat. I just want to make sure this isn't an actual living person down here with us."

My heart was racing wildly by this point and I was seriously regretting my decision to follow them down into the basement. I wanted to latch onto one of the men, but they were both operating expensive-looking equipment. Fugly wasn't helping, either, with his intermittent growls.

The woman drifted across the night vision camera screen again at the same moment Brock's thermal camera came to life. I squinted at the screen, not seeing her as clearly on his camera as I could on Montgomery's.

Brock put his finger to the screen where a dark figure moved against the dark background. "There she is and she's not glowing."

"So, so, so...she's a ghost?" I stuttered, nearly beyond the capability to form words. I don't know if I'd ever been more frightened. I couldn't even remember the words I'd been chanting earlier. Nothing in my brain was functioning any longer except for my need to run.

"She's a ghost," he confirmed. Satisfied with his experiment and showing zero unease about what we'd just witnessed, he turned in a circle and then stopped. "There's another one," he said with all the casualness he might use to tell me he'd just spotted another squirrel or an empty parking spot. He pointed to the screen and I could make out a shape hunched down inside one of the cages.

I didn't care if I destroyed his camera; I latched onto his other arm, wishing fervently I was anywhere but here. My teeth began chattering in my head and I was unable to control it..

"There are two of them down here with us?" I asked, my voice coming out in a shrill pitch.

Brock chuckled beside me, obviously amused by my reaction. "Oh darling, there's probably more than two of them. Those are the only two that showed themselves to us. The rest are probably lined up elbow to elbow, watching us."

It earned him a smack on the arm, but I still didn't let go of my death grip.

"If you're trying to scare the piss out of me, it's working."

The air was extremely stale in the basement. It had a moldy odor to it, reminding me of my grandmother's basement. But unlike my grandmother's basement that was once filled with canning jars of vegetables, this one had scary iron cages and apparitions that moved around us, unseen and unheard.

I kept my flashlight moving around me, terrified something was going to sneak up and grab me. Every horror movie I'd ever seen flashed in my mind as I imagined all the ways these ghosts could murder me. There was so much I didn't know and it allowed my mind free reign to fill in the gaps.

Out of nowhere, the silence was pierced by a blood-curdling scream.

It wailed for five or six seconds, bringing to mind all sorts of horrific images. It sounded like a woman being murdered. Both men turned their cameras and began walking towards it. Since I was still latched onto Brock's arm, I followed them.

Something bad was going to happen. I could feel it.

The air prickled with anticipation.

My ears began ringing wildly, but not with the sound I heard when Bertha was around. This sound was lower in pitch and swirled around me like smoke. The feeling it gave me was anything but friendly.

"Nothing's going to hurt me," I tried again, but my words missed their mark.

As we got closer to the area where we saw the woman, we came to an opening in the wall. Words were printed on the wall, but were covered in a heavy coating of dust.

Montgomery reached out and wiped away the dust, revealing a word that nearly sent me to my knees.

"Morgue," he read aloud.

Just when I thought it was as bad as it could get, it just got worse.

I wasn't sure how much more I could take.

Chapter 28

The room was exactly how I expected a morgue to look. It was about the size of a large home kitchen. An old stainless steel table with a nasty looking drain at one end sat in the middle of the room and was surrounded by waist-high cabinets and shelving filled with dusty jars and bottles. Another wall contained nothing but cabinet doors. Old, decrepit light fixtures dangled dangerously above us on the ceiling, looking as though they could crash to the floor any second.

I walked over to the shelves and beamed my light at one of the jars. I wasn't sure what I was looking at, but it looked fleshy and disgusting as it floated in an amber-colored liquid. I turned away before I ended up hurling all over it.

"This is amazing," Montgomery said from behind me, choosing the very last word I would have used to describe the room. I would have picked something closer to morbid, vomit-invoking or maybe just terrifying, but never amazing.

He progressed around the room, catching everything on film. I watched him for a moment, fascinated by the process. He zoomed in on the jars and then walked down the row before panning out to take in the rest of the room. The cabinet doors drew his attention, so he pulled on one of the doors and aimed the camera at the maw. Inside was a metal tray where a dead body could be stored prior to autopsy.

He sat his camera on the metal table and pulled on the table, trying to dislodge it. It gave a mighty shriek of metal against metal before rolling out into the room. I nearly died on the spot, just looking at it.

"Climb in there, Shelby, and I'll film it," he suggested with a snarky laugh.

"Why don't I just kill you and we can do it for real?" I countered.

Being around Montgomery was like having an older brother who enjoyed torturing me. I didn't mind his antics, but given the location, I could have done without them at the current moment.

"I'll do it," Brock offered.

I backed up against the far wall to make sure I wasn't in the shot. I still wasn't convinced my hair wasn't one big frizzy halo, which was the last thing I wanted to see on TV. Montgomery picked up his camera and gave him some room.

"Three, two, one…go," Montgomery said.

"I'm here in the basement of the Parkesburg Insane Asylum. We've been walking around in the dark for almost an hour now and we finally found the morgue. I'm here with Montgomery, who is filming, and Shelby Moore, who is our location researcher. What do you think about the morgue, Shelby?" he said, and Montgomery panned the camera in my direction.

I'm pretty sure I began shooting laser beams out of my eyeballs, but covered it quickly with a fake smile for the camera. "It's pretty creepy down here, Brock. Now, turn the camera in the other direction," I said. I would have thrown in a swear word or two to make sure it didn't show up on television, but knew they'd just bleep it out and then I'd have to explain what I said to my mother later.

Brock chuckled as Montgomery turned the camera back around to him.

"As you can see, this wall is filled with morgue trays." He pulled open another door to show the camera what it looked like inside. "We already pulled one out and I'm going to climb inside to see what happens. Montgomery and Shelby are going to leave me here for a few minutes, which might give the souls an opportunity to communicate with me."

I felt myself suck in a lungful of air. The man had balls. I'd give him that.

As promised, Brock hopped up on the table and positioned himself so his head was near the cabinet door.

"Okay, Shelby. Push me in," he said. I rolled my eyes, knowing full well he was doing this on purpose.

I still had Fugly on his leash, so I pulled him over to the wall where Brock waited.

"I'll get you for this later," I whispered, my face inches from his.

I couldn't see his expression in the shadows, but I did hear his low laugh. "I'm counting on it," he almost purred.

This warranted him another eye roll as I gave the tray a mighty shove. In my mind, one mighty shove should have done it, considering it was fueled with an atomic cocktail of adrenaline, anger and fear, but it was harder than I imagined. I had to put my back into it and really push before it began rolling. Metal shrieked against metal as it went in, giving my friends some amazing sound effects for their television show.

Montgomery redirected the camera back at me.

I blinked for a moment, confused by the series of events. Suddenly, I was the show's host? Was he expecting me to take over where Brock left off?

Without a doubt, I was going to kill these guys for real later.

I'm pretty sure he was hoping I'd say something to the camera and lead him back to the scary room with the screaming woman, but he was wrong. I moved aside and allowed him room for passage, then hung as close to the back of him as possible.

Just outside the morgue door was a set of double doors similar to the banshee doors. Montgomery didn't initially see them, so I called to him and he panned the camera back in my direction.

"I wonder where these go," I mused.

"Let's find out. Lead the way, Shelby," he said. He didn't follow it with a laugh, but I could hear the amusement in his voice. A lot of people would be thrilled to be in my position, but I wasn't one of them. I had no desire to be on television, especially not knowing what I currently looked like. When I signed the waiver, I knew I would be filmed for the show on occasion. In my misguided delusions, I thought it would consist of short interviews about the history of the location, something that happened after my hair and makeup were done. This was bullshit. They could have filmed me when I first crawled out of bed and I wouldn't have been more mortified.

I started to move out of the way to allow him to go first but he stopped the camera.

"Come here for a second," he told me.

I walked to where he stood, and he motioned me to come around behind the camera.

"I have five sisters, so I kind of know what's going on here. Take a look at what I've filmed so far. You look fine. You look more than a little pissed off, but you look fine. See for yourself," he said and rewound back to when he first aimed the camera in my direction.

It was a sweet gesture, one I didn't expect from him. As I watched, I could see myself coming into frame and I quickly began picking myself apart. I didn't look as bad as I thought I did though. My posture could use some improvement and my hair was a bit on the wild side, but the night vision camera blurred a lot of it out.

"Thank you," I told him with all sincerity. I don't know why I've always been so pessimistic about the way I look. Some people didn't seem to mind, but it bothered me a lot.

I've never considered myself a pretty girl. I might have grown into one, but my mind was firmly latched onto the gawky, frizzy-haired girl of my youth, the one who never knew the right thing to say and often tripped over her own feet. My peers found me to be an easy target for their amusement, setting me up for a lifetime of mistrust. It's one of the reasons why I went into journalism. It gave me a voice that didn't necessarily come with an image. My words were front and center, not my face. I could hide behind my keyboard and allow the real Shelby to emerge without worry. This situation made my face the object of attention and I wasn't thrilled by it.

"You ready to continue now?" he asked. The light from the camera screen illuminated his face, showing me warm, concerned eyes. If I'd dismissed him as a brat early on, I changed my opinion on the spot. He did have a touch of humanity. If I ever met those five sisters, I'd be sure to thank them because I was fairly certain they were the reason why he turned out like he did.

"Yeah. I think so." I walked ahead of him, pulling Fugly along for the ride. He was being unusually quiet. Before we started filming again, I took a moment to assess what was going on with him.

I knelt down beside him and stroked his wiry coat. He was trembling like he did when I brought him to the vet.

"I'm sorry I got you into this, boy. It's going to be okay. I'll be right here," I said.

He licked his lips and gave me an adoring gaze. I'd make sure he got a big juicy hambone as soon as I could find one. I also needed food for me and wine, lots and lots of wine. Before I could finish compiling my grocery list, I stood back up and found my way to the scary double doors.

I pushed through them, not certain what I was seeing.

The doors led to a concrete tunnel that dipped down into the ground. My light didn't extend very far, but it looked like it went on for a distance. As Montgomery came in behind me, I heard him inhale sharply.

"Oh my God. It's the body chute!" he said.

I wasn't sure what a body chute was, but it definitely didn't sound like something I wanted to experience. Knowing the camera was on me forced me in a direction I wouldn't have taken otherwise. I thought about my mother and all my old high-school friends who would be watching the show when it aired. I didn't want them to see me as a coward, someone who screamed and ran every time something scary happened. Nothing had hurt me yet, right? I took a step into the tunnel.

It smelled strongly of fungus and decay, the air as stagnant as the rest of the basement, maybe even more so. It was completely possible no one had been down here in decades, unless the giant also roamed the basement. For all I knew, I was the first person here in years.

"What was this used for?" I asked Montgomery.

He put the camera down. "I want to film this with Brock, so you're safe for now," he said, setting my mind at ease a bit. "Back in the days when this was a tuberculosis hospital, patients were dying off by the dozens every day. When the other patients saw them being carted off on gurneys to the hearses parked outside the front doors, it made them kind of realize the score. If those people were dying, they'd probably be right behind them," he said, letting his words hang for a moment.

"So they built a tunnel to bring the bodies out through?"

"Yeah. That way, the hearses could meet the attendants at the bottom of the hill where nobody would see them," he said soberly.

"Did it help?" I asked.

"No, not really. You saw the potter's field cemetery. Over five-thousand people are buried there and those are just the ones who didn't have family members to pay for a plot in a regular cemetery. I'm sure you'll dig this up when you start researching, but I think over ten-thousand people died here before they found a cure."

The number was staggering. It was more than the total population of the town I lived in.

It also made for a lot of ghosts.

As the thought swept through my mind, we heard a loud bang, followed by a scream.

It sounded like Brock.

We turned and ran in the direction of his voice.

Crazy Dead People

Chapter 29

Nothing makes me move faster than a screaming human or a barfing dog. In this case, both happened simultaneously. As Montgomery ran ahead to see what was wrong with Brock, I stood there in the dark, scary body chute where thousands of ghosts probably hovered, watching my dog ralph up something he shouldn't have eaten to begin with.

I held onto his leash and looked around, taking in the way the darkness seemed to press in on me. It was almost like a living thing, growing like a vine with long tentacles. Fugly heaved one more time, spitting out a stream of something foul -smelling I probably didn't want to know the origin of.

"Are you finished?"

He looked up at me and wagged the tip of his tail.

I wasted no time getting through those double doors. Hopefully what he threw up would just mix in with all the other gross stuff on the ground and nobody would notice. More than likely though, I'd be the one to step in it later. That was usually the case when I failed to do the right thing.

We came into the morgue to see Brock attempting to pull himself out of the body tray. He had managed to get his head and arms out, but was struggling with his torso. For his part, Montgomery was filming him and laughing.

"Come on! Help me get out of here, dude! I'm telling you, something happened while I was in there," he pleaded.

It was enough to dislodge me from my spot by the door. I ran over, giving Montgomery a healthy elbow to the ribs on my way, and helped Brock dislodge himself. I grabbed him under his arms from behind and pulled with all my might. He must have been pushing with his feet because we both went tumbling backwards, with him landing firmly on top of me.

"Oh my God, that was brutal," he said, rolling off of me.

"You should have been the one on the bottom. It was a lot less fun being squished."

He leaned over and offered his hand. Under normal circumstances, I would have gotten up on my own, thank you very much, but I was eager to get out of the basement. I accepted his help as I attempted to determine if I'd broken anything in the process.

As I got to my feet, everything seemed to be in working order. I was immensely thankful for the small favor. Trying to get out of here with a broken leg wasn't on my bucket list.

I'd let go of the leash during the fall, leaving Fugly up to his own devices. His newfound freedom had apparently led him out of the room because I couldn't find him.

"What happened in there?" Montgomery asked, still filming.

"Thanks for the help, ass wipe. I'll remember that the next time we need to check out a crawl space." He dusted himself off and pulled several impressive cobwebs out of his hair before he turned to me. "Are you okay? I didn't hurt you, did I?"

His concern seemed genuine, but I was still unnerved by the entire situation at hand. I didn't want to stand around exchanging pleasantries. I wanted to find my dog and then leave.

"I'm fine, but I don't know where Fugly went. Can we walk and talk at the same time? I don't want him to get too far away," I said.

"But what about the body chute?" Montgomery asked.

"You found the body chute?" Brock asked, his voice high and reedy with elation.

I heaved the world's largest sigh. "You can look at the body chute another time. I really need to find my dog and get out of here," I said, leaving nothing to chance with my tone of voice.

The expression on Brock's face faded fast, euphoria turning to despair in one fell swoop. He recovered quickly though. I had to give him props. A lot of guys would have insisted on "just a quick peek" that would have turned into an hour of close inspection, my problems getting moved to the back burner.

"Yeah, sure." He turned to his friend. "Let's get her out of here. We can always come back."

We headed for the door with me in the lead this time. As I swept my flashlight around the room full of cages, I realized how different the room felt. I hated to say the morgue had a good vibe about it, but it felt safe somehow. Stepping into the cage room was like pushing through a wall of thick air. I immediately felt like someone was watching me, hanging just out of my vision.

"Fugly!" I called as loudly as possible.

I stifled a giggle as both men jolted at the sound of my voice.

"So what happened in there?" I heard Montgomery ask. I was mildly curious myself, so I paused in my Fugly search to listen.

"Oh my God, man! It was awful. I could hear you two in the body chute and then I heard footsteps walk into the room. I couldn't turn and look because the space is way too tight. I called out, thinking it was one of you, but nobody answered me. Then something at the bottom of the tray grabbed my ankles and started pulling. It was like it was trying to pull me into the wall. I ended up all the way down at the end, wedged in tight."

It sounded terrifying, but my mind was fixated on finding Fugly. I left them chatting, catching a word here and there about how they'd try to recreate it, only with Montgomery on the tray and how it was freaking awesome and scary as hell. Their voices trailed out as I got further away.

On the other side of the cages, I could see a doorway that led to another part of the building. I stopped beside the last cage in the row and listened.

"Fugly!" I called out.

I thought I heard the sound of toenails on concrete, so I returned to the guys, who were still arguing about who was going in the morgue tray.

"Hey guys? I think I found Fugly. Can you come with me?" I asked as sweetly as possible. I would have batted my eyelashes at them for good measure, but it would have been a fruitless effort in the dark. I walked back over, thinking they were right behind me, but they weren't.

The guys finally came meandering over, in no particular hurry. I thought about belting out a bloodcurdling scream to help them pick up the pace but didn't want to be known as a screamer.

I pointed towards the doorway. "I think I heard him in here."

Brock shined his light into the doorway, but we couldn't see anything more than concrete floor and more darkness. He stepped inside, sweeping his light across the broad expanse. It appeared to be nothing more than a big, empty room. The temperature was several degrees cooler than the other room for reasons I didn't want to know about. I wrapped my arms around my body, wishing again for a warmer jacket.

"Can you use your thermal camera, Brock?" I suggested. "If he's sniffing around in a corner, ignoring me, we will be able to see his heat signature."

"That's a great idea. Hold up, Montgomery." He rooted through the pack again until he came out with the camera.

In another situation, I might have been more fascinated with his camera. I'd seen them used on news programs where they were trying to find escaped prisoners on the run, but never had the opportunity to see one close up.

Brock swept it around the room. "Nothing here."

"Hey, there's another doorway on the other side," Montgomery said, looking at his night vision camera. "It's directly in the middle of the wall. Just keep walking straight."

It took about thirty steps to cross from one side of the room to the other, making me wonder what they used it for. Based on what I'd seen so far, it could have been anything. At this point, it wouldn't have surprised me to find shackles on the walls. I didn't see any, but then again I didn't look very closely. I just wanted to get out of there.

We found the doorway and passed through it with Montgomery and his night vision camera in the lead. Brock and I flanked him, hanging just behind him, fanning our flashlights back and forth to take in the room.

"What is that?" Montgomery said, staring into the camera.

We crowded in around him for a better look.

It looked like metal boxes lined up similar to the way the cages were. There didn't appear to be as many, but their appearance in the basement was startling.

We headed in that direction, not stopping until metal gleamed back at us in the darkness.

The boxes were about four feet high and enclosed on four sides with thick metal. There was a metal lid with a hole in the middle on top of each of them. Brock lifted one of the lids and stood back so Montgomery could film inside it.

"What do you see?" he asked. Even close up, we couldn't see much with our flashlights.

"I don't know, dude. It's so weird. There's a little metal stool inside, right beneath the hole. People must have sat in these," he said.

"Oh my God. It's a hydrotherapy chamber!" Brock said, his voice rising in excitement. "They would put them inside with buckets of ice water. They used it as treatment for manic depressive patients."

The thought was sobering. No wonder this place was so haunted. If I'd gone through what the patients here had endured, I'd haunt the hell out of the building too.

I'd truly had enough. Actually, I'd had enough about five minutes after stepping into the basement. Everything else was just more fallout from the original bad decision. As fascinating as the hydrotherapy chambers were, I just wanted to find my dog.

"Fugly!" I called out, my anxiety beginning to climb. All the 'what ifs' began piling up in my mind, stacking on top of one another like a mammoth game of Jenga.

What if I didn't find him?

What if he fell in a pit?

What if we had to leave without him?

"Fugly! Treaty treats!" I called out. It was how I got him inside sometimes and it usually worked. If he was within the sound of my voice, he'd come running for a snack. I stopped and listened, but didn't hear a response.

"Hey, there's another door," Montgomery said.

The basement was like a maze full of rooms that made no sense. Doorways appeared out of nowhere, leading to other rooms with doorways. If we found our way out, it would be a miracle. Somehow my fear of ghosts had been replaced with a brand new horror.

I pulled my cell phone out of my pocket and discovered I didn't have any service in the basement. Plus that, my battery was dangerously low. We couldn't even call for help and, even if we could, we'd probably be arrested for trespassing. How did I get myself into these situations?

We passed through the room and came through the open doorway. Ahead of us, across the long room, was a staircase. It glowed with a tiny bit of natural light. As we started towards it, a man-shaped shadow crossed the light and walked up the stairs.

Brock aimed his thermal camera at it and a red and yellow image appeared on the screen.

"Someone's down here with us," he said.

Without pause, the guys took off towards the stairs, leaving me with two choices. I could either stand there in the darkness, terrified at the prospects of another living person being in the depths of hell, or I could run after them.

I ran after them.

Crazy Dead People

Chapter 30

The guys took the stairs two at a time in their pursuit of the elusive intruder, nearly leaving me behind in their dust. Having been through a similar scenario once before, I wasn't going to let it happen again.

There isn't anything creepier than being alone in a haunted asylum, especially if you have a fear of the dark. Being an over-imaginative person didn't help matters either. I could easily envision a hoard of invisible entities racing behind me, their fingers reaching out and barely missing the back of my head.

My legs burned as I raced up the stairs behind them, thoughts of Fugly still emblazoned in my mind. My only hope was Fugly had somehow made his way up the stairs, too. I wasn't solid on my convictions, but they were all I had to cling to at the moment. There was no way I was staying in that basement by myself to look for my rotten dog.

The men bypassed the first floor door and continued up to the second floor. Weak light filtered through the open doorway, highlighting the edges of the stair treads. I climbed them quickly and found myself in a hallway similar to the east side of the building. The only thing missing was the veranda.

As I raced down the passage, my feet slapping loudly on the old linoleum, I caught glimpses of the interiors. Bare walls were dappled with black splotches of mold reminiscent of Rorschach cards. The ceilings were stronger on this side, providing the rooms with protection from water damage. Most of the ceilings were intact and the floors were relatively free of debris. The most notable difference between the two wings was the bars on the windows, telling a story unto itself. In one room, I saw a slip of gray fabric hanging from a window, the last remnants of curtains used to block the relentless sun.

Sunset was only minutes away, painting hazy rectangles on the floor. My feet landed on them like a sloppy game of hopscotch. If Brock was right, the mentally ill patients were kept on this side of the building, incarcerated like criminals. I hadn't seen a courtyard yet, so it was likely they spent their entire existence locked up in the building. The only sunlight came through the barred windows.

Modern psychiatric medications could have tempered many of their conditions, but hadn't been discovered yet. Instead, they probably brought them down to the damp, dark basement for ice baths and isolation when they became violent. If that didn't work, I was sure there was a room set aside for frying their brains with electricity or shoving ice picks through their skulls. If nothing else, history showed us just how brutal our species could be.

Some of the rooms were cast in deep shadows because the ivy outside had grown over the window opening. In several cases, it branched out into the room, covering the interior walls as thickly as it covered the outside of the building. I caught the glint of metal in several rooms, making me think there must still be the remnants of beds in the rooms. More than likely, they had been rotted down to nothing more than bedsprings, but it would be a historian's delight to witness it.

The asylum was trapped in a time capsule. It looked like they locked the doors and boarded up the windows before the thrill seekers and vandals could get inside. I remembered the library assistant, Kiki, telling me how she sometimes snuck in with her friends and was chased out by the giant. If that were the case, he must have spent most of the day roaming the hallways while he guarded the building

I had to wonder what he must have seen over the years. We'd only spent a matter of hours here and endured a living nightmare. I couldn't imagine being here for years on end, willingly subjecting myself to the hostile environment. It certainly gave me more insight into his psyche and helped me understand why he changed so much.

I didn't have time to pursue the thought because the guys sprinted down the hallway and onto the next set of stairs. My leg muscles burned and my lungs were nearly turned inside out. The only running I normally did was when I was being chased by bears, which translated to basically never. I might walk fast on my way to my car when it was raining or when I was chasing after Fugly when he slipped off his leash, but running just wasn't a part of my life. I was beginning to regret my decision.

"Hey guys! Wait up!" I called, but they were like wolves in pursuit of prey. They were so caught up in the moment; they either couldn't hear me or were ignoring me. I finally just gave up and stopped.

I eventually became so winded, I couldn't move another step. I bent over at the waist and put my hands on my knees, working on controlling my air intake. The edges of my vision began darkening, signifying my brain wasn't getting enough oxygen, so I stood back up and simply focused on pulling air into my lungs. The end of the hallway wasn't far away. If I could just make it there, I might be able to crawl up the stairs. I managed to make it to the steps and decided to sit down instead.

I couldn't fully comprehend everything that had happened to us. It almost felt planned, like a guided trip through a fun house. It started with the spider stampede, which led us to the potter's field cemetery. Seeing those lights floating in the darkness did something to me. It made me see the spirits as beautiful, harmless entities, giving me the motivation to follow the guys into the dark basement, which was something I wouldn't normally do.

What were the odds of all those things happening to us in one night? I only watched two or three episodes of Paranormal Warriors and nothing like this had happened. They were lucky if they heard a door slam in an empty room. Was it the asylum or was it something else?

A dawning came to me. If my theory about everything happened for a reason was correct and the spider incident was nothing more than a vehicle to get us to the potter's field, then what was this? Was this an attempt to separate me from the guys? Was this the purpose of them leaving me behind? If that was the case, I probably needed to find them quickly before something bad happened.

As I started to rise, I heard the distinct sound of Fugly barking.

I froze, trying to pinpoint where the sound was coming from. It sounded close, but muffled. It happened again, so I followed it, tracking it down to the wall beside the stairs. Was he on the other side in the east wing?

"How in the world did he get there?" I whispered, trying to make sense of it. According to the guys, there wasn't a doorway between the two wings.

Fugly barked again, so I left the stairwell and began exploring the wall beside it. It was getting too dark to see properly, so I turned on the flashlight and directed it onto the wall, my mind spinning.

Boards and trash were piled up high beside the stairwell door. I walked around them and was amazed to find an opening in the wall. I knelt down to get a better look. It was about three feet high and two feet wide. I wasn't sure how it got there, but the erosion of the building might have had something to do with it. Along the ground in front of it were dog prints in the dust.

"Oh, Fugly..." I sighed. "Why do you do these things to me?"

Getting down on my hands and knees to crawl through God-knows-what wasn't high on my bucket list either, but I really needed to get out of the asylum before it became fully dark. As I crawled through on my hands and knees, I realized I knew how to get out of the east wing. I'd look for my dog, but if I couldn't find him, I could at least escape the asylum.

I squeezed through, taking huge chunks of plaster with me, and came out the other side, finding myself in familiar territory. The long hallway stretched out before me, looking as creepy as it had the last time. Even though the east and west wings were laid out nearly identical to one another, this wing gave me an instant burst of anxiety. I felt as though I was being watched.

It wasn't hard to imagine them, standing in the open doorways leading to their old rooms, watching me, planning my demise. Even though this should be the friendlier of the two wings, it didn't feel that way. It felt as though everything lingering here wanted to hurt me.

I began thinking about the crawler and wondered if he was the reason for my sudden apprehension. Was he lurking just out of sight, waiting for me to come within his grasp?

My dog barked again and the sound seemed to come from the stairwell. I didn't give the second floor another thought. If the crawler was hiding here, he could have the whole damn floor to himself as long as he let me leave. As I turned to find the door, I began hearing the distinct sound of voices down the hallway. I paused, initially thinking it was Brock and Montgomery, before I realized several of the voices were female. I froze in place, my heart hammering.

I couldn't make out what they were saying. I could only pick up the cadence of their voices. The conversation sounded urgent, as though they were making a crucial decision. They grew louder, as though the conversation was moving in my direction. It was enough to break me out of my paralysis.

The stairway was darker than I would have liked. Knowing it led to an even darker first floor made my legs tremble. I slipped down the stairway, trying to be as quiet as possible, so I could listen for my dog.

"Fugly?" I called out, hearing my voice echo in the stairwell.

He barked in response, but the sound was fainter than before. He must have already made it to the first floor.

Unlike the first time I'd been there, the first floor door was propped open. I pointed my flashlight at it and it seemed to completely absorb the light. The light barely made a dent in the darkness.

There was nothing I would have rather avoided. Every cell in my body begged me to turn around and find another way out, but then Fugly barked again, closer this time, and I was helpless to resist the pull. Escape was perhaps fifty feet away at the end of the dark hallway.

I gathered my courage and simply bolted down the hall, ignoring the flashes of movement on either side of me. I didn't look to see what was moving. I just kept my eyes focused on the tiny beam of light from my flashlight as it bounced on the worn tile floor ahead of me.

Something crashed in one of the rooms and I let out a short scream, but I didn't stop. They could only get me if they could catch me. I wasn't falling victim to their tricks to distract me.

The banshee door was also ajar, caught on a chunk of debris. I hit the door with both hands, the flashlight clanking against the metal with a sound that nearly sent me jumping out of my skin. With a mighty shove, I pushed it the rest of the way open and stopped short.

Fugly was standing in the middle of the room. The light from my flashlight caught him and I could see his wiry gray coat and his tail tucked firmly between his legs. He was fixated on something in front of him.

I aimed my light higher and saw brown pants legs.

A man was standing in the same place where the giant hung himself and he had a rope in his hands. As I watched, he swung the rope upwards, catching it on the chandelier. It took me a second to realize who it was. Once I did, I did the only thing I could think of.

I tackled him and knocked him to the ground.

Crazy Dead People

Chapter 31

"Jimmy Bob! What the hell are you doing?" I screamed as he scrambled to get back up. The rope was still grasped tightly in his hands as he attempted to pull himself to his feet.

My flashlight rolled to the middle of the room and landed with the beam highlighting him. It sent long shadows across his face, similar to when Brock put the flashlight below his chin.

Something about him was wrong. His eyes were dazed as though he was dreaming.

I slapped him on the face as hard as my hand could handle, but he didn't wake up. Was he dreaming? Was it even possible? I grabbed onto his legs as he rose and managed to knock him back down, but it was a losing battle. Jimmy Bob was much stronger and overpowered me in an instant.

What I needed was Brock and Montgomery, but I had no way of reaching them. Even though we all had cell phones, we hadn't exchanged numbers yet. The only person I knew who could get a hold of them was Beezer.

As much as I hated to hear his voice, it was my only option. I managed to trip Jimmy Bob one more time and pinned him down with my body. Fugly jumped in to help by growling and latching onto his pant leg. For him, this was great fun, attacking a man in uniform together. He probably expected me to help him with the mailman as payback for the favor.

I wrapped my legs around Jimmy Bob's legs and locked them at the ankles. While he bucked and attempted to turn over, I managed to squeeze my fingers into my pocket and extract my cell phone, praying I had service. I had two bars. Thankfully, Beezer was one of my last calls, so I found his number quickly.

"Shelby! Hey, babe! How's it..."

"Beezer! I have an emergency. Call Brock and tell him to get down to the lobby NOW!"

Jimmy Bob managed to roll over, taking me with him. I did a dive off the side of him and watched with horror as he climbed to his feet, the rope still clutched in his hands. He was hell-bent on hanging himself.

Was this what happened to the giant? Did something overcome him and force him to take his own life?

I tried to tackle him again, but he pushed me off, swinging his arm wildly, landing a solid hit on the side of my head. My head snapped backwards with the impact, the pain blistering downward like an explosion.

"Why are you doing this, Jimmy Bob? You need to stop!" I screamed at him, but it was as though he couldn't hear me. He took the rope and swung it back up towards the chandelier.

His throw fell short and the rope tumbled back down, slipping from his hands. It landed in a coiled heap on top of his feet. I rolled over and lunged for it, but before I could grab it, Fugly raced in and snatched it away.

"Good boy, Fugly! Bring it outside!" I yelled, pointing towards the door.

Jimmy Bob turned and tried to grab it, but Fugly was faster. He raced gleefully outside with the rope, perhaps listening to my command for the first time in his life. I'd like to say he was having a Lassie moment, but he wasn't. In his mind, he was playing keep-away, something he did every time I tried to play fetch with him.

My head was spinning from the solid blow he landed, and everything was becoming blurry. I grabbed onto his leg and tried to wrestle him back down to the ground, but he just pulled his leg free as though it were being held with tissue paper.

I wasn't sure what he was going to do next, but I needed to get him outside. Something in this asylum had a hold on him and getting him outside might be the only way to break the spell.

Abruptly, Jimmy Bob turned and glared at me. The expression in his eyes was pure madness. His brow lowered in a glowering frown and his lips lifted in a sneer that would haunt me for the rest of my life. It was as if he suddenly got a new order from whoever was controlling him. If he couldn't kill himself, he'd kill me instead.

"Aughhh!" he screamed and came for me.

I rolled over several times, finding my knees on the second turn. I managed to get my feet below me and was halfway up, when he was on me. There was no fighting him. He was so much stronger than I was. My every effort was blocked with sheer strength.

I could hear footsteps pounding down the hallway, but I didn't know if they'd make it in time.

"Brock!" I shrieked as loudly as I could. The sound of my voice drew Fugly's attention and he abandoned the rope to race back inside and latch back onto the deputy's leg again. It wasn't enough to stop him, but it drew his attention away from me for long enough to allow Brock and Montgomery to push through the banshee door.

They came to an abrupt stop, trying to make sense of the scene in front of them.

"Get him outside! Something in here is controlling him!" I told them, as he reached down, intent upon putting his large strong hands around my throat.

My words prompted them into action and they grabbed the deputy by his arms and began pulling him towards the doorway. He was bigger and stronger than either of them, but their combined efforts were enough to get him outside.

I was so exhausted. I just rolled over and laid there for a moment. Fugly came up to me and gave my cheek a wet lick, something that usually got a reaction out of me. When I didn't move, he curled up beside me and wiggled in as close as possible. I wrapped my arm around him, feeling the comforting cadence of his breath rising and falling.

I heard footsteps in the doorway, but was too mentally and physically depleted to lift my head to see who it was. I only hoped it was Brock or Montgomery. If it was Jimmy Bob back for round two, I was done for. I didn't have any more adrenaline to burn. My tank was below empty.

"Shelby? Are you okay?" Brock said, rushing to my side. He rolled me onto my back and stared down at me, his face lost in shadows. I didn't have to see it to know he looked concerned. I could hear it in his voice.

"Yeah, I think so. Can you help me up?" I asked.

He hooked his arm beneath my shoulder and helped me get to my feet. As soon as I was vertical, the world tilted on its axis and I nearly tumbled back down again, but Brock caught me, holding me tight.

"What happened in here? We got him outside and he seems fine, but seriously Shelby, I thought he was going to kill you when we first came in," he said, his words running together as the reality of the situation raised its ugly head.

His body was warm against mine. I could smell the faint drift of cologne and his musky natural scent. I wanted to just put my head on his shoulder and let him take care of me for a little while, but I pushed the thought away.

"I think it was the crawler," I told him. "He knows how to get into people's heads. He got to the caretaker and now Jimmy Bob. We have to do something about him before he kills someone else."

"Yeah, yeah. We will. Trust me...we will, but we need to get you taken care of first," he said, turning me so he could get a better look at me in the light. "You look like hell," he said with a laugh.

"Maybe you should get the camera. Make sure the world sees this," I said dryly.

He pointed up to the corner by the doorway. "We installed a camera yesterday and kept it running, so we have it all on film. I'm just not sure how much of it we'll be able to use," he said, regret filling his voice before he had the decency to realize how bad it sounded. "But, you're okay, so that's all that matters. Let's get you outside, too."

We came outside to find Montgomery and Jimmy Bob sitting in chairs under the command center tent. Montgomery had given the deputy one of our bottled waters from his magic backpack and he was looking worse for the wear. His face and clothing were plastered with dust and dirt from the asylum floor, covering him like a deadly second skin. His hair stood up in fifty different places, which immediately made me put my hand on my own hair to smooth it down.

Brock pulled up a chair for me and I gladly used it.

"Are you okay, Jimmy Bob?" I asked.

He gave me a hang-dog look. "I'm so sorry, Shelby. I don't know what happened. It was like I was in the middle of a dream and his voice was in my head controlling me. He told me I needed to hang myself or he'd come after everyone I loved and then he wanted me to kill you. He said you were the enemy and if I didn't kill you, you'd kill everyone else."

I reached across the table and laid my hand on top of his. "It's okay, Jimmy Bob. I know it wasn't you trying to kill me." I glanced up at Brock. "I think the crawler is controlling people. He probably got inside the caretaker's head and then he got inside of Jimmy Bob's head. If I hadn't heard Fugly barking, I wouldn't have made it back in time to stop him."

As I said his name, Fugly came around and pressed against the side of my chair, looking up at me with loving eyes. I stroked his head, pulling his long bangs out of his face so I could see his eyes better. I loved my dog, but I've probably never loved him more than I did in that moment.

"How did Fugly get over here to begin with? We found a way over from the fourth floor, but I'm not sure he had time to get all the way up there and get back over here in time." Brock asked.

I explained about the opening on the second floor and the doggy footprints I found in the dust.

"But how did he know Jimmy Bob was over here? We followed him to the fourth floor. He must have crawled through the opening we found up there. Fugly crossed over on the second floor and got to him faster."

My ears began ringing with a familiar tone and I saw an old lady in a rocking chair in my mind.

"I think he had some help and it might be what we need to get rid of the crawler," I said, feeling goosebumps break out on my arms.

If I was right, my plan would be dangerous. But, if it worked, we could put an end to the nightmare encompassing the asylum and stop the crawler before he became more powerful.

I looked up at the asylum, feeling dread wedge in my stomach like a round, hard stone.

"Let's get away from this place. Let's go back to my cabin and we can talk there," I said, pulling myself to my feet.

We squeezed into my Jeep and I put it in gear, sending a nice rooster-tail of gravel and dirt up behind me as I left.

I'd like to say it would be the last time I saw the asylum, but I had one more trip to make before it was all over. I just hoped I made it out alive.

Crazy Dead People

Chapter 32

A nearly full moon hung in the sky above my cabin, illuminating the darkness with a brilliance I found comforting. Everything was awash in blue shadows, making it look like an underwater scene, something that agreed with my current state.

My head was throbbing from the impact of Jimmy Bob's blow. I lifted my hand to my face and could feel the heat rising from the tender place. I'd need to get some ice on it before it swelled up like a melon. I wasn't sure of a lot of things, but I knew for certain I didn't want to appear on television looking like Pumpkinhead.

Brock insisted on walking beside me, holding onto my arm. It wasn't necessary, but I didn't push him away. It felt reassuring to have someone beside me. As we came down the path, Sonora opened her cabin door. When she saw us, probably hobbling like broken soldiers in the moonlight, she raced down her stairs to intersect with us.

"What happened?" she asked and then got a good look at the side of my face. "Oh my God, Shelby, what happened to you?"

"Let's get inside and I'll tell you everything," I told her as she cast worried glances around the group, trying to make sense of our strange collection of people. I had to give her credit though for not continuing to hammer us with questions. She just followed us up the stairs and then made herself helpful by turning on lights.

As soon as the room light came on, Frank became animated in his cage.

"What the fuck?" he said, which perfectly summed up my night.

"Yeah, what the fuck, Frank? I agree." Fugly gave his cage a perfunctory sniff, perhaps remembering we now had a bird, on his way to the couch. He climbed up and curled into a ball at the end of it without fear of the consequences for being on the couch. We'd all gone through so much in such a short period of time. It felt like we'd survived a natural disaster, minus the hurricane and flooding. The emotions were the same though. Loss and a sense of immense gratitude washed through me.

I just tucked my face in my hands for a moment and cried, the emotions more powerful than my will to stop them. I cried for the giant and for all the lives extinguished inside that horrible building. I cried for the people who were locked inside cages and made to endure ice baths, brutal primitive lobotomies and sociopathic-level neglect. And then I cried for me, for what I almost didn't survive. The reality hit me with my second wave of sobs. If Brock and Montgomery came through the door a minute later, they would have found my lifeless body lying on the ground, another victim of the asylum.

Sonora sat down beside me, with Brock sitting on the other side. I felt Sonora's hand on my knee as Brock began rubbing my back. The comfort of their touch combined with the reality of crying in front of an audience was enough for me to climb back up to the edge of my emotions and regain control.

I righted myself, embarrassed to have broken down in front of so many people. Sonora pressed a tissue into my hand and I used it to mop away my tears. I felt her rise from the couch and walk to the kitchen. She returned moments later with ice wrapped in a dish towel for my face.

The ice was cold and was a good distraction from the emotion that swelled through my body. I held it to my head as we told her about our night. Jimmy Bob sat in one of my kitchen chairs, looking like something Fugly hacked up.

He hadn't wiped away any of the dust and dirt. Tear tracks ran down his cheeks, making long stripes on his face. His deputy uniform was torn in several places and was so crusted with gunk, it was no longer recognizable. I had to wonder what he'd gone through before we found him, and also, what brought him to the asylum to begin with.

I had my mouth open to ask him about it when there was a knock on the door.

Fugly went wild, despite his proclaimed fatigue. He sprang off the couch and lunged at the door, barking for all he was worth. When he did this, people often commented how he was a great guard dog. I always laughed when they said that. As long as the intruder knocked first, I'd be safe. Otherwise, the person could walk in without any issues. Fugly would probably even show him where we kept the good stuff.

Sonora hopped up from the couch to answer it, saving me the effort of attempting to pull myself up. As she opened the door, I was immediately confused. It was Kiki, the library assistant.

She flew across the room and planted herself in Jimmy Bob's arms. He parted his legs to make room for her as she wrapped herself around him.

"Are you okay? Did you go back to that damn asylum?" she asked, pulling back just far enough to peer into his face.

He gave her his standard sheepish expression and then looked down at his feet.

"Yeah, I guess so. I don't remember much after I dropped you off for work. I'm not sure what happened. I just woke up there..." he let the rest of his words hang.

She turned to us, hoping for explanation. We filled her in on the night's events and she nearly collapsed to the floor. Sonora jumped up, ever the gracious hostess, and got her a chair from the kitchen. Kiki slid down in it as though her bones were made of rubber.

She looked at me. "When I told you how I used to break in there with a few of my friends, I didn't tell you Jimmy Bob was one of them. We'd go up there every chance we got to poke around and look for ghosts. We had a little bit of equipment and kept buying more to see if we could capture stuff like we see on TV," she said, casting a glance in Brock's direction. If she was star-struck, she didn't show it. If nothing else, she almost looked at him with resentment.

"And Jimmy Bob kept going back?" I asked. I realized I just talked about him as though he wasn't in the room, so I redirected the question to him. "Why would you keep going back there?"

He looked up just long enough to brush me with eye contact before he returned his gaze back to the ground. "I don't know. It just called to me. It was like an addiction. I couldn't stay away. Sometimes I stayed half the night there until Benjamin chased me out. I can't explain why. I know it doesn't make any sense, but I just couldn't stay away," he said, pulling his hands to his face and shuddering with sobs.

Kiki rubbed his shoulder as he cried, but remained in her own chair. She was much more subdued tonight. Instead of the wild orange plumes, her hair was pulled back into a low, thin ponytail that trailed halfway down her back.

She pushed her black glasses up to the bridge of her nose and turned her attention back to us.

"He's been going there since he was a boy. When he first showed it to me, I was fascinated by the place too, but it started wearing thin on me. It's so dark and dirty and everything there wants to kill you," she said, curling her lip in disgust. "I started doing research on it instead, studying it from a distance, you know?" she said, directing her question to me. "They say what doesn't kill you makes you stronger, but I think that's pretty much bullshit if you keep going back for more."

Her words were powerful and were something I understood fully. The asylum was more than a mere stone building. It had almost become an entity itself, filled with all the sorrow and loathing that had consumed it for most of its existence. Some of the emotion had seeped into the wood and stone, breathing life into it.

"They're planning on tearing it down soon and building condominiums on the land," Brock said, breaking his silence.

"I heard that," Kiki said solemnly. "What's it going to do to all the ghosts in there?"

Brock arched his eyebrows. "I don't know. I don't think anyone knows, but previous experience leads me to believe it won't be good."

"Remember what happened to Lakeland Asylum?" Montgomery offered.

Brock groaned and crossed his arms as though he was hugging himself. "Yeah. That was a really active location. They tore it down, just like they're planning on doing here, and built an office park, but they couldn't keep tenants at the complex. The ghosts just relocated to the new building and haunted it instead. We investigated it back in December," he said, not adding any further details. He didn't have to. Most of us had probably watched the show when it aired a few months back.

His team came in after the third suicide and second murder occurred on the property. People were abandoning the complex in rapid numbers, blaming the developers for building on such a precarious spot. Brock brought in a Shaman from Virginia to clear the ghosts from the land, but I hadn't heard any updates about it.

"Are things still calm there?" I asked.

He shrugged one shoulder. "It seems to be. I checked back with them and they said everything feels lighter there."

"Can you bring the Shaman here to do a cleansing too?" I asked, suddenly filled with hope.

Montgomery chimed in. "Nope. Beezer screwed him over on his payment. The guy worked on this for four days straight and asked for a donation in exchange for his services. I think Beezer threw him a tenner, which was a slap in the face for all the work he did. We won't see him back here again," he said.

"I mailed him more money, but I still don't think he'll be willing to help us again," Brock said, shaking his head. "So that means we're on our own this time."

I pulled the ice pack from my face and leaned forward. "I have an idea. I don't know if it will work or not, but I think we should give it a shot," I told them. As I filled them in on my plans, they watched me with rapt attention. When I finished, Brock shook his head.

"That leaves a lot up to chance," he said.

"I know, but I think it's our best hope," I told him, praying with every ounce of energy in my body it would work. He didn't seem convinced, but didn't have a better plan to replace it with.

By mutual agreement, we decided we'd had enough excitement for one night. As everyone said their goodbyes and drifted out my door, Sonora hung back.

"If you don't mind, I want to talk to you about something, "she said.

I remembered the bucket list I made while walking through the asylum. "I want to take a hot shower first. Do you still have some wine?" I asked.

"Of course! Take your shower and I'll be right back," she said, giving me a quick hug before she bound out the door.

I turned and just stood there for a moment, looking at the empty cabin, feeling the weight of the evening nearly bring me to my knees.

If everything happened according to my plan, things would be getting very chaotic, very quickly.

If they didn't, it might be the last thing I did on this earth.

I heaved a tremendous sigh.

"God Bless you!" Frank sang out gleefully.

I would have laughed if I had it in me.

"Thanks, Frank. I'm going to need it."

Crazy Dead People

Chapter 33

I don't think a shower ever felt better than the one I took as soon as Sonora left my cabin. The water was scalding hot and I let it seep into my muscles, washing away the soil and toils of the day. When I finally emerged moments later, the bathroom was so steamy, I couldn't see my face in the mirror. As I reached for my towel, I stopped short.

The water was dripping down the mirror in long stripes, forming words.

I blinked several times, making sure I wasn't seeing things, but the words remained.

Help us, it said.

I closed my eyes for a moment and took a deep breath. When I opened them, the drips had thickened and the words were too obscure to see. I knew what I saw though.

"I'll do my best, but you're going to have to help too," I told the mirror, making a mental note about how nonplussed I was over this message. Had this happened a week ago, I would have truly freaked out, but it was just icing on the cake at this point.

It was a defining moment for me. Was this how life was going to be for me? I think a part of me thought I could put this all behind me when I headed back to my mother's house, but I had to wonder. Had I opened a door? Was this going to be my life from this point forward?

I swiped my hand across the mirror, obliterating the stripes. My own worried face peered back at me, looking haunted and lost. My face was already showing the first signs of bruising from Jimmy Bob's punch. I touched the edge of it and winced at the tenderness. I'd be sporting the bruise for at least a week, making me dread having to explain it to my mother.

"You okay in there?" Sonora called out from the other side of the door.

It jolted, nearly bumping my injured head on the bathroom mirror.

"Yeah. I'll be right out."

I dressed quickly and ran a wide-comb through my hair, breaking apart the worst of the tangles, and called it good enough.

Sonora was waiting for me on the couch with two very full glasses of red wine. I normally prefer white wine, but was in no mood to complain. I'd probably drink cooking sherry at this point.

She handed me my glass and I took a sip, pleased it was a sweet wine and not a god-awful dry table wine. I wasn't a wine connoisseur, but I knew what I liked. I took another sip and found myself nearly draining the glass before I came back up for air.

"That's really good. Tastes like blackberries."

"Have you had anything to eat since the pizza earlier?" she asked, and I shook my head. "I ordered another pizza. I know it's a lot of pizza for one day, but it's the only thing we can get delivered out here."

"There's never too much pizza," I said, feeling grateful. I've never had many friends, something that stuck with me since my high school failings. People were often clingy or had ulterior motives for wanting to be around me. It seemed like every good deed came with a price that was higher than I was willing to pay. A ride home from work obligated me to attend a horrible makeup party. Exchanging phone numbers often meant I had to endure meaningless text messages that always seemed to appear at the worst times. Honestly, I was more of an introvert, preferring my own company to that of others. I had no problem being by myself. If I ever felt lonely, I always had Fugly. It had always been enough for me, which was why it was so shocking how I was so immediately comfortable with Sonora.

She didn't appear to want anything from me. She just wanted to be my friend. Of course, providing me with wine and pizza didn't hurt. I came out of my daydream to find her studying me.

"You looked really sad there for a minute. Are you okay?" she asked, topping my glass off.

I worried my bottom lip, trying to sort through all the emotions coursing through my body, but finally gave up. "I was just thinking about how grateful I am to have met you. I've never had many friends before, so I'm probably not very good at it. But, I'm just happy to have met you, so thank you," I said, feeling embarrassed for the long monologue. I was always hopelessly awkward at social situations.

I tried to hide my expression by sipping more wine, but she touched my arm, not allowing the moment to fade.

"Stop it. Really, Shelby! I don't know why you haven't had more friends. You're funny and interesting. I like hanging out with you too...and so does Brock," she said, smiling cryptically.

"Brock?" I felt the astonishment overpower me for several seconds before I shrugged it away. I felt the same way about men as I did about friends. Men always wanted ulterior motive for the relationship and it usually revolved around sex. I'd had a few semi-serious relationships, but they always fell apart in the end. More often than not, something bright and shiny caught their attention and I was discarded. I had just given up after a while, not seeing the point in the whole ordeal, especially if it ended with me on the couch crying every time.

"Oh, if you could only see the way he looks at you when you aren't aware of it. The man is clearly smitten." She shook her head and smiled. "I don't know, but if he looked at me that way, I wouldn't be wasting the opportunity."

I found her words to be amusing. There was no way Brock Daltry was looking at me in a romantic manner.

"He probably does that on every location. I'm just the easiest target," I said.

She rolled her eyes. "Oh honey, you have so much to learn. Don't believe everything you read. He's a good guy. He has an amazingly pure aura. Most people have a bit of gunk around the edges but his is as clean as they come. If he's crushing on you, don't turn him away because you don't trust him. He's a keeper."

I sat my wine on the coffee table and curled my legs up beneath me. Fugly got up from the floor with a yawn and a long, languid stretch and then climbed up onto the couch so he could rest his head on my lap. I stroked his fur, watching his eyes grow heavier and heavier until he was fully asleep.

"Is that why you wanted to talk to me?" I asked, feeling a slight tinge of annoyance.

"Oh no. Not at all. I'm just worried you're getting into some pretty serious stuff here. What happened to Jimmy Bob shouldn't be taken lightly. Have you ever felt overcome like that, even a little bit?" she asked.

I stared down at my dog, fingering through my memories. "No, not that I'm aware of."

"Then the crawler might see you as an adversary. He's already tried to scare you off with the bat thing," she said, sweeping her hand in the air at the area he flew through. "And the way he made Jimmy Bob come after you was pretty frightening. I'm just saying…" she paused, looking down at her lap as though searching for the right words. "There's no shame in walking away from this. It isn't your battle. This has been going on for decades. You just walked into it. You don't have to fix it."

I gave her words a moment to sink in. A part of me truly did want to just walk away and leave this to someone else, but something else pushed the thought right out of my head. "I've never walked away from anything in my life. I have to do this," I told her.

She sighed. "They probably called to you because of who you are. You're a stubborn woman, Shelby Moore," she said, finally smiling.

I matched her smile with one of my own. "I've heard that a time or two."

"The Universe works in mysterious ways. I think you know this. Sometimes things are set into motion years before they happen. As much as I hate to say this, you were probably meant to be here. Everything in your life lined up to make this possible."

The realization of her words swirled around me for a moment. I've never been a huge fan of the concept of fate and destiny, but what she said made perfect sense. I lost my job nearly six months ago and hadn't had any luck finding anything to replace it with. Every opportunity fell through, sometimes at the last minute. I'd have a good interview, but then someone with better qualifications would apply and I'd be back to the beginning again. Had this job been sitting there, waiting for me so I could help those lost souls at the asylum? It seemed preposterous, but I couldn't discount it, no matter how hard I tried.

"You are such a babe in the woods with all of this. Have you connected with your angels and spirit guides?" she asked.

"No." I had read about spirit guides, but had never felt mine. According to what I read, they are around us all the time, helping us. Sometimes, I thought mine might be more prone to tripping me than helping me.

"Just do me a favor. If you're ever in a situation that terrifying again, reach out to them and any loved ones you might have lost. They will help you."

As she finished, a vision floated into my head of my father, standing beside his Shelby Cobra, smiling. I didn't know if I truly believed in spirit guides or angel assistance, but I did believe in my father.

"Will do," I told her and let it drop.

A yawn overtook me before I could suppress it. I rode it all the way through to the end, feeling the satisfying effects of the wine burbling through my system.

"You need some rest. Do you want me to sleep here? I can just crash in the spare bedroom?" she asked.

While the thought had some nominal appeal, I really craved some alone time. I'd even risk crawlers and mirror ghosts for the chance to just collect my thoughts and sleep.

"Thanks, but I'll be fine. I'll call you if anything weird happens."

She rose from the couch, collecting our empty wine glasses. "I'll have my phone right beside me." She carried the glasses and empty bottle to the kitchen sink and headed for the door. "I'll be mad if something happens and you don't call. Just remember that."

I waved. "I will. Don't worry. I'm too big of a chicken to handle that alone," I told her. "Get some rest and I'll see you in the morning."

As soon as she left, it dawned on me the pizza had never arrived. When I heard a tentative knock on the door, I rose, thinking it was the pizza man, but I was sadly mistaken.

It was Brock.

Crazy Dead People

Chapter 34

Brock smiled, holding a pizza in his hand like a waiter with a tray.

"I saw the pizza man heading this way, so I intercepted. I hope that's okay?" he said, waiting on the doorstep for me to invite him inside.

I didn't know why he was there, but I was pretty sure nothing good could come out of us being alone. My entire world had been turned on its axis. The last thing I wanted was romance right now. To be honest, I wasn't even sure I wanted company.

"Thanks, Brock," I said and stepped back to allow him room for passage. He walked to the coffee table and sat the box down. Fugly, who had slept through the door knocking, jolted awake at the smell of pizza. He lifted his nose to the air and followed the scent to the box full of heaven that had landed directly in front of him. Even Frank got in on the action.

"Frank is a good boy!" he told us.

"Welcome to the zoo," I said wearily and returned to my warm spot on the couch, wishing I could just curl up there and not budge until sunlight graced the windows. Having company was the very last thing I wanted, even from a gorgeous television star. All I wanted was eight hours of blissful rest, followed by another shower and a power breakfast at Sonora's table.

Brock followed me into the living room. To his credit, he chose the chair beside the couch instead of plopping down beside me. I silently gave him points for it.

"Aren't you exhausted after everything we went through?" I asked.

"Oh yeah, but I wanted to make sure you were okay. You looked pretty rattled earlier."

I reached forward and lifted the lid on the box. Hamburger mushroom deliciousness greeted me. I pulled myself up from my nest on the couch with a groan and retrieved paper towels from the kitchen.

"Help yourself," I said, lifting a cheesy piece of goodness from the box and bringing it back to the couch with me.

Brock patted his stomach. "I really shouldn't. I have to watch what I eat or they'll start memes on the internet about me," he said with a short laugh. I tried to laugh along with him, but fell short. There was just too much on my mind.

I bit into the pizza, allowing my entire world to revolve around the mingling of flavors in my mouth. Nothing else mattered for the fifteen seconds it took me to chew and swallow. I didn't care about the ghosts at the asylum or the handsome man with a possible agenda sitting beside me. It was a nice break from reality, but it ended far too quickly. I looked up to see him watching me.

"I'm worried about your plan," he said, throwing cold water on my moment. "I've been to a lot of haunted places and I can tell you the souls there are often caught in a kind of limbo. I know you're hoping they're going to jump up and help us, but I just don't think they can. They might want to, but something holds them back. We need more help. If I can have a few days, I might be able to find a psychic medium or an energy worker who can help..."

"We don't have time, Brock. This is all coming to a head. Can't you feel it?" I told him about the words that appeared on my mirror.

"Did you get a picture of it?" he asked in all seriousness.

I rolled my eyes. "Of course not. I wiped it off," I said as he started to rise from his chair. "It was a message for me, not something to put on TV." I took another bite of my pizza and barely tasted it this time. I pulled myself off the couch and headed to the kitchen for a glass of water, suddenly thirsty from the pizza. "Want some? I'm sorry, but it's all I have to offer you," I told him.

As soon as the words left my lips, I regretted them. Another guy would twist them around and turn them into an innuendo. I waited for him to follow suit, but he just waved me off, telling me he was fine.

"I've dealt with entities like the crawler before. I don't think you understand how powerful they really are. If it can get into people's minds and take them over, it can kill you, Shelby. Are you prepared to die for all those ghosts trapped in the asylum?"

I plopped back down on the couch, no longer interested in the rest of my pizza.

"Bertha helped me once. She chased the crawler out of this room and I think she led Fugly down to the lobby. Why wouldn't she help me again? Plus, there must be a thousand others who would like to see him gone. Surely, some of them will help."

As I said the words aloud, they felt almost silly.

"He's stronger at his home base. I believe he pulls energy from the other lost souls there, making him even more resilient." He paused to let his words sink in before continuing. "Even if they wanted to help, I'm not sure they can. There is a hierarchy system in place, just like everywhere else. The stronger, more powerful ones control what's going on. The weaker ones might not like what's happening, but they can't do anything about it. If he's become strong enough to control living people, they don't stand a chance against him."

"What do you usually do to clear a haunting?"

The line of his lips tightened as he arched his eyebrows. "There's usually nothing we can do. If it's a residential haunting, we'll try to get someone in there to help them, usually a Shaman or a really good psychic medium, but even they have problems with crawlers and shadow people. They are a notch above regular ghosts. It's really difficult to remove them."

"So, you just go in and film for your show and then leave?" I said, my words coming out with a bit of heat attached to them. Irritation flashed across his face for several seconds before he could stop it. I'd obviously hit a nerve.

"We document it. It's our job. That's what we're paid to do." His voice sounded remorseful as he said it and I felt some of my anger fade away.

"If you could do more, would you?"

"Of course I would. I'd clear every haunted building we visit and leave it better than I found it, but it's out of my range of capabilities," he said, clearly growing frustrated with our conversation. He rubbed his face with his hands and then looked at me with a weary expression. "We try to be respectful, at least. We don't go in and provoke them just to get a reaction because we don't want to rile them all up and then walk away. We've had a few cases where we've brought in a minister to bless the building, but I'm not sure it's ever really helped. The haunting started well before we ever walked into the buildings and keeps on going long after we leave. All we do is go in and document it. If someone else wants to try their luck, they're welcome to it, but we can't do much," he said.

I got up from the couch and went to the kitchen table to retrieve the books. Frank eyed me curiously.

"Who farted?" he asked me in all seriousness.

I was in no mood for Frank's jokes. I grabbed the pile of books and brought them back to the couch. I flipped through them until I found the book with Dr. Crask's photo in it. Something about the anger in his eyes made me queasy.

I flipped through the book until I found a listing with his full name, Dr. Morris Eugene Crask. I pulled my phone out of my pocket and did a quick search for him. His obituary was the first thing that popped up, so I opened it. What I found wasn't surprising.

"Dr. Crask was a doctor at the Parkesburg Asylum from 1964 until it closed its doors in 1974, and then stayed on after it was converted to a nursing home. He died at the age of 53 and was preceded in death by his wife, Eve, and his daughter Samantha," I said. I did another online search and found an article about their deaths. "They were killed in a house fire. Dr. Crask was the only survivor because he was working at the asylum when it happened."

Brock leaned forward and put his elbows on his knees. "Does it mention his address?"

"No, but I'm sure I can find it," I said, digging back into my online searches. After less than a minute, I had it. I stared at the address, confusion muddling my overtired brain.

As I put two and two together, I was almost incapable of speech.

"What is it?" Brock asked.

"His address is the same as the caretaker's," I told him, watching as the realization hit him as hard as it hit me. He stood up and reached out for my hand.

"Are you up for one more adventure tonight?" he asked.

Fatigue weighted my body and I knew I should decline his offer, but there was no way I could sleep with this knowledge. I'd just lay in bed, staring at the ceiling, thinking about everything we learned. With one more hearty sigh, I took his hand and allowed him to pull me to my feet.

"Let's do this," I said, hoping my words wouldn't come back to haunt me.

Chapter 35

Fugly jumped up onto the passenger's seat, eager to go for a ride.

"Sorry, buddy. You need to sit in the back," I told him in no uncertain terms, pointing to the backseat. He pretended he didn't hear me until Brock came to the door.

"Oh…" he said, when he saw my dog. "Do you want me to sit in the back?"

I laughed, even though I didn't think it was possible to find humor under these circumstances. The expression on his face was so earnest; I knew without a shadow of doubt he would have climbed into the backseat if I told him to. It earned him quite a few more points.

"No, you can sit up front." I turned my attention to my dog, who was clearly ignoring me. "Fugly! Get in the backseat!" I snapped my finger and pointed for good measure, but he continued to stare out the windshield as though he hadn't heard me. His hearing was often selective. If it included his favorite words, like treat, walk or ride, he was all ears, but other than that, he usually ignored me.

With a sigh, I grabbed my purse off the floorboard and dug around inside of it until I found the sandwich bag full of his favorite dog treats. I tucked several of them in my pocket in case I needed them later and tossed two more into the backseat.

"Treaty treats!" I sang in a high-pitched voice, like I always did when I was trying to manipulate him with his cookies. Fugly was a glutton for his favorite treats, so it always worked. It was his kryptonite, just like pizza and wine was mine.

As expected, Fugly scrambled over the center console and hopped into the backseat. Brock looked at me with pure amazement on his face.

"Nice trick! I wish I could use that on Montgomery."

"Try pizza and wine," I said, laughing inside over my private joke.

"More like weed and beer." He climbed in beside me and snapped his seatbelt on. "Speaking of Montgomery...we should really have him with us. Can you swing by the room so I can grab him?" he asked.

"Sure. Just as long as he brings his magic backpack that seems to always have exactly what we need in it," I said, which garnered me a chuckle.

"He's always a good Boy Scout. It's his biggest redeeming quality."

I pulled up to the parking lot and stopped in the general vicinity of their room. My headlights splashed against the front of the building, highlighting the fake wooden façade. Brock hopped out and was gone for a few minutes before returning with his friend. Montgomery's eyes were red and hooded, making me wonder if he had indulged in one of his own Treaty Treats.

"Hey..." he said as he climbed into the backseat.

I wasn't necessarily against pot smoking. I didn't partake in it myself because I hated the way it made me feel. I tended to get paranoid and far too introspective. The last time I smoked, I hid in a closet and counted all the shoes on the floor until the buzz wore off.

"Is he going to be okay?" I whispered to Brock.

He turned and glanced back at his friend. "Yeah. He does his best work when he's stoned. He'll be fine. Besides, he'll come out of it by the time we get there."

As we drove, I began thinking about everything I'd learned and it all began making sense.

The asylum had a way of calling to people. It lured in the giant and then it did the same thing to Jimmy Bob. I didn't fully understand how haunted locations could do that, but there was a lot I didn't know about the paranormal world. I was beginning to respect the power the dead had over the living.

I tried to piece it together in my mind. The giant grew up in the area and probably knew about the asylum since he was a boy. More than likely, he was one of those kids who regularly broke in to explore it. As an adult, he must have purchased the property after learning it once belonged to Dr. Crask.

My mind went numb as the pieces came together. Dr. Crask's house burnt down, killing his entire family, and the same thing happened to the giant. Their lives had followed a very similar path.

It couldn't have been a coincidence. Everything was too much the same. Had Dr. Crask come back from the grave to inflict the same torture on the giant? If so...

"I think Dr. Crask is the crawler," I said, as the realization hit me. It made sense on so many levels. I explained my theory to the guys and Brock surprised me by agreeing with me. "I think you might be right," he said, piercing me with his clear blue eyes. "Ghosts take different shapes all the time. They don't always appear like you'd expect them to, especially if they were already fairly evil when they died. He probably takes a shape he knows will scare people and then he feeds off their fear, becoming more powerful over time."

I filled Montgomery in on how both houses burnt down, killing their families.

"Wow, man. That's crazy!" he said.

"It's too similar to be a coincidence," Brock said, mimicking my own thoughts.

More pieces of the puzzle began knitting together.

I knew in my heart Dr. Crask was probably the one responsible for locking those people in those cages. He was one of the doctors on staff when it was an asylum and then continued working there after it became a nursing home. It wouldn't surprise me if he used some of those antiquated torture devices on the elderly, as well.

"I wonder if Dr. Crask was evil before his family died," I mused aloud, not really expecting an answer.

Montgomery chimed in from the backseat. "From what we've seen over the years, nasty ghosts usually start off as evil bastards in life. He was probably a schoolyard bully as a kid and grew up believing he could push people around when he wanted."

The idea resonated with me, but there was no way of documenting it without actually talking to someone who was there. One thing seemed to lead to another without time to even recover from the first experience. I wondered if that was their way of wearing us down. Were they hitting us with multiple encounters so they could weaken us? The only thing I had to go from was the photo in Bertha's album. It was nothing more than a moment captured on film, but the heat radiating from his eyes wasn't something I imagined. It spoke volumes.

I found the road the giant had lived on and turned down the rutted lane. My Jeep bounced and clawed its way through the muddy path, bottoming out several times as we went through some deep ruts.

The moon hung above us, bloated and all-seeing, serving as our witness. I was thankful for it as I stopped at the end of the driveway and we climbed out of the Jeep. It was so bright, we almost didn't need flashlights.

Montgomery handed them out anyway and I gladly took one, turning it on the minute it hit my hand. I pointed it in front of me, lighting up the spooky sight ahead of me.

The giant's yard looked more frightening than it had before. The rusted junk sent long shadows into the darkness, creating a perfectly terrifying foreground for the cabin behind it. The air smelled like dried grass and rusty metal, making me want to sneeze. I pinched my nose to ward off the urge and stepped away from the safety of the Jeep.

"Here goes nothing," I mumbled to myself.

I led the group up the path through the tall weeds, not missing the irony of this moment. When I first came here, I reluctantly followed Sonora, petrified to take my next step. Now, here I was leading the pack. Fugly hung closely at my side.

"Just be careful, fur face. There's a lot of sharp things in the grass," I told him, knowing I should have just left him in the Jeep.

The porch steps creaked beneath my feet, providing the perfect sound effects. My hands were trembling as I pushed open the creaky door and located the light switch. Being here once was bad enough, but I was probably pushing it by returning again. If the crawler found me once, he could find me again and this would be the perfect place for a reunion.

The light came on with jarring intensity, shocking my system with the sudden change. I blinked a few times, willing my eyes to adjust as I looked at the boxes and piles of papers filling the interior of the cabin. It was almost like watching a movie for the second time. You pick up details you missed the first time.

The boxes weren't standard boxes. They were the kind meant to hold file folders. Some of them were brown, while others were a deep shade of green. Most of them were showing the tolls of age and moisture, causing the stacks to lean in various directions. I initially thought the giant had a compulsive hoarding issue, but as I stared at them, I had to wonder if he was protecting them from further deterioration instead.

Was this his way of protecting their histories?

"Holy cow!" Brock said as he came in behind me. "Talk about hoarders..." He walked around and lifted several lids, shining his light inside the boxes. "There must be thousands of patient files in here. Is this where you got those files at your cabin?" he asked.

"Yeah. We were here briefly. This is where we found the bird, Frank."

"What the fuck?" Montgomery said with a laugh. His words pretty much summed up the interior of the cabin.

How many years had the giant lived here, surrounded by boxes full of patient files? I couldn't imagine having to squeeze sideways through the tunnel of boxes on my way to the bathroom in the middle of the night or completely losing sight of my living room.

"Why would the contents of these boxes have been so important to him?" Brock asked.

I caught his eye and held it for a moment. "Maybe he was trying to save them from becoming ruined by the mold and mildew at the asylum."

"Or he was researching them," Montgomery said from across the room. He flipped through the folders in one of the boxes. "Every one of these files has a disciplinary punishment written on it." He pulled out a file. "This patient from 1957 had a tendency to bite people, so they removed all of her teeth." He tossed the file back in the box with disgust and pulled out another one. "This one from the same year went through hydrotherapy to treat her bipolar disorder. I'm sure if I dug through these boxes, I'd find more evidence of abuse." He tucked the file back into the box and shook his head. "It was a different world back then," he said.

The documentation in the files painted a very clear picture of what must have gone on in the basement. If I had simply read the files, I might have had a different mental vision of what happened down there, but seeing the actual cages and tubs changed everything. Those people were tortured, plain and simple. There was no other word for it and anyone who was a part of it had to know what they were doing.

"Sadistic bastards," I said. I felt the shudder of a sob trying to take root in my chest just thinking about what those poor people endured. They were prisoners in the asylum, forced to endure whatever torture their captors felt like delivering. The idea that many of them still lingered in spirit form made it even worse. They couldn't escape the madness until somebody did something about the crawler.

I needed some air. The smell of moldy boxes and stagnant air was getting to me. I walked to the kitchen and found the door that led to the backyard. I could hear toenails clicking on the linoleum floor behind me and turned to find Fugly following me. He wasn't his normal happy-go-lucky self. Something in the house was affecting him too. I grabbed the metal doorknob and turned it, relieved when the door opened easily. The sweet smell of dried grass and cool air greeted me and I breathed deeply for a moment, trying to calm myself.

"Let's check out the backyard and see if we can find the foundation to Dr. Crask's house," I called over my shoulder to the guys, who were still picking through the boxes.

I stepped through the doorway into total darkness. I just stood there for a moment, willing my eyes to adjust to the light while the guys finished up what they were doing. By the time they came outside, I was beginning to pick out murky shapes in the moonlight.

It struck me that I should have felt more fearful, considering where I was. The hair on my arms should have been standing at full attention and my senses on high alert, but they weren't. It felt normal, like stepping out onto my mother's back porch. If something was here, watching me, I didn't feel it.

Fugly pushed through the doorway ahead of me and paused on the concrete stoop, his ears pricked. He honed in on something in the darkness as the hair on his ruff began to rise.

"What do you see, boy?" I asked, confused at his reaction. What was he seeing that I wasn't? Was he watching a horde of apparitions parading across the field or was it nothing more than a bunny hiding in the brush?

He looked up at me and wagged the tip of his tail for a moment before turning his attention back to the overgrown field behind the giant's house.

The guys came through the door behind me and stood beside me. Montgomery swept his flashlight across the yard, giving us a better perspective.

The yard was filled with more cast-off debris. I could see more rusted pieces of metal and junked cars in the tall weeds. He aimed the light higher and I could see the hulking remnants of an old building several hundred yards back in the field.

"Is that what I think it is?" I asked.

"Let's find out," Brock said and took off into the back yard.

I followed along behind him, feeling the first sense of apprehension come over me.

I wasn't sure what we were going to find back there, but it was too late to turn back now.

Chapter 36

We were getting close to something. I could feel it with every breath in my body.

It was as though something changed in the atmosphere that was far greater than a drop in the barometer. The air nearly tingled with current, heightening my anxiety. I wanted nothing more than to run home and hide under the covers.

The asylum obviously had long-reaching arms. It wasn't just the building and grounds that were haunted. It had a way of flowing out like a sea of lava and encompassing everything in its path, swallowing it whole and growing bigger and stronger in the process.

Once you allowed it into your life, it grasped on tight, claiming you in a way you'd never want to be claimed.

The light from my flashlight bounced with my shudders, sending haphazard bursts of light across the field. I only saw small details at a time. Spiky meadow grass, clumps of soil that had once been part of a field, spears of rusted metal that were slowly becoming part of the earth. Ahead, I could make out the outline of a dark building, blocking out a portion of the moonlit sky. A thousand stars surrounded it as though holding it prisoner.

"Be careful," Montgomery said, shining his light into the tall grass where an old plow blade rested. "There's a lot of junk in the yard."

I followed behind him, being careful not to trip over anything, but it was difficult to watch the ground when the building was so close. It felt like a slumbering monster, waiting for us to get within attack range. I wondered if the guys were experiencing any of the same trepidation I was feeling. It just felt like the closer we got, the more dangerous it was becoming.

One thing was clear to me. The crawler didn't want us to know his secrets.

He tried to fill us with terror with his demonic disguise, but underneath the cloak he was nothing more than a dead doctor with a really bad attitude. By destroying his costume, we removed his power and subsequently eliminated his ability to hurt us. If Brock's theory was right, our fear was feeding him and making him stronger. If we weren't afraid of him, then he would become nothing more than a ghost in an abandoned asylum.

I took a deep, cleansing breath and attempted to purge out the terror that filled me whole. I tried to remind myself I was strong and my heart was pure. Good was more powerful than evil. It had to be. My life depended on it. I remembered what Sonora taught me and grounded myself before building a huge imaginary bubble of protection. I wasn't sure if it would help me or not, but it certainly couldn't hurt.

We finally reached the old building and I stopped for a moment to take it all in. It felt like something with a conscience, watching us as we stood before it.

The building was tall and stoic, nothing more than a husk held together by ashes. It was surrounded by thick, thorny bushes. We walked all the way around it, but there was no clear way through the bushes without getting torn up by the thorns. I found myself studying the shadows.

Was the crawler here, watching us from the darkness, waiting for a chance to pounce? I edged closer to Brock and Montgomery, not wanting to be in the back of the pack where something could sneak up behind me.

Montgomery directed his light on the building, giving us a better look at the details.

It was a modest-sized two-story house, built of wood and stone. Most of the walls were still standing, to one degree or another, but the roof was long gone, having collapsed during the fire. A tall fieldstone fireplace and chimney climbed one wall, bringing to mind happier times that might have occurred there. The remaining walls were scorched black and the windows were nothing more than empty maws.

"I don't see any way in there," Montgomery said finally.

"And even if we did get in, I'm not sure it would be safe. The roof must have fallen into the interior of the building," Brock added, sweeping his light along the side of the structure.

His words cascaded through me with a calming effect. I really didn't want to go inside.

In the next second, I caught the scent of cheap perfume and heard a tone coming from behind me. It sounded exactly like the ear-ringing sound I heard when Bertha was around. I turned with a start, fully expecting to find her standing behind me, smiling her old lady smile that simultaneously set me at ease and creeped me out.

Nothing was there.

I tried to open my mind and pull her in, but nothing happened. Either I wasn't skilled enough to do it or she was too weak to make the connection. What she did to save me from the crawler must have taken a lot of energy. Maybe she wasn't capable of more right now. I shone my light across the field behind us, hoping to catch a glimpse of her. I didn't see any ghostly apparitions, but my light glimmered as it passed across several white stones.

"Hey guys...what's that?" I asked and they both turned around to look.

As if by spoken agreement, we all started walking towards it. My stomach tightened as my feet crunched through the dry leaves. There was no doubt in my mind what I was seeing. They were gravestones.

Was Bertha trying to guide me towards something?

Once we reached them, Brock knelt down and pulled some of the tall grass aside so we could read the names.

"Crask," he said, turning to look at us with astonishment. "It must be an old family cemetery."

I joined him in front of the first grave. "Elizabeth Crask...born January 7, 1898 and died February 15th, 1961." Beside the grave was another similar stone. I pulled the grass away. "William Crask...born September 15th, 1896 and died May 27th, 1963." I sat back on my heels, trying to make sense of it. "That must be Dr. Crask's parents."

Since their death dates were different, they obviously weren't killed together in a tragic accident. It made me wonder what they would have thought of their son. Did they know what he'd done at the asylum? Would they have been shaken by his sociopathic behavior or would they have made excuses for him? As I was internally musing, Montgomery moved down to the next three stones.

"Here's Dr. Crask's grave, along with his wife's and daughter's graves," he said, sweeping away the grass.

We all stood in front of Dr. Crask's grave, reading the inscription. Dr. Morris Eugene Crask was born in 1925 and died in 1977. I did the math in my head. He was only fifty-three when he died. I thought I remembered Kiki saying he died of a heart attack, but it seemed young to me. Maybe the asylum got to him too before it absorbed him into it. I moved down to the next two stones.

"Eve and Samantha. Eve was born in 1938 and died in 1963. The daughter, Samantha, was born in 1959 and died the same year as her mother," Brock read aloud.

"My God, she was only four years old when she died," I said, feeling sadness sink into my soul. I closed my eyes and could see a fire enveloping a house. The flames roared as they burned through the building. Samantha was small and blonde. She was trying to pull her mother by the arm when a tremendous crash happened above her. Then everything went black.

I allowed myself to fall backwards on the ground and just sat there hugging my knees, stunned by the clarity of the images that played in my mind.

She was so scared. I could feel it as though it were my own emotion. I saw her eyes, wide and blue as she tried to pull her mother to safety. If she'd let go of her mother's arm, she could have made it out of the house before the roof collapsed, but she hadn't. She was nothing like her father. She would sacrifice her own life to save another.

Tears streamed down my face as her loss somehow became my own. I was unable to stop the tears if I wanted to. I tucked my face against my knees, wanting nothing more than to cry my eyes out for her, when I was jolted by the sensation of someone touching my back. It came from a small hand. I turned to look, but no one was there, at least not visibly. I knew otherwise, though. Samantha was showing me what her death had looked like.

The guys had moved further away, so I took a chance and tried to talk to her. "You have to help us, Samantha.

Your father is doing some pretty bad things and we need to remind him he was once loved," I told her.

The air swirled around me like a tiny harmless tornado, carrying the sweet aroma of honeysuckle. With it came a sense of calm and joy that filled me to the bottom of my soul. I smiled into the darkness as my face was brushed with a gentle caress.

In that moment, I knew she would try. I just wasn't sure if it would be enough.

"Thank you, Samantha," I whispered into the faltering breeze, feeling the tears stream down my face. The message she delivered was nothing but pure love and light, making me feel as though I wasn't facing the darkness alone.

The encounter shook me unlike anything I've ever experienced. If I shared my story with other people, they probably wouldn't believe me, but I knew without a trace of doubt I just spoke with the spirit of the child who died in the house.

It brought me back to an earlier conversation with Sonora when she told me how I had a sixth sense. Had it been lying dormant for all years, waiting for the chance to emerge? It made me think about the imaginary friend I had as a child. I remember seeing her as clearly as I saw living people. Was this going to be my life from here on out? Were dead people going to start flocking to me to tell me their stories? I wasn't sure I was up for the challenge, especially considering not all of the dead were good.

The guys returned to where I sat, pulling me out of my internal conundrum.

"Are you okay?" Brock asked, extending his hand to help me up from the ground.

"I'm fine. Just taking a break," I said, ducking my head as he pulled me to my feet so he couldn't see my tear-streaked face.

He turned me by my shoulders until I was facing him. "This is a lot to take in, Shelby. It hits me too."

I kept my face turned to the ground, not wanting him to see how emotional I became. It was a moment meant only for me and, selfishly, I didn't want to share it with anyone, not even him. He touched my chin with his finger and tipped my face upwards, so he could see my eyes. If he was surprised by my tears, he didn't react.

"I know I'm supposed to be angry at Dr. Crask for being so evil," I told him, my voice choked with tears. "But seeing this really changes things for me. I can't imagine what it would have been like for him to lose his entire family so tragically. Do you think this is what made him evil and turn into the crawler?"

He studied me for a long moment, his eyes taking in my face from eyes to lips and back again, as though trying to memorize my face. There was something warm and languid in his expression, making him feel familiar and safe. "Most people don't look for the reason and I love that about you, Shelby. We just see the hatred and we react to it, not digging any deeper. You're probably right though. Something like this might have changed him forever."

He continued to stare at me, his eyes telling me all the things my mind refused to believe. At the moment when he would have leaned forward to kiss me, something happened to prevent it.

Montgomery called out from the shell of the building.

"Hey guys! I think I just found a bulkhead," he said.

Brock and I stared at each other for a moment. All roads led to this and we both knew it.

"Let's do this," he said.

I took another deep, grounding breath, but it had no impact. We were heading into the belly of the beast and we both knew it.

I said a little prayer and followed him to the bulkhead.

Chapter 37

The bulkhead was hidden in a thick clump of bramble. Thorny branches encapsulated it like a fortress, keeping it invisible to the outside world. A small path had been carved out directly in front of it and appeared to be well attended, making me wonder if someone used it regularly. The ground in front of it was hard-packed and worn.

I walked around to where Montgomery stood to get a better look at it.

The bulkhead was nothing more than two wooden doors set at an angle with metal handles screwed into the front. It looked old, as though it had been there since before the house burned down.

"What is it about bulkheads? Does this make sense to you?" I asked, hearing the tremble in my voice.

Montgomery reached down and grabbed onto one of the wooden doors covering it. It lifted easily on well-oiled hinges, showing us nothing more than a pit of darkness below.

"They were used pretty frequently back in those days. The caretaker must have used this a lot," he said, shining his light down into the depths.

I let the thought sink in for a moment. Why would the giant need to access the basement of the old house? Surely, he didn't use it to store more boxes. The moisture alone would have reduced them to pulp within a month.

I leaned around him to get a better look. A myriad of cobwebs dangled from the ceiling. Dead bugs and bits of grass clung to it like morbid decorations. Below the cobwebs were a set of concrete stairs. They looked wet and slippery, not something I'd willingly utilize.

"Should we check it out?" Montgomery asked, leaning around me to make eye contact with Brock, his eyes bright with excitement.

Brock hesitated, probably balancing the dangers against the intrigue. Apparently, the intrigue won out. "Yeah, let's give it a quick look. I doubt we're going to find anything down there, but we should look anyway, considering the caretaker has obviously been down here recently."

Montgomery pulled his video camera out of his bag and began rolling. He ducked his head beneath the cobwebs, leaving me to contend with them. I started down and paused, terrified a large arachnid would pounce on my head.

"Here, let me get those for you," Brock said, ever the gentleman. He grabbed a large stick from the ground and swept the webs away, giving me a clear path down the creepy stairs. If I were still counting points, it might have scored him a few more.

"Thanks," I said, making brief eye contact with him. His blue eyes were flirty and playful, telling me more than words ever could produce. I stopped myself just shy of an eye-roll, pushing my pounding heart back into my chest where it belonged before I started down the steps.

I would have made an old lady proud with my cautious steps, but I navigated down them without falling, which had to count for something. As I reached the bottom, the temperature had fallen at least ten degrees, leaving me chilled. I swept my light around in an arc, trying to figure out what I was seeing.

It appeared to be long and narrow with stone walls and a dirt floor. It was completely empty, except for the cobwebs gracing the ceiling. As I studied them, I noticed a path had been sliced through them. I moved my light in that direction, jarred by what I saw. It looked like a tunnel carved into the wall. I barely had a chance to acknowledge it before Brock made his way down the steps behind me.

"Whoa! What's that?" he asked, merging his light with mine.

"It looks like a tunnel," I said, feeling the trepidation take a firm hold on me. I directed my flashlight further into the opening, taking in the same fieldstone walls lining the basement. The ceiling looked like it was made with old railroad ties. I looked down to see large footprints in the dirt floor. The giant must have used it, but for what?

A dawning came over me, giving me head-to-toe goosebumps. "Where are we in relation to the asylum?"

Before anyone could answer, the sound of a dog whining drifted down the stairs. I sighed. Fugly wasn't crazy about stairs, especially stone steps that led down into dark, scary places.

I went back to the doorway and shined my light up the steps. Bright eyes glowed back at me from the darkness. Even though I knew it was just my dog, it still gave me a start.

"Come on, boy," I called, but he stood his ground.

I rolled my eyes and fished in my pocket for one of his biscuits. "Treaty treat!" I sang out, which were the magic words. Fugly scrambled down the stairs without a second thought. I gave him one but saved the rest of them in case I needed them later.

I returned to the group and found the guys staring at Montgomery's phone. As I edged up beside them, Brock pointed to the screen.

"We're not far from it." He pointed to a dot on the screen." This is where we are," he said, moving his finger to another spot on the map. "And here's the asylum. I'd say it's only about a quarter of a mile away. If this tunnel leads to the asylum, it cuts beneath those trees that ring around the building, just to the right of the old potter's field cemetery.

Thoughts of the cemetery lights flashed in my mind, reminding me of our goal. If we found a way to get rid of the crawler, we might be able to release all those poor lost souls. I only wished it would be as easy as that. Somehow, I didn't think the crawler was going to go without a fight.

"Okay, let's do this," Brock said for the second time that night. I tried to remember if it was one of his catchphrases for the show, but couldn't retrieve the information. My brain was nothing but mush after the night we'd had.

Before we started down the tunnel, he got in front of the camera and explained what we were doing. I only hoped the footage would air on their show and not turn up as "found footage" later after we disappeared into thin air. I shuddered again, just thinking about it.

Brock led the way with Montgomery following behind him with the camera. As I crossed the threshold of the doorway to the tunnel, my light flickered on something metal beside the door.

I stopped to look at it.

"Hey guys. There's a key hanging here," I said, and they joined me at the doorway.

As Montgomery zoomed in for a close-up, Brock narrated the findings.

"Shelby just noticed a key hanging on a nail beside the door." He reached out and took the key from the hook and held it up for the camera. "It appears to be an old-fashioned skeleton key. I don't know what it goes to, but I think we'll bring it along in case we need it at the end of the tunnel."

I felt another tremor wrack through me as I considered the key. Did it unlock a door at the other end of the tunnel? Apparently, Dr. Crask hadn't been worried about anyone finding the tunnel from this end because the opening didn't even have a door on it. What would we find on the other end?

The guys had already started down the tunnel, so I jogged to catch up with them, not wanting to be left alone in the darkness.

Fugly found a space between us, leaving me with my back to the darkness. I swiveled around several times, thinking I heard something behind me, but never found anything. Just more darkness and a whole lot of creepy tunnel.

I've never been claustrophobic, but the walls seemed to be closing in on us. The path was only wide enough for one person to pass and seemed to narrow in places where the walls bulged inward. It probably wasn't safe. One good tremor and we'd be buried alive, something that made my heart pound a little heavier.

While the guys plodded ahead of me, chatting for the camera, I turned my mind inward. Why would Dr. Crask build a tunnel between the asylum and his house? It truly made no sense to me. If the asylum was as close as the guys said it was, why would he need to travel underground to get there? And who built it? Did he use the patients from the asylum? I wanted to ask Brock's opinion but didn't want Montgomery to point his camera in my direction. I'd barely run a comb through my hair after my shower and had allowed it to air dry, which was a surefire recipe for hair disaster.

After we'd walked for about fifteen minutes, my flashlight picked up the glint of metal on the wall. I paused and knelt down to get a better view. It appeared to be a metal hook.

"Hey guys! Come check this out," I called, unnerved to realize how far ahead they'd walked.

As they turned, I could see the red light from Montgomery's infrared camera beaming in my direction, looking like a one-eyed monster in the darkness. As they got closer, I could hear Brock's commentary on the situation. I wasn't happy we were now in TV show mode, but there wasn't much I could do about it, except try to stay out of their frame.

I pointed to the wall, where the rusted hook protruded.

Montgomery stepped around Brock to get a close-up of it.

"Shelby just noticed a metal hook in the wall," Brock said to the camera. "I'm not sure what it was used for, but the implications are jarring. Was it used to restrain someone or was it simply a hook to hold their digging implements?" He left a pregnant pause before continuing. "We don't know for sure, but we might find out more as we travel further into the tunnel." He gave Montgomery a throat-slashing gesture, telling him to cut the camera.

"Do you really think it was used to restrain people?" I asked, breathlessly.

Brock shrugged. "I have no idea. Someone had to build this tunnel, though, and I can't imagine Dr. Crask doing it by himself. It would have taken him a decade and judging by the photos, he didn't have the body type for hard labor."

"He probably used the patients," Montgomery offered.

We stood there for a moment and stared at the hook, probably reviewing the same images in our minds. I could easily see Dr. Crask pulling the stronger men from their cells and forcing them to work. They'd come back to the asylum dirty and exhausted, only to be treated to a piece of bread and a cup of water for their efforts, forced to repeat it again the next day. The hook spoke volumes about the resistance he must have faced. If he had to chain them to the wall, they weren't doing the work willingly. If we looked, I bet we'd find even more hooks on the wall.

"Let's move on," Brock said, finally. He gave Montgomery another hand signal and the camera was turned back on for round two of filming.

I hung back a few steps, just far enough to be off camera, but not far enough to be alone. Fugly dropped back too, heeling beside me like a well-trained dog. I glanced down at him, not surprised to see the happy-dog gait gone from his steps. His tail was hanging low and his eyes were fixed on the tunnel ahead, sure signs he was ill at ease.

I heard a pop behind me that almost sounded like a rock being thrown. I spun around and aimed my light at the dark tunnel behind me, not seeing anything that could have caused the sound. Fugly turned too, a low growl emanating from his throat.

"What do you see, boy?" I asked.

He continued to stare at the space behind us. He acted as though he was seeing something I wasn't. I beamed my light at the ceiling, terrified at the prospects of being stalked by the crawler. I didn't see anything, but it was enough to nudge me forward again.

I was dismayed to see the guys had continued on, leaving about thirty feet between us. Fresh chills washed over me. I picked up the pace, nearly jogging to catch up with them.

Another pop sounded just beside me. It was enough to make me yelp. I pointed my light at the ground and saw a round, dry rock sitting in the mud. Someone was definitely throwing rocks at us. I started walking again, terrified to be very far away from the group. I'd barely taken three steps before another rock glanced off my shoulder and hit the ground.

I turned with a sharp shriek to discover strange shadows lumbering across the wall behind me. They were tall and thin, looking very much like people following behind me. I was frozen in place for several seconds, watching them grow closer, until I regained my ability to move.

"Come on, Fugly," I whispered and took off. We ran as fast as the mud would allow us, making our way back to the safety of the group. I touched Brock on his shoulder and pointed behind us.

He turned, but there was nothing there. The shadows had vanished.

"What did you see?" he asked.

"Shadows. They looked like people."

Montgomery turned his camera in that direction and filmed for a moment, but it was clear the shadow people were gone. After a moment, we continued on.

My heart thumped in my chest like a pounding fist. I kept turning every few steps to look behind me, certain I'd see ghosts and phantom shadows looming there, ready to reach out and grab me by my hair. By the time we reached the end of the tunnel, I was verging on total meltdown.

Brock and Montgomery were standing in front of an old metal door. Brock tried the doorknob, but it was locked. With a smile for the camera, he produced the key from his pocket and held it up.

"I think we just found the reason for the key. Let's see if it works," he said, leaning down to put the key in the lock. It turned with a snap and the door creaked open, sounding similar to the banshee door in the lobby.

I crowded close behind them and peered over their shoulders.

The doorway opened into the basement of the asylum.

We stepped forward, our steps cautious and measured. A stillness lingered in the space, speaking volumes. The hair on the back of my neck stood up as my ears began ringing with a thousand tones.

We'd barely taken three steps when all hell broke loose.

All at once, our flashlights cut out, leaving us in the darkness. Before we could even tap them to get them to work, a tremendous roar echoed through the room, growing stronger as it got closer.

The world faded out at the edges until it was gone completely.

I opened my eyes, moments, or maybe hours later, only to discover I was all alone.

Everyone was gone.

I was all alone in the dark, deep inside the haunted asylum.

Chapter 38

I scrambled to my feet and spun in a circle, trying to find a source of light to show me where I was. All I could see was pitch blackness.

I reached my hands out, batting the air, but they swung freely, not hitting anything that would give my location away.

Where was I and how did I get here?

All I could remember was coming through the door and then our flashlights went out.

Did I fall and lose consciousness?

I was with the guys though. Surely they were still with me.

"Brock? Montgomery?"

I held my breath, trying to listen for telltale sounds, but heard nothing but silence.

Where had the guys gone? And where was Fugly?

"Brock! Montgomery! Fugly!" I called out louder, repeating their names over and over, my voice getting louder and sharper with every repetition.

I suddenly remembered the flashlight. I dropped to my knees and crawled frantically around the ground, sweeping my hands out in front of me. All I felt was dirt and dry things I didn't want to think about.

The flashlight had to be there somewhere. I had it in my hand when I lost consciousness.

I turned around and began skimming the ground behind me, completely blind in the darkness. I was near a panic state. I touched my pocket, feeling the familiar shape of my cell phone. With shaking hands, I pulled it free and pushed the button, but nothing happened. The battery was completely dead. My heart raced so wildly I could feel it in my temples. It was my worst fear come to life.

"My worst fear," I whispered as the thought resounded. Brock said they fed on fear. It made them stronger.

But how would they know what my worst fear was?

When it came to me, I nearly cried out in shock. They could read our minds. There was no other way to explain it. I hadn't talked about it at all at the asylum. In fact, I thought I'd been rather brave walking into the basement to begin with, considering my fear of darkness.

Thank God there weren't spiders, too.

As the thought hit me, I clamped my hand over my mouth in horror.

Oh my God! Were there spiders? Had I just given them more ammunition?

A small squeak came from my chest, and I had no knowledge of making it.

Please, God. Don't let there be spiders.

I jumped up from the ground and frantically swiped at my jeans and shirt. I didn't feel anything moving, but it didn't mean they weren't on their way. I imagined masses of them, marching in a pack, heading directly towards me. They would climb up my legs and engulf me in seconds.

"Please, God. No," I whimpered.

I began hyperventilating, the breath coming in and out of me faster than my pounding heartbeat. I was on the verge of passing out again when I heard a sound in the distance.

I forcibly slowed my breathing. It sounded like something scraping against the concrete floor.

What was that?

It happened again. This time, the sound was more pronounced. It was something metal.

My mind spun out of control again as visions of apparitions dragging bloody axes filled my head. They would find me in the darkness and begin chopping me up into small pieces my mother would have to later identify.

All thoughts left me as I took off running away from it.

I couldn't see, but I could run.

"Brock! Montgomery!" I screamed again, as loud as my voice could handle.

The sound continued to follow me, growing faster and louder. The harder I ran, the faster it came. Then, it was joined by another sound just ahead of me.

It started with a low wail, growing slowly to a full blown howl.

I stopped in my tracks, looking wildly around me but seeing nothing.

They could be right in front of me and I'd never know it.

I took off in a different direction, or at least I thought I had. I ran towards where the door we came through should have been, but there was no wall. I slowed down to a walk as my mind helpfully provided the possibility of open pits and stairwells. If I fell in a pit, I'd be lost forever. No one would ever find me.

A sob escaped my body. My mother would fall apart with worry. She'd spend every last penny hiring investigators to find me.

I finally stumbled into a wall, my hands hitting it seconds before my face would have plowed into it. I stopped and felt my way down it, shrieking as I touched cobwebs. Images of long-legged spiders filled my mind and I batted the webs away, desperately trying to get them off my hands.

"Somebody help me!" I called out. "Anybody!" I stopped and tried to reel myself in.

Fear feeds them. I'm just making them stronger.

I closed my eyes, even though there was no difference, and tried to count to ten in my mind. I once read a book about self-relaxation. I'd been having a hard time falling asleep at night and found the book at a local bookstore. It said you have to occupy the mind so the body can drift off to sleep. Counting often helped. It also helped with anxiety attacks.

I let go of my panic and counted to ten in my head, trying to slow my breathing down with every number. By the time I got to ten, I was still trembling wildly, but I was no longer hyperventilating.

After a few long seconds, I began following the wall again, using my foot to kick it instead of patting it with my hands. When my foot failed to connect with a wall, I reached out and was amazed to find an opening.

As I stepped through it, something shifted on the ground right behind me.

I barely had time to turn and react before someone wailed again, right in my face.

I couldn't stop the panic racing through my veins this time, no matter how hard I tried. I bolted forward through the doorway, my hands pawing out in front of me.

"Fear feeds them, Shelby," my father's voice sounded in my head. It was so clear and so real, it felt as though he were inside my head with me.

"Daddy?"

If he was there for a second, he was now gone. The only thing I could hear was my own pounding heart. I continued forward, trying to get a grip on myself.

Fear feeds them. Don't feed them and they won't chase you.

You've been down in the basement before. You know the layout.

"Think, Shelby! Think!" I said aloud, my voice sounding high and thin.

The room I was in was large. I walked more than fifty paces and never hit another wall. The only room that matched it was the room with the stairwell. Something grabbed onto my arm and I yanked it away, the fear suddenly transforming into anger.

"Leave me alone, you bastard! You can't have me!" I screamed with all my might.

I wasn't sure if anger was a good substitute for fear because both were strong emotions, but anger felt a hell of a lot better. I latched onto it and let it fill my body.

"Get away from me! I command you! Go back to where you came from!"

Someone chuckled directly beside me. The voice was male.

I took a swing in that direction, but my hand swept through nothing but air.

I started walking forward again, trying to put some distance between us when my ears began ringing. It was the same tone Bertha made.

"Bertha?" I whispered.

The tone grew louder, coming from directly in front of me. I took a tentative step towards it, praying it wasn't a trap leading me to a pit in the floor. The ringing continued.

I took another step and another until my foot connected with something solid. I reached out with my hands and connected with a rail.

The stairs!

I grabbed tightly onto the railing, ready to race up them when I heard the chuckle again. It was right behind me. The air suddenly grew even colder, like a breath of winter sweeping through the basement. I could feel it tingling against my ankles, creating goosebumps on my flesh. Before I could move, rough arms grabbed me, pinning me in place.

"Help me!" I screamed, hoping my voice would travel up the stairwell and someone would hear me.

A hand clamped over my mouth before I could scream again. It was rough and dry, smelling strongly of rot and decay, like the hand of a dead person.

Rooted to the spot, I couldn't even flinch when I felt the unmistakable sensation of something being lowered over my head.

As it touched my bare neck, I felt the rough bristles and knew what was happening.

It was a rope.

He planned to hang me just like he did with the giant and Jimmy Bob.

Chapter 39

I could not fight an invisible being with unimaginable strength.

The smell of death surrounded me, gagging me as I stood frozen to the spot. It smelled like meat rotting in a dumpster, stewing in its own juices. The cold draft seemed to intensify, freezing me nearly solid. My teeth rattled together and I had no means to stop them. I wanted to wrap my arms around my body for warmth, but couldn't move them.

Phantom voices began lilting around the room, sounding like an orchestra of the dead. Their voices rose and fell in conversations I couldn't understand. They moved in closer, numbering in the thousands. My head nearly exploded with the surge of energy surrounding them, making the air almost unbreathable.

I would have never believed a ghost was capable of physical violence like this, but the arms around my body were as real as anything made of flesh and bones. I tried to still the fear inside me so I would stop fueling his anger, but it was impossible. He had a grip on my mind as well as my arms.

As the rope was tightened around my neck, my mind simply separated from my body. The fear became a hatchet, disconnecting me from the physical world.

A vision came into my head of my father. It was late summer and we were at the park near our house. There was a large metal slide, but I was too afraid to climb the ladder. I was only four years-old and the ladder looked as tall as a skyscraper.

"Go ahead, Shelby. You can do it," my father told me, smiling calmly.

I turned and stared back up the ladder, panic gripping me like a vise.

"It's too tall. I'll fall," I told him, and he knelt in front of me.

"Shelby, as you get older, you'll see a lot of tall ladders in your lifetime. Some of them will seem to be so high, you'd never be able to climb them, but here's the trick: you still have to climb up. Once you get to the top, you'll realize it wasn't as bad as you thought it was. Sometimes, you just have to be very brave."

The sun slanted from the late afternoon sky, reflecting on his sunglasses. I could smell freshly cut grass and hear the distant sound of a lawn mower. A bird flew down and landed on the top of the ladder. It looked down at me quizzically, making me giggle.

"Go get the bird," he told me. "The bird isn't afraid because he knows if he's careful, he'll be safe. Just hold onto the rails tightly and climb. You can do it, sweetheart." He put his hand on my shoulder. "Nothing is ever as bad as it seems."

My tiny body trembled, but his words gave me strength. I could do it.

Something stubborn rose up inside me. Before I could change my mind, I grabbed onto the ladder and started to climb. I didn't look down. I just kept my eyes on the next rung until I made my way all the way to the top.

The view was astonishing, even to my four-year-old eyes. I could see the entire playground and even the street and neighborhood beyond it. I wanted to stay up there forever and just look. I felt free, like I did when I swung on the swing set and flew like a bird.

As I looked out beyond the edge of the playground, I saw a small blond-haired child running through the tall grass where the groundskeeper hadn't mowed yet. She raced towards a man wearing a long white coat. A doctor.

My mind refused to make the connection until he turned, and I could see his face. He was tall and dark-haired. Instead of the scowl I saw in Bertha's photo, this man was smiling a father's smile, beaming at his daughter. There were crinkle lines around his eyes as he grinned at her. It was clear he loved the little girl very much.

I came back to myself. I could feel the rope around my neck, but I was still paralyzed. My arms refused to budge from my side and the smell of death still surrounded me.

There was nothing left but words.

"Dr. Crask?" I said tentatively.

The hands tightening the rope around my neck paused as he heard his name. It made me realize he probably hadn't heard his name for decades. So much time had passed since he left his human persona behind and became the crawler. It seemed to jolt him for a moment, possibly unleashing thousands of memories.

I took a deep breath for courage and continued, praying I didn't say the wrong thing.

"I know you started out as a good man. You were a devoted father and probably a great husband, too. Samantha still loves you. She's waited for you to help you find your way to Heaven. You have to let go of the anger and remember the love," I said, my voice sounding like a prayer.

The hands holding the rope fell away.

I became aware of a soft light drifting towards us in the darkness. It was the size of a soap bubble, lit from within by a pale pink light.

"Samantha? Is that you?" I called out, trying to keep the tremble out of my voice.

The light grew closer, growing larger but not manifesting into a recognizable form. It was as though she was uncertain about the situation. Was she seeing her father or the evil crawler he had turned into?

I pulled the image of the blond-haired girl and her father to the forefront of my mind. If they could read minds, they might see this. I focused on it, hearing her burbling laughter as he picked her up under her arms and swung her around in a circle.

"I'm flying, Daddy!" she sang out, her voice as pure as an angel.

The wailing woman yelled out again in the distance, the sound growing closer as though she was mesmerized by our conversation. This was quickly followed by shuffling footsteps as the dead drifted even closer.

My ears began ringing again with a thousand tones. I could hear Bertha's sound swirling amongst them. The souls of the asylum were drawing near.

"Please, come closer!" I pleaded. "Help me!"

I could feel them pressing in tighter, crowding side-by-side, making a circle around us. I couldn't see them, but I could feel them. Samantha's light grew brighter, reflecting against the cement floor below her and brightening the room like a sun.

Her love washed over me, pure and warm. It felt like sunshine on my skin on a beautiful summer day.

The others seemed attracted to her light, like moths. Her energy was so beautiful and untainted. They wanted to be close to it because it brought them solace. I don't understand how I knew, but it was true. Without their bodies, all that was left was emotions. Her love was something they hadn't felt in a long time.

Like Dr. Crask, they had been reduced down to their greatest feelings, clinging to the fear and hatred like a lifeline. As Samantha's light grew brighter, I could feel the energy changing.

They too could feel the love.

I pushed away the fear and anger and tried to really visualize him as a man in pain. It was easier to see him as the distorted creature who roamed the hallways, leaving a wake of terror behind him. It was far more difficult to peel away the mask to reveal the man behind it. It was easier to wallow in the misery than it was to rise above it.

"Samantha, lead your father to the light," I told her, praying she would listen to me.

Her light bobbed in the darkness for a moment before it shot to the ceiling and filled the room with its intensity. It was so bright, it hurt my eyes to look at it, but I did so anyway. Like the others in the room, I was helpless to resist.

I could make out shapes, standing around us. They were no more than shadows. As her light grew brighter, they came in closer, but they didn't go into the light. Dr. Crask was still holding them back.

"Dr. Crask, go to your daughter. Find the peace and love you deserve," I said softly, knowing he was still right behind me.

"Daddy?" a small voice rang out and I felt him move away from me. He drifted upwards towards her. I watched in stilled silence as he transformed from a monster back to a man. When he reached her, the light became brilliant, mixed with a rainbow of colors. And then he was gone.

The shadows followed suit. One by one, they lifted from the ground and disappeared into the light Samantha had created, finding their way to Heaven.

I fell to the floor in a heap, unable to move. The cold of the concrete penetrated my skin, chilling me in an instant. I didn't even try to pull myself to my feet. It was more than I could handle. I just wanted to lay there and drift away to a place where nothing could ever touch me again.

As I began the slow tumble towards unconsciousness, I heard the distinctive sound of toenails on linoleum. It was enough to pull me from the depths.

"Fugly?" I whispered, raising my head from the hard concrete ground.

He whimpered from the top of the stairs.

Fugly never liked stairs.

With a shaking hand, I reached into my pocket and pulled out several of his biscuits. I couldn't hold onto them and they fell to the floor beside me.

The world began fading out at the edges, but I held tight for one more moment. I lifted my head from the cold floor again and looked up towards the staircase.

"Treaty treats!" I sang out as loud as my voice would allow.

Seconds later, I heard the sound of footsteps on the stairs.

I felt the brush of fur on my arm and knew everything was going to be okay. Fugly had found me.

He then did the most amazing thing. Instead of wolfing down his biscuits, he began barking. He didn't stop until the sound of footsteps thundered down the stairs in front of me.

Crazy Dead People

Chapter 40

The light from two flashlights bounced down the stairs, accompanied by the sound of thundering feet. The world faded in and out for me. I caught moments, interspaced by darkness, making me feel as though I was seeing the world through a strobe light.

Brock knelt down beside me, his face taut with worry. His hair looked like he'd been through a windstorm and his face was smudged with asylum dirt, telling his story for him. He swept his flashlight down my body, probably looking for visible injuries before touching my arm.

He finally met my eyes and I was taken aback by the panic trapped inside them. They were wide and worried, searching my face as though he hadn't expected to find me alive.

"Are you okay?" he asked, reaching up to smooth a piece of hair from my face.

I gave him a weak smile, caught between emotions. I wanted to laugh, cry and fall into a thousand pieces simultaneously. "I will be, eventually," I said, feeling a wave of contentment come over me very abruptly, despite the cold floor and the lack of energy. I was safe. Finally safe.

I'd lived through a near-death experience, but it wasn't one I could ever validate or fully explain. If I told people what had happened down in this basement, they'd look at me with skepticism etched in their eyes. Only a handful would believe me, and the rest would wonder about my mental state.

I, too, was worried about my mental state. My mind reeled back and forth between past and present as I tried to focus on what was in front of me. My eyes must have fallen shut again because Brock patted my cheek.

"Stay with us, Shelby. We need to get you out of here."

I opened my eyes with a start and tried to concentrate on his face. He faded in and out of focus until I was able to gain control. It felt like a lifetime had passed since I last saw him.

"What happened to you guys?"

Brock looked confused. "What happened to us? What happened to you? The flashlights cut out and the next thing we knew, you were gone. Where did you go? We've been looking for you for hours," he said, firing questions at me one after another, not giving me a chance to respond.

"I don't know. I just woke up in a pitch black room," I told him. He helped pull me to a sitting position. My head spun for a second but then settled down. "Do you have any water in your magic backpack?" I asked Montgomery.

He passed me a bottle and I nearly drained it in one long pull. After I finished, I felt a little better. What I needed was to get out of the basement, but I had to tell them what happened first.

"I crossed him over," I said simply, watching the confusion march across his face.

"Who?"

"The crawler…Dr. Crask," I said and then filled him in on the experience.

He looked around as though expecting to see some evidence and then regarded me with wary eyes. "Are you sure he's gone?"

"Pretty sure. He wouldn't have let you find me if he was still around." I shifted on the hard floor, suddenly noticing the aches and pains, and he helped me to my feet. I was wobbly at first, but felt better once I got my hand on the railing. The fresh memories rushed back to me as I stood in the same place I'd been when the rope went around my neck. I looked down at the stairs, searching for the rope but didn't see it.

"Are you looking for this?" Montgomery asked, holding up a long brown rope.

I stared at it, instantly feeling a phantom prickle of the crawler lowering it over my head. It would probably take me years to get past this, but I was alive. That counted for a lot. I left his question unanswered and continued up the stairs.

As we walked down the dark hallway, I had something else I needed to do.

"I need to talk to Bertha," I told them, leading them to her room on the third floor.

A lot of souls crossed over after Dr. Crask went through the light, but I had a feeling Bertha had hung back. I held up my hand to the guys. "Stay here for a minute, okay? I just want to talk to her by myself." I nailed Montgomery with narrowed eyes. "And no filming me!"

He put up his hands in surrender and the two of them took a few steps backwards, giving me the space I needed.

Her room looked exactly like it had the last time I was there. The floor was covered in moldy plaster and the walls were peeling. In my mind's eye, I saw it like it used to be, back when Bertha lived there.

She was in the corner rocking and smiling her old-lady smile at me.

"I just want to thank you for helping me. You probably saved my life by leading me to those stairs," I told her. For a second, I could see a wavering in the shadows as though she was attempting to manifest into a visible form, but it passed quickly.

In my mind, I saw her rising from her chair to give me a hug. As our bodies connected, I felt an electrical shiver in the places where she touched.

Information came to me, transferred into my mind in a psychic wave. Helping me had taken every ounce of her energy and she didn't have much to start with. The crawler kept them there as hostages, pulling energy from them to make himself more powerful. He used them like batteries, draining them nearly dry.

It explained a lot to me. I had repeatedly asked her for help and she gave what she could, but wasn't able to provide as much as I needed. I was thankful for what she'd done. Her last favor had led me to the stairs.

"I think you should cross over now and be with your family," I told Bertha and she nodded. She faded bit by bit until I couldn't see her at all. In her place was a tiny bubble of light, similar to what we saw in the potter's field cemetery. As I watched breathlessly, it rose slowly and then shot through the ceiling. As it disappeared, something floated to the ground.

I leaned over and picked it up. It was the photo of Bertha sitting in her rocking chair with needlepoint on her lap.

She was gone.

I felt a tear leak from my eye, but I suppressed the shuddering sobs that wanted to follow. I had to hold it together for just a little bit longer. I rejoined the guys in the hallway.

Brock gave me a hopeful look. "Done?"

"Almost," I said, reaching down to pat Fugly. "We have one more thing to do."

"Lead the way, darlin'," Brock said with a grin. It was impossible imagining finding a moment of pleasure in the middle of the hell we were wading through, but there it was.

I led them out of the asylum, closing the banshee door behind us for the very last time. The guys would remain and finish shooting their show, but I was heading home in the morning. I didn't care if Beezer fired me on the spot. I needed my own bed, familiar walls surrounding me and a whole lot of comfort food. It would probably be a while before I was able to sleep again, but home called to me, pulling me there with an invisible string.

We picked our way down the steep hill to the ring of trees. I borrowed another flashlight from Montgomery's magic bag and led the way down the dark narrow path to the potter's field cemetery.

As we stood at the edge of it, all I could see was a blanket of stars overhead. The field was trapped in shadows.

I closed my eyes and said a prayer. "You can all go home now," I whispered and the field immediately lit up with tiny, colorful lights. It reminded me of my youth, when my father would plug in the lights on our Christmas tree, except these didn't remain stationary. They bounced and danced in the darkness as though filled with jubilation. And then, one by one, they rose to the sky and disappeared.

Tears streamed down my face as the last one departed.

"That felt really good," Montgomery said, surprising me with his words. I thought he was nothing more than weed, women and magic backpacks. Apparently, there was more to him than what met the eye.

Brock linked arms with me, his body so close to mine, I could feel every breath he took.

"That was beautiful," he said, meeting my eyes.

I had resisted him since the moment we met, but I found myself letting go of the hesitation. I allowed myself to fall into their depths, feeling all the emotions I'd held back for so long. Every bad relationship and hurtful rejection that had molded me into the person I'd become fell away like dust. I wasn't sure what tomorrow would bring, but I stopped worrying about it and focused on the moment instead.

He wrapped his arm around my shoulders and kissed my forehead, pulling me closer so I could press my face into the front of his shirt. He smelled like sandalwood mixed with fear sweat, but it was the sweetest scent I've ever encountered.

I allowed him to walk me out of the forest.

It was done.

Truly done.

Chapter 41

"Shelby, do you need more chicken and dumplings?" my mother called from the kitchen.

Sweeter words have never been spoken.

She came into the living room and ladled another scoop onto my plate. Fugly edged close to me, hopeful for a spill, nearly sending my TV tray tumbling to the floor. I steadied it and shot him a warning glance he understood clearly.

He backed away and lowered himself to the floor, steadily staring at me from under the fringe of his long gray bangs. I had no delusions of what would happen to my plate if I left the room and he made no promises about resisting temptation. If he left me alone, he'd be allowed to lick my plate. If I was feeling especially generous, I'd leave him a few hunks of chicken.

"What the fuck!" Frank called out from the kitchen, which was followed by my mother's scolding him for his bad language. Montgomery was going to take him, but needed more time. So I was Frank's temporary caretaker, something my mother was definitely not happy about.

A month had passed since I limped home, wounded and mentally battered. My mother didn't understand my fatigue and I didn't try to explain it to her. The things that had happened to me were monumental and life altering, but they were largely beyond most people's comprehension. My mother probably thought I was just tired from walking around the huge asylum, and I didn't bother to correct her.

"Oh, it's coming on!" my mother exclaimed as the Paranormal Warriors logo filled the TV screen. I held my breath through the intro, watching the opening clip of Brock and Montgomery walking through haunted buildings, looking far cooler than they were in real life.

I'd be remiss if I said I didn't feel a twinge when I saw Brock's face on the screen. He tried to call me several times after I left, but I let them all go to voicemail. Healing was a long process and I wasn't ready to deal with him. I did meet Beezer in Louisville again to tape several interviews about my experiences, but neither Brock nor Montgomery had been there. They'd already moved onto the next location, one I was given a breather for.

Beezer had been enthusiastic about the episode and already had my next assignment ready and waiting. I had fully planned on telling him to shove it in a really dark, narrow space, but then he surprised me. Since I had participated in the filming of the episode, he was doubling my salary and giving me a sizeable bonus to boot.

Reliving the experience through the eyes of a camera was vastly different from the live version. As I watched the calendar, mentally counting down the days before the segment aired, I felt a sense of dread in the pit of my stomach. I'd finally gotten to the point where I stopped watching ceilings and could now sleep without every light in my room blaring. I did add another nightlight, but it didn't help me with the nightmares.

I saw the crawler in every dream. Sometimes he stood in the background, looking like Dr. Crask. Other times, he leaped out from the dark shadows in full crawler mode. I jumped at the slightest things, always on edge. I hoped in time I'd learn to deal with it, but a part of me wasn't sure it would ever completely go away.

As I watched the show, I was impressed with the way they pieced it all together. Montgomery had managed to pull several seconds of footage from the lost crawler scene, where he ran away from us on the third floor. It was incredible, something they had never captured on film before. The scenes of the tunnel and basement experience set my teeth on edge, but the field full of lights made me smile. Since much of it wasn't caught on film, they hired actors to do recreations and I wasn't completely displeased with the actress they hired to play my role. She was younger, thinner and prettier. If I could have traded bodies with her, I would have.

As I clicked off the TV, my mother carried our plates to the kitchen. Fugly came up and put a paw on my leg. I looked down at him and smiled. He certainly wasn't much to look at and he could be the orneriest dog on the planet, but he was my best friend, and nothing would ever change that.

I patted my lap and he jumped up.

"Wanna watch it again?" I asked him, and he licked my face.

I hit the button and Brock's face filled the screen.

I wasn't sure what the next location was going to bring me, but I knew it was bound to be eventful. I just hoped with all my heart there wasn't another crawler.

Fugly licked my face and I smiled.

But if there was another crawler, at least I'd have my worthless guard dog by my side.

I couldn't ask for anything more than that.

The end

To My Readers

Writing this book was truly a labor of love that started almost twenty years ago. My characters, Shelby and her dog Fugly, were in the first full-length novel I ever wrote, *Indiana Insanity*. When I couldn't find an agent, I put the two books I'd written about them on a shelf and moved onto writing the next book, the one that would be good enough for an agent.

When I was writing the third book in the series, I had a message come through that gave me faith that I would one day see my dreams come true.

While my kids were little, I worked part time at a local pizza restaurant. It was really hot inside the building, so we propped a door open for air circulation. As I was tossing a pizza, I saw a scruffy dog walk through the doorway. I stopped, my mouth hanging open. The dog looked exactly like how I'd imagined Fugly.

As I got closer, I realized the dog had a recent run-in with a skunk, which was even more astounding. In the chapter I just wrote that afternoon before leaving for work, Fugly also got skunked. I ended up bringing the dog home and bathing it. I put up "lost dog" flyers and received a call a few days later. It broke my heart to hand over the dog, but it was the right thing to do. As I walked away, it occurred to me that I didn't know the dog's name.

"What's the dog's name?" I asked.

The woman smiled at me.

The dog's name was Destiny.

I carried this story around inside my head for eighteen years, knowing that somehow it would all work out.

If you enjoyed this book, please, please, please write a reader's review on the site where you purchased this book. Readers often look for a book with a generous amount of good reviews and it will help me go onto write the next book about Shelby and Fugly.

Thank you for all your support over the years. It truly means the world to me.

Joni

About the Author

Joni Mayhan is a paranormal investigator and the author of nineteen books. After spending thirty years in Massachusetts, she recently relocated to her home state of Indiana where she operates Haunted New Harmony Ghost Walks and Investigations.

A self-described Facebook addict and a lover of books and nature, she is also the sane version of the crazy cat lady, with five felines muses and a dedicated canine at home.

She is currently working on her 20th book, Hanover Haunting, and will appear on the Travel Channel's *A Haunting* in its 100th episode the summer of 2019.

To learn more about Joni or her Haunted New Harmony Ghost Walks, check out her website: JoniMayhan.com

Books by Joni Mayhan

True Paranormal Non-fiction
Haunted New Harmony
Ghost Magnet
Spirit Nudges: Allowing Help from the Other Side
Signs of Spirits – When Loved Ones Visit
Ruin of Souls
Dark and Scary Things – A Sensitive's Guide to the Paranormal World
Ghost Voices
Bones in the Basement – Surviving the S.K. Haunted Victorian Mansion
The Soul Collector
Devil's Toy Box
Ghostly Defenses – A Sensitive's Guide for Protection

Paranormal Fiction
Lightning Strikes (Angels of Ember Dystopian Trilogy– Book 1)
Ember Rain (Angels of Ember Dystopian Trilogy – Book 2)
Angel Storm (Angels of Ember Dystopian Trilogy – Book 3)

The Spirit Board (Winter Woods – Book 1)
The Labyrinth (Winter Woods – Book 2)
The Corvus (Winter Woods – Book 3)